The Making of A Surgeon

William A. Nolen, M.D.

Mid-List Press
Minneapolis

Published by Mid-List Press, 4324 12th Avenue South, Minneapolis,
Minnesota 55407-3218. Visit our website at www.midlist.org.

Originally published by Random House, Inc. Chapter II was first
published in slightly different form in Esquire *magazine.*

Library of Congress Cataloging-in-Publication Data
    Nolen, William A., 1928–1986
        Making of a surgeon / William A. Nolen
                p.   cm.
        ISBN 0-922811-46-6
        1. Nolen, William A., 1928–1986. 2. Surgeons–Minnesota–
        Litchfield–Biography. I. Title.
    RD27.35.N64A3   1990
    617'.0092—dc20

Printed in the United States of America.

My father was a lawyer.
When I was a boy he said to me,
"Billy, if you're smart,
when you grow up you'll be a doctor.
Those bastards have it made."
I took my father's advice,
and I dedicate this book to his memory.

Contents

Foreword

A few weeks before my father died, he said to my brother Billy, "I'm a doctor first, a writer second." I was surprised. As an aspiring writer myself, I knew how much writing meant to my father, and I admired his dedication. He wrote eight books in all, among them: *A Surgeon's World*; *Healing: A Doctor in Search of a Miracle*; *Surgeon Under the Knife*; and *Crisis Time*.

But as I read *The Making of a Surgeon* again, and consider the man who wrote it, I see the truth of his statement to his son. I wonder how I ever could have thought otherwise.

It isn't just that Dad wrote about his profession. Writers must write about what they know. It's more than that. Simply put, he lived to take care of people; he was a "born doctor."

Dr. William Nolen shouldered the burdens of many people and did so with a devotion that often went unremarked. He was tall and strong. There seemed no way this man could falter. He kept his vision clear. He possessed a friendly, easy manner that complemented the determination in his gait. Family, patients, colleagues, and friends relied on his strength and relaxed in his company.

Anyone else having written an international bestseller might have thrown aside previous goals, previous career, previous life. Not Dad. He wasn't immune to the attractions of fame and money. But it was in Litchfield, Minnesota, a town of five thousand people in the middle of the midwestern prairie that he resumed his real identity: "Doc Nolen."

Near the end of his life, Dad became discouraged about what he increasingly perceived as the shortcomings of the medical profession. Once I even heard him say that he wasn't sure he could encourage young men and women to pursue medical careers. He seemed tired and disillusioned then. Besieged with health problems, he couldn't keep up the grueling routine he had established for himself. I thought about all of the young men I had met (a great introduction to young doctors, being the daughter of William Nolen, M.D.)—men who chose medicine because of *The Making of a Surgeon*. Dad gave urgency to their idealism by stating the truth as he knew it. He always had been able to push past disillusionment with his considerable wit, wisdom, and honesty.

I remember the times he would take us to the hospital when he made his rounds. Or on an emergency visit to a farm. Helping the sick and injured had been his mission in life, his driving force. Glamour and money were merely accidental and not at all necessary to him.

Dad died young, barely fifty-eight, at the same age and from the same disease (genetic coronary heart disease) as his own father. My grandfather had died suddenly. But Dad endured two bypasses, and continued to work with constant pain for the last three years of his life.

As he wrote in *Surgeon Under the Knife*, my father didn't like being a patient. He was used to being in charge.

The day before he died at the University of Minnesota Hospital, I told him that he had been offered another book contract. His proposal for a book on the changing face of American medicine had been accepted by a publisher. Dad nodded weakly. It wasn't writing a new book that he would miss most dearly.

He was lying down while his doctors conferred about what to do next—another bypass? a transplant? Dad turned to me, noticed my hand was bandaged. I'd cut my palm at work the day before, a deep slice, requiring stitches. Dad had always performed the honor of fixing his kids in the past.

"Jody, let me see it," he said.

I held out my hand. He studied the workmanship, the wound so tightly sewn.

I had never had to take care of anything, not really, not with Dad around. My father was a doctor, a healer, a caretaker. He was also gifted with words, These are the words he used to express how he felt about the life he'd chosen.

The details of surgical apprenticeship have changed over the years. Certain procedures, taught as standard medical practice when my father learned his profession, are no longer performed. The spirit behind his story remains strong and inspiring. The practice of medicine—like life itself—grows, changes, and endures.

Jody Nolen
Minneapolis, Minnesota
March 1990

Introduction

How do you make a surgeon? Not by the preliminaries, the four years of college and four years of medical school that have to be gone through to earn an M.D. degree, but by the five, six or seven years that a man spends after medical school learning the surgical trade. Exactly what happens in this apprenticeship period that transforms him from a helpless, frightened medical school graduate into, hopefully, a capable confident surgeon?

It's not an easy question to answer. The transformation is a slow process marked by a little more dexterity on one case, a slight improvement in judgment on another, a bit more confidence on a third. Not big jumps, just small steps forward. But when it's all over and the new surgeon is turned loose to practice his art, somehow he's ready. He has to be.

Every would-be surgeon travels the same general path. It's known as the residency system, a plan originated in 1895 by William Halsted, a professor of surgery at Johns Hopkins Hospital, and one which has persisted, with minor modifications, since that time. Any hospital which is authorized by the American Board of Surgery to train surgeons must have an approved program which follows this plan.

Briefly, the program consists of five years of training: one year as an intern, two years as an assistant resident, one year as first assistant resident and a final year as chief resident. In each succeeding year the trainee assumes more responsibility in every phase of patient management. In the final year he takes full responsibility for surgical patients in everything but name. The chief of the surgical service, or one of the attending surgeons, always shares the legal responsibility for any patient treated by a resident.

Internships are assigned, nationally, through a system known as the National Intern Matching Plan. Every medical student applies, in the fall of his senior year, to the hospital or hospitals at which he would like an appointment. He may apply to one hospital only; he may apply to ten or more. It's up to him.

There is a wide variety of internships available: rotating internships, during which the intern spends a month or two on each of the specialty services; mixed internships, six months of medicine and six of pathology; straight internships, all surgery or all medicine. If a student has not decided in what field of medicine he wants to specialize, or whether he wants to specialize at all, he'll probably pick a rotating internship. If he has made up his mind—subject, of course, to the possibility of a later change of heart—he'll take the appropriate specialized internship. I had decided that I wanted to be a surgeon, so I had applied for a straight surgical internship.

Sometime during the winter, after his marks have been submitted to the hospital chief of staff, the student will be asked to visit the hospital. He may be interviewed by one or several attending physicians—an attending physician being a doctor in private practice who holds a staff appointment at the hospital and who helps supervise the internship-residency program. Usually he will be interviewed by the director of the training program as well.

After the interviews are completed, in the early spring, the future intern makes up a list of the hospitals to which he has applied, with his number-one choice at the top, his last choice at the bottom. All the participating hospitals submit similar lists of the students they have interviewed. The lists are then gathered at a central office, fed into a computer, and pairings are made. The senior student gets an appointment at the hospital highest on his list that wants him.

This program, instituted in 1952, saves a great deal of chaos and anguish. Before that time neither students nor hospitals knew where they were at until the last moment. Hospitals like Massachusetts General and the New York Hospital—prime popular training centers—could leisurely pick and choose among the students. Other hospitals, not quite as well known, could not get commitments for internships until the students had found out whether they were rejected elsewhere. Worse, some students would accept an offer and then welsh on the agreement if a more attractive opening came through. Good hospitals often found it necessary to guarantee appointments to second-rate students just to be certain they had a full quota of interns. By the same token, top-ranking students who late in the year learned they hadn't made it at the General would find that the only available appointments still left were at third-rate hospitals. The matching system remedied all this.

Surgical training programs, though generally alike in that they must follow the residency system, may differ greatly from hospital to hospital. In university hospitals, for example, where the emphasis is on academic training and research, and where there may be qualified surgeons practicing full time in the hospital, supervision is maximal and responsibility, at least until the last year, is minimal. In city hospitals, on the other hand, there may be no full-time surgeons on the staff. Supervision is minimal, responsibility is great, beginning with the internship year. Private hospitals, without university affiliation, run the gamut from one extreme to another.

There is a great difference of opinion among practicing surgeons as to which type of training produces the best surgeon. Usually the views are prejudiced by the training the individual has had. University-trained surgeons argue that the man who has trained in a city hospital doesn't have the knowledge of physiology and biochemistry—the "book learning"—a compleat surgeon should have if he is to operate intelligently. They maintain that all the city-hospital-trained surgeon can do is take orders from the internist, function as a technician, and remove the organ or do the repair that the medical man says is necessary. The city-hospital-trained surgeons, on the other hand, claim that even though the university surgeon may know all there is to know about the serum sodium, he can't cut his way out of a paper bag. The fact is that either type of program produces excellent surgeons. Both systems work.

I took my surgical training at Bellevue Hospital in New York, a city hospital which was associated with three different medical schools. The First Division belonged to Columbia University; the Second to Cornell; the Third to New York University. A fourth surgical division belonged to Postgraduate, which is not a medical school but rather, as the name implies, a center which offers postgraduate training. Each of the four divisions ran a medical and surgical service, and each functioned separately within the hospital. We cooperated, and competed, with one another.

The division to which I had been accepted was the Second (Cornell) Surgical Division. Our immediate responsibility was to run the three surgical wards: L4 and M4 (male) and M5 (female). We also took care of any surgical problems that arose on the Second (Cornell) Medical Division, on the Cornell Neurological or Neurosurgical Division, or on the Second (Cornell) Genitourinary Division. In addition to providing surgical consultations to these allied services, the interns and assistant residents on our surgical division rotated through the neurosurgical and genitourinary divisions both to gain experience in these subspecialties and to supplement the house staff needed to run them.

The subspecialties were parceled out among the four divisions. New York University had the gynecology service,

Columbia the chest service, Cornell and Postgraduate the genitourinary service, and so on. The general policy was to assign a man to a subspecialty after internship, then bring him back to general surgery for the next six months. There were several possible services to which an assistant resident might be assigned: genitourinary surgery, thoracic surgery, neurosurgery, laboratory, pathology, etc. Wherever he went, the assistant resident stayed for six months; it took at least that long for him to master the technique he was expected to learn. Then off to another subspecialty and back again to general surgery. Thus, in his two years as an assistant resident he would become reasonably well trained in two subspecialties as well as in general surgery. He would then be ready for the job of first assistant resident. The assignments were made by the chief resident and approved by the chief of surgery.

As far as advancement is concerned, the chief of surgery can arrange his hospital training program in one of two ways. If he chooses to establish a "straight up" system, the interns who begin in the program planning to go through the entire residency, have no problems. If the hospital takes four general surgical interns, it has room five years later for four chief residents. The intern base is broadened by accepting interns who have already decided to go into some subspecialty. The four top jobs are created by dividing the surgical service into four separate parts and letting each chief resident supervise each part for three months.

On our division at Bellevue we had what is known as a "pyramid" system. We started with seven interns on general surgery, and five years later one would become chief resident. The pyramid was narrowed by several methods. Some of the interns might decide to go into one of the subspecialties, and after two years of general surgery, required by most subspecialties, they'd move into a different program. Others in the starting group would decide that the pace at Bellevue was too hectic and the competition too great. They'd drop out after a year or so and enter a private or a V.A. hospital with a "straight up" program. Some of the starters would be fired. If the guy was obviously a goof-up, this wasn't too painful; but if he was a nice fellow who just wasn't quite as good as the man with whom he was competing, it was sad.

Bellevue has been around a long time. It was founded in 1736 as a six-bed infirmary in New York's "Public Workhouse and House of Correction." At that time it was located near what is now the approach to the Brooklyn Bridge. In 1811, because of the expanding population, it was necessary to enlarge the hospital facility. The city acquired a farm in the area occupied by the present Bellevue, now bounded by Twenty-fifth and Thirtieth Streets and First Avenue and the East River Drive. Part of the farm purchased at the time was known as "Belle Vue," and the name, contracted, was kept for the hospital.

The hospital occupies several buildings. The main ones are the outpatient department, the nurses' residence, the psychiatric building, the morgue, and the general-hospital and administration building.

The general hospital wasn't built all at one time. Wings were added to the central portion, so that all areas are not of the same height; some sections have six stories, others seven. The central portion, in its front half, contains the administrative offices on the first floors, and the intern and resident quarters on the upper floors. The back of the building, bordering the East River Drive, contains on its ground floors the emergency ward and the blood bank. The doctors' dining room is in the basement.

The various wards are designated by letters. For example, on the ground floor of the southernmost wing of the hospital are A and B—medical wards—with A2 to A5 and B2 to B5 on the other floors of the buildings. The L and M wards are in the northernmost wing, with C through K, in alphabetical order, in the main section between them.

Every ward is assigned to one specialty or another. All the A and B wards are medical wards; all the L and M wards are surgical. I4 and K4 belong to the Second Genitourinary Service. F and G are male and female neurological wards. Pediatrics, gynecology and the other specialties each has its own ward or wards, the number depending on how active the service is.

Despite its medical school affiliations Bellevue was not, in any sense of the word, a university hospital. It was and is a city hospital. So the surgical training and experiences that this book deals with are those of a city-hospital-trained surgeon.

And, of course, Bellevue is not exactly like any other city hospital. It compares in size and patient types with Cook County in Chicago, Kings County in Brooklyn and Los Angeles General, but it has a personality of its own, and that personality influences the training of any resident who spends five years within its walls.

Which brings me to a point I want to make. This is the story of the making of a surgeon. It is the story of a "universal" experience in one sense, since the program I went through conforms to the general plan all surgeons, not only in the United States, must follow; but it is also the story of a unique experience, since it is the story of a particular surgeon, trained in a particular program at a particular time. I am hopeful that the experiences I relate will, in general, convey to the reader a sense of what must happen to any man before he arrives at the time in his life when society, and he, are willing to call him a surgeon.

Several years have elapsed since I completed my surgical training. It may, of course, be possible that the whole system of training has changed in that time. Things may be different now.

They may be—but they aren't. I am now, and have been for the past few years, an attending at a county hospital with a surgical training program associated with the University of Minnesota Medical School. I know the interns, the residents, the patients of 1970. The names and faces have changed; the problems haven't.

It is still difficult to get a patient transferred to the psychiatry service, impossible to find enough blood. Interns often have trouble tying knots, and residents lie awake nights worrying about their decisions. Addicts still stumble in with abscesses at two o'clock in the morning, and operating on broken hips is no less hectic. The essentials of surgical training are unchanged.

All that has really been added to the life of the would-be surgeon is more problems. With the advent of organ transplantation, the intern now has to worry about permits to "harvest" organs in addition to obtaining autopsy permits; the resident must keep in mind the need for a kidney or a heart when he decides to turn the respirator off on some vegetating body. And sometime in his five years he must also master the techniques of this new field of surgery. Surgical advances have complicated rather than simplified the making of a surgeon.

Now, watching young men enter training as inept interns to emerge five years later as capable surgeons, I still find it impossible to mark exactly the points of transition. I can only reaffirm what I said at the beginning—there are no giant steps. The making of a surgeon is a tedious, painstaking, laborious and time-consuming process. The man that suffers through it will never forget it. I never have.

The Making of a Surgeon

1

Bellevue: Breaking In

Bellevue is not an attractive hospital. The old buildings, all of brick and stone, are grimy with years of accumulated New York soot. The new buildings, also of brick, are rapidly getting that way. There are no lawns or trees to brighten the surroundings. It's all brick, asphalt and cement.

When you walk into the hospital through the front entrance you find yourself in an auditoriumlike waiting room with walls of chipped plaster. There are only a few hard wooden benches for patients and visitors. No bright colors, no comfortable seats. The total impression when I arrived for my interview was that of a railroad station lobby, complete even to the derelicts slumped and sleeping in the corners. All it lacked was the newsstand, and even that was partially compensated for by a portable rack being pushed slowly down the hall by a young man with cerebral palsy. I found the entire scene depressing.

My original plan, when I decided that I wanted to go into surgery, had been to apply for an appointment to a surgical internship at the Albany Hospital. The professor of surgery at Tufts, my medical school, resigned during my junior year and went to Albany as an associate professor. I admired the man. He was a rough, outspoken, somewhat vulgar individual, but he was an original thinker and a damn good operator (I really couldn't tell a good operator from one who was all thumbs, but interns and residents said he was and of course I believed them). I thought I'd enjoy training in his program.

But in November, when I looked into the internship and residency volume of the *Journal of the American Medical Association* to review the pertinent data—how many patients, how many operations, how many autopsies each year—for the Albany Hospital, my eye fell on the Bellevue Hospital listing just beneath it in the New York section. I had heard of Bellevue, of course—who hadn't? And, just for the hell of it, I applied. I chose the Second (Cornell) Surgical Division, rather than the Columbia, New York University or Postgraduate divisions, because I thought Cornell might be "classier" than any of the others. I really didn't give it much thought. I didn't think I'd get the appointment, and I didn't think I'd accept it if I did.

In February I started my interviews. Since Tufts is in Boston, I went first to its New England Medical Center, then up to Albany. At both hospitals I was treated very well and was favorably impressed. The hospitals were clean, the interns were well dressed, the intern quarters were comfortable, and no one seemed harried or tired. Now I was at Bellevue and the contrast was overwhelming.

I was interviewed by Dr. Russell Stevens, chief of surgery on the Cornell Division. I don't remember if he asked me any questions—he certainly didn't ask me anything about surgery. I have the impression now that we just talked in generalities while we looked each other over. The interview couldn't have lasted much more than five minutes. But when I left the office I understood quite clearly that the job was mine if I wanted it.

When my interview was ended I was delivered by Dr. Stevens' secretary into the hands of the chief resident, whose job it was to show me the wards where I'd be working, if and when I took the job at Bellevue.

Dr. Jerry Baker looked, to put it mildly, like a very sick man. He was slumped over and had huge bags under his eyes. He looked as if he hadn't been to bed in a week. After every statement he made, he would give a nervous little cough. I was afraid he was on the verge of collapsing. His white coat and pants looked as if they had been slept in. His shoes, which had been white at one time, were covered with a reddish-brown mixture that I could only assume was a combination of blood and dirt.

My God, I thought, if this is the chief resident, what must the interns look like?

We walked through a corridor which reeked of urine—the genitourinary ward—over to one of the male surgical wards. As we stopped at the entrance, Jerry gave a weak wave of his hand and said, "This is one of the wards where you'll be working, if you come here." He looked as if he wanted to add, "You're nuts if you do."

I looked—hard. It was quite a sight.

This ward, like all the other Bellevue wards, was nothing but a big rectangular room. There were eight beds perpendicular to each of the two long sides of the room, and another fourteen beds, in two rows, each head to head, in the center. There was a bedside stand, chipped and dirty, next to each bed. Otherwise there was nothing to separate one bed from another. There was no privacy.

At the front of the ward, near the nurses' station, lay a man who, even to my unpracticed eye, looked very sick indeed. He had tubes, it seemed, running in or out of every orifice, and he was moaning and tossing. He had kicked off his covers and I could see a huge bandage, partially soaked with blood, covering his abdomen.

"What's the matter with him?" I asked.

"Who?"

"That man over there. In the first bed."

"Oh, him," said Jerry, "we took his stomach out this morning. He had a helluvan ulcer."

"He seems to be having a lot of pain," I said. "Shouldn't somebody be doing something?"

"He'll get a shot," Jerry said, "as soon as Sharon finishes her coffee. Come on—let's have a cup." And he led me into a dingy kitchen just off the end of the ward.

Two nurses were sitting at a battered wooden table covered with an oilcloth. They were drinking black coffee out of huge mugs. Jerry introduced me, walked over to the stove and poured us each a cup. We sat down.

"How's Gonzalez doing?" Jerry asked Sharon Avery, the head nurse.

"Fine," she answered. "He moans a lot but he's all right. I'll give him a shot when I get back."

"How about Nielsen?"

"Which one?"

"Ralph, the one with the leg ulcer. The big boy in bed six."

"Nothing but trouble," Sharon answered. "Unless we stand right there he won't take his aureomycin. The other day I caught him holding the thermometer against the radiator when he thought I wasn't looking."

"We've got to get that guy out of here," Jerry said. "I think he picks at that ulcer at night. I'm going to tell him we'll bug him if he doesn't behave." (To "bug," in Bellevuese, meant to transfer to psychiatry.)

He turned to me. "Nielsen's from the Bowery. He likes it here and he'll do anything to stay. I wouldn't mind, but we need the bed."

The nurses said good-bye and left. We finished our coffee and got up.

"I'd show you the rest of the place," Jerry said, "but there isn't much point. The other male ward is just like this one.

The female ward's the same, only worse. You either like this hospital—or you hate it. I don't want to try to talk you into anything because, I warn you, if you come here you'll work your ass off. If you don't like the idea, go somewhere else.

"Nice meeting you," he said, sticking out his hand. "I've got some work to do," he added and slouched off down the hall. It took me twenty minutes to find my way out of the building.

I went back to Tufts, thought it all over for the next month, and when I submitted my list of preferences, I put Bellevue at the top.

I was eager and anxious to go to work; I couldn't imagine any hospital that would offer more of a challenge than Bellevue. Besides, strange as it may seem, I had been favorably impressed by Dr. Stevens, the chief of surgery, by Jerry Baker, the resident, and by Sharon Avery, the charge nurse. None of them wasted any time; none of them put on a show for my benefit. They were simply professionals, doing their job. They implied that if I wanted to help them with their horrendous task they'd welcome me; if not, they would go it alone. Jerry hadn't merely implied it; he had stated as much.

I asked myself, Why are they at Bellevue? Why is Dr. Russell Stevens—an eminent surgeon who has a fashionable and lucrative private practice with all the patients he could possibly need—sitting in a dingy office in Bellevue interviewing an applicant for an internship? Yet there he was, devoting many hours of his time to the care of the indigent at Bellevue, when he could have chosen to spend this time in leisure activities or working on the care of affluent patients. Why?

And why was Sharon there? With the perennial shortage of nurses she could certainly have taken a position at a white-tower hospital where she might have worked in attractive surroundings, at a more leisurely pace, on cleaner and more co-operative patients. Why was she sipping coffee in that grubby kitchen at Bellevue, when she might have been drinking it in an immaculate coffee shop at any one of innumerable other hospitals?

And Jerry, who looked as if he might collapse at any moment. Why hadn't he gone off to some training center where he could get eight hours' sleep a night, where he could earn a living wage, where he'd have a patient load that would leave him with time to read and study?

Why? I know the answer now but I suspected it even on that first day: because Bellevue, despite all its monstrous problems, offered the ultimate in challenge to anyone in the medical profession. If you climb to the top of Mount Everest you know that you've accomplished something; if you get to the top of some grassy knoll the feeling isn't there. Bellevue was like Everest; the white-tower hospitals were the grassy knolls. I was young and fresh and idealistic. I wanted to join Dr. Stevens, Sharon and Jerry and take a crack at conquering Everest.

When the results of the Intern Matching Plan were published, I had my appointment. On June 30, I entered the hospital to begin what turned out to be a seven-year hitch.

When I arrived at Bellevue, this time to stay, and took a close look at the place, I was somewhat less than ecstatic over what met my gaze. My previous visit had been sort of a lark; this time there was no turning back. I was committed for at least one year. The thought was something short of a cheerful one.

Suitcases in hand, I found my way to the proper office, signed in and asked for my room key. The secretary looked at her list, found a key and handed it to me, saying, "I'm sorry, Dr. Nolen, but for the moment we're a bit crowded. I've had to put you in the lounge on the fifth floor. It will only be temporary. We'll get you a room of your own as soon as we can."

I took the elevator to the fifth floor and found the lounge. It was in the front of the building, looking out on First Avenue. It couldn't have been much of a lounge. There wasn't anything in it except an old leather couch, two or three card tables (the kind with the checkerboard tops) and a few scattered chairs. No television set; not even a radio.

But if it had been a seedy lounge, it was a worse bedroom and an even worse dormitory. There were four beds, one in each corner of the room, each with a bureau beside it, and there were two clothes racks of the portable type in the middle of the room. There was no privacy at all. Brother, I thought, I really got the green banana! I got my release after two months of constant pleading with the hierarchy when a resident was transferred to another hospital. I was the third of the original four roommates to get his own room.

The last fellow, the one I left behind, is worth a short note. I had found him already established, in the best bed, of course, when I arrived. He apparently had been living in the lounge for some time, so I assumed he must be a resident rather than an intern. His name, he told me, was Dr. Schwartz.

He was, to put it plainly, a real pain in the ass. He worked on a neurological ward and was called two or three times every night he was on. When I wanted to read, on my nights off, he'd insist on talking to me about bizarre neurological diseases that I had never heard of. When I'd try to go to sleep he'd turn on his radio. I would have liked to tell him off, but since he was obviously a resident and I was an intern, I didn't dare, even though we were on different services.

When I got a private room before he did I couldn't understand it. I couldn't believe he actually preferred the lounge, but why else would a resident be left behind while I moved? I finally inquired of an intern I had met who was in neurology as to why Dr. Schwartz, the resident, was still living in the lounge.

"Schwartz? The resident?" my friend said. "You must be confused. The only Schwartz that I've ever seen around here is a second-year medical student who works as a flunky in the lab. A real bullshitter. No one can stand him. We ignore him."

"No," I said, "this must be a different Schwartz. He must work on another service." I was so mad I was livid, but I couldn't admit to this friend that some two-bit medical student had been stealing my toothpaste, keeping me awake and virtually driving me nuts for two months. I had been "taken" at Bellevue; it wouldn't be the last time.

Less than one minute after I put in an appearance the day after my arrival, I got the first chewing out of my Bellevue career.

"I'm Eddie Quist," said a doctor who was sitting at a small metal desk at the front end of M5, the female surgical ward, my first assignment. "You must be Bill Nolen. Where the hell have you been?"

"Eating," I answered. I had just finished a leisurely breakfast in the doctors' dining room.

"Around here we eat after we draw the blood. Where do you think you are, at the New York Hospital?"

"Gee, I'm sorry, Dr. Quist, I didn't think I was supposed to be here till eight."

"All right, all right," he said. "Don't worry about it. Grab that syringe and start drawing blood. Jean will show you who you've got to hit. This is Jean Swanson; Jean, Dr. Nolen."

A cheerful nurse, with a clean white handkerchief tucked into her uniform pocket, said, "Very nice to know you, Dr. Nolen. If you'll come with me, I'll show you which patients need to have blood drawn."

She walked down the row of beds, pushing a small table on rollers on which there were syringes and tubes, until she came to one in which a very obese woman, about fifty years old, was sitting. "This is Mrs. Pica, Dr. Nolen," Jean said. Then, after looking into a little red book next to the syringes, she added, "We need fifteen c.c.'s of blood." I picked up the tourniquet and put it on Mrs. Pica's arm. Then I looked through the needle supply for a #18, a relatively large bore needle, to put on the syringe which Jean handed me. "I can't seem to find a number eighteen needle, Miss Swanson," I said after a few seconds.

"There aren't any," said Miss Swanson.

"There aren't any?" I echoed. "Why not?"

"Central Supply didn't send us any today," she said.

"Why not?" I couldn't let it drop.

"Probably they're just out of them. That happens a lot. But there are plenty of number twenties."

I decided not to pursue the point in front of Mrs. Pica. I put the #20 needle on the syringe and looked at her arm. Please God, I silently prayed, "let her have nice big fat veins."

I looked down. The bulging blue line that I was hoping to see was nowhere in sight. "Maybe we should try the other arm," I said, reaching for a tourniquet.

"The other arm's worse, Doc," Mrs. Pica answered. "You better use this one."

I decided she was probably right and I felt in the ante-cubital fossa, the pit of the front of the elbow, for a vein.

There was something there, all right. I took the syringe, said another silent prayer and plunged in the needle. The blood practically gushed into the syringe.

"Nice going, Doc," Mrs. Pica said. "Dr. Ramsey, the one who left yesterday, he always had to stick me at least twice."

It's impossible to imagine how delighted I was with myself. I had only drawn blood once before, as a junior in medical school, and then I had stabbed my victim three times. I knew all about serum sodium, potassium and calcium, the things in Mrs. Pica's blood that we wanted to study, but the simple mechanical process of drawing the blood was something I had never learned. Which was, of course, why I was an intern.

The internship year, for an aspiring surgeon, is the one in which he acquires the basic mechanical skills that he will polish and perfect in the subsequent years as assistant resident and, hopefully, resident. But medical school graduates are all long on theory and very short on practice. We could discuss rheumatic heart disease with the professors, but we didn't know how to attach the electrocardiogram wires to the patient; I could recite the proper treatment for a fracture of both bones of the forearm, but I had never manipulated a bone, taken an x-ray or wet a roll of plaster. I had a long, long way to go.

We moved on to the next patient. "This is the only one left," Jean said. "Dr. Quist drew all the others. Mrs. Luchow, she cries a lot."

Sure enough, as our little contingent wheeled up to the bed Mrs. Luchow, a fat, dark woman with hair in the wildest disarray I have ever seen, burst into tears. "Oi," she said, pounding her hand to her forehead, "not again. Please, I beg you—let me die in peace."

"Now, now, Mrs. Luchow," Jean said, patting her on the hand, "don't you talk like that. We just need a very little blood, and Dr. Nolen is very good at getting it. Didn't you see how easy he was on Mrs. Pica?"

Mrs. Pica, who had been listening attentively to all that was being said, shouted from her position three beds away, "That's right, Sophie—don't you worry. This doctor's a good one. A helluva lot better than the one that left."

With that Mrs. Luchow stopped crying and stuck out her arm. I put on the tourniquet, turned and fixed the syringe, and when I looked back I smiled. There, bulging forth like a relief map of the Rhine River, stood a vein as big as a lead pencil. A cinch.

With all the confidence of the ignorant I stuck the needle through the skin and on into the vein. But nothing happened.

That's odd, I thought to myself, and pulled back more vigorously on the syringe. Still nothing. I stared down at the arm. The entire area around the vein was rapidly becoming black and blue.

"Dr. Nolen," Jean whispered, "you've gone through the vein. You'd better take it out and try again on the other arm."

As I pulled out the needle the blood poured forth from the hole I had made, all over Mrs. Luchow's gown and onto the sheet. Jean reached up and quickly released the tourniquet, which I had forgotten to do, and the blood stopped.

Mrs. Luchow, who had kept her head averted through the entire procedure, now looked around. "It hurt," she said, "but not too much. You're not bad, Doc." She thought the job was over.

"I'm afraid I'm going to have to stick you just one more time, Mrs. Luchow. There was something wrong with that vein," I lied.

"No, no," she shouted, pulling back her arms, "not again!" Every patient in the ward was now watching us.

"Please, Mrs. Luchow," I pleaded, "just one more time?"

"All right," she sobbed, sticking out her arm, "but just this once."

I put the tourniquet on her left arm, picked up the syringe and looked down. This vein was just as inviting as the other.

But now I moved cautiously. First through the skin, then gently into the vein. This time I was certain I was in, and not through the vein. I drew back on the syringe. It wouldn't budge.

"Damn it," I muttered to Jean, "this syringe is stuck."

"Did you flush it out?" she asked.

"No," I said, "why should I? Isn't this a fresh syringe?"

"No, it's the same one you used on the other arm."

"My God, you mean you gave me a used syringe?"

"Of course," Jean said. "How many syringes do you think we have? They only sent us four today and one of those leaked. We had to draw blood from eight patients."

I resigned myself to the situation. "Have you got another syringe I can slip onto this needle?" I asked.

"I'll get you one out of the sink," Jean said. She rushed

to the front of the ward, picked up a syringe, came back and
flushed it out with the saline solution on the cart. Gingerly
I wiggled the plugged syringe off the needle and quickly
hooked the cleansed one on. I was relieved to see the blood
flow smoothly into the barrel.

"Ten c.c.'s," said Jean. I drew it off, loosened the tourniquet and withdrew the needle.

"Bend your arm, please, Mrs. Luchow," I said. "We're
all through."

"Thank God, thank God," said Mrs. Luchow, opening
her eyes. "Please—tomorrow no blood."

"Not if I can help it," I said, and I certainly meant it.

After I had finished my blood-drawing chores—credita-
bly, I thought—I walked back to the front of the ward and
asked, "What do I do next, Dr. Quist?"

"First," he said, "cut out the Dr. Quist bullshit. Save the
'Doctor' routine for Dr. Stevens. My name is Eddie." He
looked at his watch. "We've got about five minutes before
rounds. Let's have a cup of coffee and I'll fill you in."

We walked back to the kitchen—a small room with a
stove, a battered table, a refrigerator and a few chairs. "Mary,"
Eddie said to a big Negro woman who was cooking something
on the stove, "this is Dr. Nolen, one of the new interns. We'd
like some coffee."

"Help yourselves," she said, smiling. "Glad to know you,
Dr. Nolen. Hope you like it here."

We poured ourselves coffee and sat down.

"Now listen, Bill—it is Bill, isn't it?" I nodded and Eddie
continued, "In about five minutes Ron or Ernie will arrive.
Probably Ron today, because Ernie is operating this morning.
Ron's the chief resident. He runs the whole show. What he
says goes. You'll meet him officially this afternoon at four
when we all meet for card rounds." These, as I soon found
out, were the late-afternoon meetings of the entire surgical
staff of the Second Surgical Division. They took place at four-
thirty every afternoon—sometimes at four if the operating

schedule had been a light one. At these meetings either Ron Miller or Ernie Gallow or George Walters would review with each assistant resident all the things that had happened on his ward during the day.

Each assistant resident made out a 4″ x 6″ card on every patient on the ward, giving his name, hospital number, date of admission and diagnosis. The assistant resident always kept these cards in his pocket and at these evening meetings he would hand them to whichever of the senior men was running the session. He in turn would go through them one by one. In this way they found out what new patients had been admitted during the day and what progress each patient had made since morning rounds. This was also the time when the results of the work assigned during the morning were reported. What was Mrs. Pica's hemoglobin? Did the proctoscopy on Rodriguez show anything? Where were Mr. Flanders' stomach films? It was a system which allowed a check on the assistant resident's and intern's work. At the same time it kept the first assistants and residents up to date on all their charges.

"Anyway," Eddie continued, "when Ron comes, you and I and Jean will make rounds with him. You push the chart rack, Jean will carry the order book and I'll take the scut book—that little red volume you saw on the table out there. That's your bible for the next twelve months.

"Ron will want to know anything that's new about each patient. I'll answer his questions today because you don't know the ward. After tomorrow you do all the talking. Then, if he wants any work done, I'll write it in the scut book. Any new orders, medicines or such, you write in the order book. Got it?"

"Got it," I said.

"Okay, let's get to the ward."

We arrived almost simultaneously with Ron Miller, the chief resident of our general surgical wards. How to describe him? Dynamic is all I can think of. Average height, medium build, hairline receding, about thirty years old. His eyes looked right through you. I never met anyone who could stare him down. Energy seemed to burst out of him. "Okay, kiddies, let's go." This was the greeting I was to hear almost every morning for the next twelve months.

Those first rounds remain a hazy memory. It was all new to me and I had difficulty keeping things clear. But they were, I suppose, like all the other rounds that year. We'd spend one minute, maybe two or three, at each bed. Ron would say, "How are you today, sweetie?" to big fat Sophie Luchow. And Mrs. Luchow would practically drool on him. "Wonderful, Doctor, just wonderful!" Ron knew how to make them smile.

Then he'd turn to Eddie—or me after the first day—and ask, "What's Sophie's last hemoglobin? . . . When was it done? . . . Is she on any iron?" Bark, bark, bark, and brother, you'd better have the answers. If you had to thumb through the chart looking things up, Ron would gaze off into space, drumming with his fingers on the end of the bed as if to say, "Jee-sus! What a stupid intern!" Then, if the hemoglobin hadn't been done for two weeks, he might say, "Get one," and down would go the order in the scut book and off we'd all go to the next patient.

That might be Mrs. Rodriguez, who had had her stomach out the day before. "Hello, beautiful," Ron would say, taking her hand and feeling her pulse, "how are you this morning?"

"No good," Mrs. Rodriguez would murmur. "No good today."

"Well, don't you worry," Ron would answer, patting her hand, "we're going to make you well."

Then would come the barrage: "Is the stomach tube working all right? . . . How much urine has she put out in the last twenty-four hours? . . . Did you draw a serum potassium this morning? . . . How much does she weigh?"

At first I didn't always have all the answers, but damn

soon I learned that I had better have them—or one helluva good reason why I didn't. It was amazing how much information I learned to keep in my head, or so I thought then.

After rounds, on the first morning, when we got back to the front of the ward, Ron said, "Okay, boys, I need a quick cup before I hit the next ward." He headed for the kitchen. Eddie and Jean behind him, and me behind them. They sat down and I grabbed a chair. I was about to lower myself into it when Ron looked up. "Say, Bill, you must be one great intern if you think you've got time for a cup of coffee. I'd like to stick around and see you work. You must move like the wind."

My face flushed and I started to get up. Ron laughed and said, "Don't let me scare you. Sit down. You've got a lot to learn, that's all. Have some coffee now. By tomorrow I think you'll find you won't have time to sit. You're on a treadmill Bill, but you don't know it yet. Relax while you still think you can."

Ron was right, of course. Time, as I quickly learned, was the secret of getting through a surgical internship. You learned how to do your work quickly and efficiently, or you didn't get anything else done. This included eating and sleeping— because eating and sleeping were luxuries for an intern. He ate and slept only as he deserved to eat and sleep; leisurely meals and long hours in bed were never for the intern, but if you hustled you could at least bolt two or three meals a day and find five hours for the sack.

When we finished our coffee Eddie and I went back to the ward and Eddie showed me what he had written down. It hadn't sounded like much when we were flitting from bed to bed, but now I could see what I was in for. I don't remember the exact load for that first day, of course, but I lived with that scut book for twelve months and I can compose a representative page without much difficulty. It might look something like this:

1. *Check hemoglobin and urine on Pica*
2. *Find upper G.I. films on Lane*
3. *X-match three units for Frost*
4. *Remove stitches from Rollins*
5. *Proctoscope Flanders*
6. *Chest film on Johnson*

Even written down, the list didn't seem as formidable as it was. But in Bellevue even the simplest of tasks was complicated by the shortage of help and lack of equipment. The first day, or week, the list would probably have taken me most of the day to accomplish. Partly because I was inept, it's true, but also in part because I hadn't yet learned anything about efficiency.

I would have done each task as listed, without any regard to the other jobs. I would have gone all over the hospital looking for the lost stomach films, and then gone to the x-ray department later to take Mrs. Johnson for her chest film. This lack of foresight would have cost me hours and miles that I later learned to conserve.

Since there is no lab technician to check hemoglobin and urine on Mrs. Pica, at least not on our division, I have to run to the lab on the floor below, the Second Surgical interns' lab, to get a pipette with which to check the hemoglobin. Of course, the laboratory is a shambles. It's always a shambles. Neither I nor my fellow interns ever clean it till Ron, on one of his periodic rampages, walks in and sees what a sight it is. Then we clean it on our evening off.

I have a terrible time finding a pipette. The ones in the sink are either plugged with blood or broken. I look in our favorite hiding places and none are there. Finally I lift up the centrifuge, on a long shot, and lo and behold, a clean pipette. One of my fellow interns has hidden it there. I grab it and run. (Of course, on my first day I wouldn't have known the ropes; I'd have spent half an hour looking for a pipette and finally would have had to bring Eddie down to find one for me.)

Now I dash back upstairs and track down Mrs. Pica. I stick her finger with the needle and quickly apply the pipette. I suck on the tube and up comes the blood, too high. Fortunately it doesn't get in my mouth. I let a little out. Too low. I try again. Too high. On the first day I would have fooled with this till the pipette clotted and I'd have had to begin all over again. At the end of two weeks as an intern I'd suck it up and if I got too much I'd say, "To hell with it," and use it. When I compared the mixture with the standard color, I'd have dropped the value, mentally, a small amount. Not perfect, but close enough, I'd figure. (After one month as an intern I'd be able to hit the proper level on the pipette almost automatically, and the first time. Just one example of how, by constant repetition, the surgical intern learns what he needs to survive, and to care for patients.)

The urinalysis is somewhat less of a problem. On the male ward I grab a urinal, hand it to the patient and stand there until he gives me a specimen. But on the female ward, I soon learned, what you did was to track down Lena—a nurse's aid who really knew how to work—and she'd take a bedpan to the patient and get a specimen for you. If you asked one of the student nurses it might take all morning to get the specimen.

Provided the proper reagents are in the laboratory, the urinalysis can be done in a few minutes. If they aren't there, you would have to run over to the medicine lab in the A and B building, two blocks away, to do the urinalysis. After one trip like this, you and your fellow interns learned to keep the proper reagents in your own little lab.

As for finding the upper G.I. (gastrointestinal) films on Mrs. Lane . . . Now, after all these years, my stomach gets jumpy at the mere thought of this task. Just the fact that Ron asked me to get the films means that they must be lost, and what a problem that creates! Needles in haystacks are far easier to find than lost films at Bellevue.

I can't even begin to count the hours I spent looking for

films during that first year at Bellevue. First I'd look through the x-ray files on the ward in the hope that the films had been alphabetically misplaced. Then I'd check our other two wards. Next I'd go to the x-ray department in the I and K building; then over to the C and D building, a city block away. This took time and lots of it; and when I had done it all I still might not have the films. If they were "interesting"—films that showed an unusual stomach tumor, for example—one of the radiologists might have lifted them for an x-ray conference, or worse, for his own personal collection. Either way, there was nothing left to do but put in another request for films— which might be done in a week or two, depending on how heavy the x-ray schedule was.

When I was at Bellevue, cross-matching blood was one of the intern's jobs. It isn't any longer, except in emergencies, and it damn well shouldn't be. I think it's fine for an intern to know how, but, practically, it's best left to technicians who can do the job carefully and regularly. I was the fastest cross-matcher on the division after the first two months, but I wasn't the most accurate. Fortunately none of the patients I cross-matched ever had a major reaction, but I have only the Lord to thank for that. My technique certainly didn't offer them much protection.

Removing the stitches from Rollins was a cinch, provided there were any scissors on the treatment cart. If there weren't, then the job might have to wait till the next day.

One incident might well be mentioned here, since it shows just how impractical-minded we interns were at the beginning of the year.

On rounds one day, early in the internship year, the resident, or possibly the assistant resident—told one of my fellow interns to "Take out half the stitches on Mr. Ross," a patient who had had his gall bladder removed a week earlier.

Taking out "half the stitches," to the assistant resident, meant taking out alternate stitches. This is sometimes done when a wound is almost healed but is possibly not quite strong enough to stick together without some support. Of course what the intern did was to remove every stitch from half the wound. The skin edges promptly separated on that half, fortunately not a serious complication. But it demonstrates how, despite all our medical school knowledge, we were not exactly on a par with Socrates when it came to logic.

Proctoscoping Flanders involved putting him on a stretcher, wheeling him into the side room and examining his lower bowel through a long metal pipe. This was not a difficult task either, as long as the proctoscope bulb was working —and once you had mastered the technique. Another one of the mechanical procedures an intern had to learn.

To get a chest film on Mrs. Johnson was one of those jobs that would be easy at most hospitals (just write the order and all sorts of ancillary help would come to your assistance), but at Bellevue it was much more difficult. It meant, if you wanted the film that day, that you would load Mrs. Johnson onto the stretcher yourself, wheel her to X-ray, and pick her and the film up later. Again, it took time.

It didn't take me long to learn the ropes and to use any and all shortcuts I could muster. Looking at the list even now, I automatically block out a plan: first, I'll remove the stitches, before anyone swipes the scissors. It's early, so I'll get the cast change done while the fracture room is empty. I'll proctoscope Flanders next, because that has to be done in the side room near the lab, and while I'm down there I'll pick up a pipette so that I can do the hemoglobin on Pica when I get back.

By this time it's almost eleven. I look quickly for Mrs. Lane's films in our own files and when I don't find them I load Mrs. Johnson onto the stretcher. But before I take her to the x-ray department, I draw some blood from Mr. Frost.

I wheel Mrs. Johnson to the elevator and drop her off at the x-ray department on the first floor to have her films taken. While I'm there I look for Mrs. Lane's films and I find them. Then I walk to the blood bank, on the first floor just above the doctors' dining room, and I set up a cross-match on Mr. Frost.

Now it's eleven-thirty and the doctor's dining room is open, so while the cross-match incubates, I slip downstairs for a quick lunch. Fifteen minutes later I come upstairs, read the cross-match, walk back through X-ray, pick up Mrs. Johnson and her chest film, and return with it to the ward. All neat and efficient—the only way for any intern to work if he wants to survive. Some interns never could learn to think of the economical approach to their work. Not only did the internship year almost kill them; they never did become "good" interns.

An intern isn't expected to be a whiz kid. It's accepted that if he was bright enough to get through medical school he isn't a dunce, but no one counts on him to contribute anything cerebral to the running of the division. There are plenty of others to provide the brainpower. What is needed from an intern is muscle and stamina. As a former professor of mine used to say, "I don't give a damn about the intern who got straight A's; give me the one who will get out of bed at night."

But on our division, though it was true that I wasn't expected to come up with anything brilliant and that I could call for help any time I needed it, it was also true that once I had learned to do something, it was permissible for me to just go ahead and do it the next time the occasion arose. There was no point in utilizing the time and energy of two men in situations where one could do the job. There was too much to be done to allow any duplication of effort.

Eddie Quist made this very clear to me during my first few weeks as his intern on the female surgery ward. We had one patient, a Mrs. Simpson, who had cirrhosis of the liver—a very common disease among Bellevue patients—and every few days when her abdominal cavity was filled up with fluid, she would have to be "tapped." Technically, this procedure is known as a paracentesis. With the patient sitting on the edge of the bed, the doctor injects the abdominal wall with a local anesthetic and then pushes a trocar—a pointed metal tube about one fourth of an inch in diameter—into the abdomen. After all the fluid has leaked out into the basin or bottle which is held beneath the open end of the tube, the trocar is withdrawn and a bandage is placed over the hole.

I had never witnessed a paracentesis while I was in medical school, so the first time Ron suggested that it was time to tap Mrs. Simpson and Eddie told me to go ahead and do it, I told him I didn't know how, that I had never seen it done.

"Okay," Eddie said after rounds, "run up to Central Supply and get a paracentesis set and I'll show you how."

"Running up to Central Supply" was a trick I had learned quickly at Bellevue. If I had asked the nurse to order a paracentesis set I'd have gotten one, all right—maybe in half an hour, maybe in half a day. It would have depended on how soon she could find an aide to make the trip. I saved time by running this sort of errand myself.

I got the set and put some curtains around Mrs. Simpson's bed; then Eddie came over and did the tap while I watched. A few days later, when Mrs. Simpson's belly had refilled with fluid and we were told to tap her, I again got the set, brought over the curtains and called Eddie. He was busy at the front desk filling out x-ray requisition cards.

"You don't need me," he shouted. "Go ahead."

So I did. I was nervous about it, but Eddie was right. I didn't need him. It was a relatively simple procedure, and after watching him once, I could do it alone and from then on I did.

During my first few weeks as an intern I learned to do a number of things that I had never done before. I learned to take out stitches, to draw blood, to change dressings using sterile technique, to proctoscope patients. I even became reasonably adept at sewing up minor lacerations, which were a dime a dozen at Bellevue. And as soon as I had shown that I could do these things I was on my own. It gave me a feeling of great power and a wonderful sense of accomplishment.

One of the dangers of this system, and one to which I succumbed, was that of deciding prematurely that you had some technique mastered. It was a trap into which I fell not once but dozens of times in the course of my surgical training.

My first experience with this pitfall remains indelibly stamped on my mind. It was a stupid error to make and I still blush when I think about it.

One of our patients, a Mrs. Rogers, had had an operation on her bowel and had developed some postoperative complication—I don't remember precisely what—that made it necessary for us to feed her intravenously for almost three weeks. By this time I had been an intern for about a month and had become very proficient at sticking needles into veins, but after the first two weeks all of Mrs. Rogers' visible veins had been used. I just couldn't find another spot for a needle and I told Eddie so.

"Get a minor-surgery set," he said, "and I'll help you do a cutdown on her." A cutdown, I should explain, is a procedure whereby, under local anesthesia, an incision is made in a vein and a plastic tube inserted through which fluids can be given to the patient. It can be left in place for several days.

I had watched Eddie do a cutdown just a few days earlier, so when I brought the minor-surgery set down to the ward and he wasn't around, I decided to go ahead with it myself. I asked a student nurse to help me and together we set up the curtains and got the light plugged in. Then I put my gloves on and went to work.

I infiltrated the skin of the ankle with the local anesthetic, made a small incision, and just as I had seen Eddie do, began spreading the tissues with my clamp looking for the vein. I spread and I spread, but I couldn't find the vein. I searched for ten minutes. By this time I was beginning to perspire. The student nurse was giving me funny looks as I muttered things like "Where the hell is that vein?," "I wonder if it's clotted?" and "That goddamn thing *must* be here."

The novocaine was wearing off and Mrs. Rogers started to wince as I spread the tissues more vigorously—almost wildly, in my search for this elusive blood vessel. After half an hour, soaking wet with perspiration, I turned to the student nurse and said, "Miss Brown, please find Dr. Quist and ask him to come here for a minute."

Miss Brown, I swear, breathed a sigh of relief. She virtually ran from the bedside, and after several phone calls located Dr. Quist in the outpatient department. He was at my side about five minutes later.

"Eddie," I said, giving him a shamefaced glance, "Mrs. Rogers doesn't seem to have any veins in her ankle. What do you suggest I do?"

He took one look at my incision and said, quietly, "Put a little more novocaine in just to the inside of your incision and widen your cut."

I did as he said.

"Now spread the skin with your clamp."

I followed his directions. There lay a big bulging vein.

"Okay now?" he asked.

"Fine," I said, looking at him with what I suppose must have been the most grateful eyes in the hospital. "I can manage now."

He smiled and walked away.

My mistake, of course, was in assuming that because Eddie had made the job look easy, it would be a cinch for me. Not only that, it had looked so easy that I neglected even to "read up" on the procedure, to check in an anatomy book the location of the vein I was looking for. I had plunged blindly ahead before I was ready.

Eddie had known I wasn't ready. He had specifically told me to wait and that he'd help me with this job. But my pride—my arrogance, whatever you want to call it—got the better of me. I had injured not only the patient but the opinion

Eddie had of my judgment. I was madder than hell—at myself. It's to Eddie's credit that he never mentioned the incident to me. I guess he knew I had learned a lesson. He probably also knew that I'd have to learn it again and again, as he undoubtedly had, but he didn't add insult to injury. I'm still grateful to him for his tact.

However, it was one thing to get into trouble out of ignorance; another, of quite a different complexion, to err out of laziness. This lesson I learned, not at my own expense, thank God, but through an incident involving one of my fellow interns a week or so after my cutdown debacle.

One evening we were all assembled in the fracture room for the usual end-of-the-day discussion of our patients. Lou Thell, a fellow intern, was told by Ron to bivalve the cast on George Baden. Mr. Baden, a denizen of the Bowery, had broken his leg a few days earlier.

"Lou," Ron said as he came to Baden's card, "I think you'd better split that cast. I noticed on rounds this morning that his toes were starting to swell a little. That cast may be too tight. When we finish with rounds you'd better have a look-see." Then he went on to the next patient.

This particular evening, card rounds lasted until six-fifteen. Card rounds, while Ron was resident, had a habit of lasting late. He never gave a damn if it was your evening off. We were there to work. But Lou was off that night and he had a heavy date. After rounds he went down to his ward, looked at Mr. Baden's cast and decided to hell with it—Ron was an alarmist. The toes looked O.K. to him; he would let the cast sit till next morning.

Things got busy on the wards that night. The intern who was covering Lou's ward got tied up in the emergency room until two o'clock in the morning and never made late rounds, as he would otherwise have done. Mr. Baden didn't complain about the cast. He had a high pain threshold.

Lou got to his ward a bit late the next morning—he had had a big night—and even though the first thing he did was split the cast on George Baden, he didn't get it off quickly enough. Ron, who wasn't operating that morning, arrived on the ward just as Lou was making the last cut with the saw. He walked over to Mr. Baden's bed with Dave Kelly, the assistant resident on the ward, and stood behind Lou as he lifted off the top half of the plaster shell.

Beneath the plaster, in the middle of the leg, was a circular spot as big as a silver dollar where the skin was not only black but where, clearly visible in the center of the necrotic slough, were the two ends of the fractured tibia. Mr. Baden's cast had been too tight.

The chances are that if Lou had bivalved the cast the previous evening, the sight would have been the same. The fracture had been a bad one, and the skin barely viable from the beginning. All this was irrelevant, of course. Lou had goofed off. He had put himself ahead of his job, and that was simply not tolerable.

"Dave," Ron said "get the intern from M4, and put Mr. Baden in traction. Lou, you come with me." And he walked off.

Half an hour later Lou was back on the ward, white-faced and shaken. I never knew what Ron said to him. Lou never brought it up, and of course, none of us ever asked him, but from that day on we all knew that Lou had had it. He worked his tail off, but when the year ended he left Bellevue. The sin of deliberate negligence in surgery is not forgivable.

2

The First Appendectomy

The patient, or better, victim, of my first major surgical venture was a man I'll call Mr. Polansky. He was fat, he weighed one hundred and ninety pounds and was five feet eight inches tall. He spoke only broken English. He had had a sore abdomen with all the classical signs and symptoms of appendicitis for twenty-four hours before he came to Bellevue.

After two months of my internship, though I had yet to do anything that could be decently called an "operation," I had had what I thought was a fair amount of operating time. I'd watched the assistant residents work, I'd tied knots, cut sutures and even, in order to remove a skin lesion, made an occasional incision. Frankly, I didn't think that surgery was going to be too damn difficult. I figured I was ready, and I was chomping at the bit to go, so when Mr. Polansky arrived I greeted him like a long-lost friend. He was overwhelmed at the interest I showed in his case. He probably couldn't understand why any doctor should be so fascinated by a case of appendicitis: wasn't it a common disease? It was just as well that he didn't realize my interest in him was so personal. He might have been frightened, and with good reason.

At any rate, I set some sort of record in preparing Mr. Polansky for surgery. He had arrived on the ward at four o'clock. By six I had examined him, checked his blood and urine, taken his chest x-ray and had him ready for the operating room.

George Walters, the senior resident on call that night, was to "assist" me during the operation. George was older than the rest of us. I was twenty-five at this time and he was thirty-two. He had taken his surgical training in Europe and was spending one year as a senior resident in an American hospital to establish eligibility for the American College of Surgeons. He had had more experience than the other residents and it took a lot to disturb his equanimity in the operating room. As it turned out, this made him the ideal assistant for me.

It was ten o'clock when we wheeled Mr. Polansky to the operating room. At Bellevue, at night, only two operating rooms were kept open—there were six or more going all day —so we had to wait our turn. In the time I had to myself before the operation I had reread the section on appendectomy in the *Atlas of Operative Technique* in our surgical library, and had spent half an hour tying knots on the bedpost in my room. I was, I felt, "ready."

I delivered Mr. Polansky to the operating room and started an intravenous going in his arm. Then I left him to the care of the anesthetist. I had ordered a sedative prior to surgery, so Mr. Polansky was drowsy. The anesthetist, after checking his chart, soon had him sleeping.

Once he was asleep I scrubbed the enormous expanse of Mr. Polansky's abdomen for ten minutes. Then, while George placed the sterile drapes, I scrubbed my own hands for another five, mentally reviewing each step of the operation as I did so. Donning gown and gloves I took my place on the right side of the operating-room table. The nurse handed me the scalpel. I was ready to begin.

Suddenly my entire attitude changed. A split second

earlier I had been supremely confident; now, with the knife finally in my hand, I stared down at Mr. Polansky's abdomen and for the life of me could not decide where to make the incision. The "landmarks" had disappeared. There was too much belly.

George waited a few seconds, then looked up at me and said, "Go ahead."

"What?" I asked.

"Make the incision," said George.

"Where?" I asked.

"Where?"

"Yes," I answered, "where?"

"Why, here, of course," said George and drew an imaginary line on the abdomen with his fingers.

I took the scalpel and followed where he had directed. I barely scratched Mr. Polansky.

"Press a little harder," George directed. I did. The blade went through the skin to a depth of perhaps one sixteenth of an inch.

"Deeper," said George.

There are five layers of tissue in the abdominal wall: skin, fat, fascia (a tough membranous tissue), muscle and peritoneum (the smooth, glistening, transparent inner lining of the abdomen). I cut down into the fat. Another sixteenth of an inch.

"Bill," said George, looking up at me, "this patient is big. There's at least three inches of fat to get through before we even reach the fascia. At the rate you're going, we won't be into the abdomen for another four hours. For God's sake, will you cut?"

I made up my mind not to be hesitant. I pressed down hard on the knife, and suddenly we were not only through the fat but through the fascia as well.

"Not that hard," George shouted, grabbing my right wrist with his left hand while with his other hand he plunged a gauze pack into the wound to stop the bleeding. "Start clamping," he told me.

The nurse handed us hemostats and we applied them to the numerous vessels I had so hastily opened. "All right," George said, "start tying."

I took the ligature material from the nurse and began to tie off the vessels. Or rather, I tried to tie off the vessels, because suddenly my knot-tying proficiency had melted away. The casual dexterity I had displayed on the bedpost a short hour ago was nowhere in evidence. My fingers, greasy with fat, simply would not perform. My ties slipped off the vessels, the sutures snapped in my fingers, at one point I even managed to tie the end of my rubber glove into the wound. It was, to put it bluntly, a performance in fumbling that would have made Robert Benchley blush.

Here I must give my first paean of praise to George. His patience during the entire performance was nothing short of miraculous. The temptation to pick up the catgut and do the tying himself must have been strong. He could have tied off all the vessels in two minutes. It took me twenty.

Finally we were ready to proceed. "Now," George directed, "split the muscle. But gently, please."

I reverted to my earlier tack. Fiber by fiber I spread the muscle which was the last layer but one that kept us from the inside of the abdomen. Each time I separated the fibers and withdrew my clamp, the fibers rolled together again. After five minutes I was no nearer the appendix than I had been at the start.

George could stand it no longer. But he was apparently afraid to suggest I take a more aggressive approach, fearing I would stick the clamp into, or possibly through, the entire abdomen. Instead he suggested that he help me by spreading the muscle in one direction while I spread it in the other. I made my usual infinitesimal attack on the muscle. In one fell swoop George spread the rest.

"Very well done," he complimented me. "Now let's get in."

We each took a clamp and picked up the tissue-paper-thin peritoneum. After two or three hesitant attacks with the scalpel I finally opened it. We were in the abdomen.

"Now," said George, "put your fingers in, feel the cecum [the portion of the bowel to which the appendix is attached] and bring it into the wound."

I stuck my right hand into the abdomen. I felt around— but what was I feeling? I had no idea.

It had always looked so simple when the senior resident did it. Open the abdomen, reach inside, pull up the appendix. Nothing to it. But apparently there was.

Everything felt the same to me. The small intestine, the large intestine, the cecum—how did one tell them apart without seeing them? I grabbed something and pulled it into the wound. Small intestine. No good. Put it back. I grabbed again. This time it was the sigmoid colon. Put it back. On my third try I had the small intestine again.

"The appendix must be in an abnormal position," I said to George. "I can't seem to find it."

"Mind if I try?" he asked.

"Not at all," I answered. "I wish you would."

Two of his fingers disappeared into the wound. Five seconds later they emerged, cecum between them, with the appendix flopping from it.

"Stuck down a little," he said kindly. "That's probably why you didn't feel it. It's a hot one," he added. "Let's get at it."

The nurse handed me the hemostats, and one by one I applied them to the mesentery of the appendix—the veil of tissue in which the blood vessels run. With George holding the veil between his fingers I had no trouble; I took the ligatures and tied the vessels without a single error. My confidence was coming back.

"Now," George directed, "put in your purse string." (The

cecum is a portion of the bowel which has the shape of half a hemisphere. The appendix projects from its surface like a finger. In an appendectomy the routine procedure is to tie the appendix at its base and cut it off a little beyond the tie. Then the remaining stump is inverted into the cecum and kept there by tying the purse-string stitch. This was the stitch I was now going to sew.)

It went horribly. The wall of the cecum is not very thick —perhaps one eighth of an inch. The suture must be placed deeply enough in the wall so that it won't cut through when tied, but not so deep as to pass all the way through the wall. My sutures were alternately too superficial or too deep, but eventually I got the job done.

"All right," said George, "let's get the appendix out of here. Tie off the base."

I did.

"Now cut off the appendix."

At least in this, the definitive act of the operation, I would be decisive. I took the knife and with one quick slash cut through the appendix—too close to the ligature.

"Oh oh, watch it," said George. "That tie is going to slip."

It did. The appendiceal stump lay there, open. I felt faint.

"Don't panic," said George. "We've still got the purse string. I'll push the stump in—you pull up the stitch and tie. That will take care of it."

I picked up the two ends of the suture and put in the first stitch. George shoved the open stump into the cecum. It disappeared as I snugged my tie. Beautiful.

"Two more knots," said George. "Just to be safe."

I tied the first knot and breathed a sigh of relief. The appendiceal stump remained out of sight. On the third knot— for the sake of security—I pulled a little tighter. The stitch broke; the open stump popped up; the cecum disappeared into the abdomen. I broke out in a cold sweat and my knees started to crumble.

Even George momentarily lost his composure. "For Christ's sake, Bill," he said, grasping desperately for the bowel, "what did you have to do that for?" The low point of the operation had been reached.

By the time we had retrieved the cecum, Mr. Polansky's peritoneal cavity had been contaminated. My self-confidence was shattered. And still George let me continue. True, he all but held my hand as we retied and resutured, but the instruments were in my hand.

The closure was anticlimactic. Once I had the peritoneum sutured, things went reasonably smoothly. Two hours after we began, the operation was over. "Nice job," George said, doing his best to sound sincere.

"Thanks," I answered, lamely.

The scrub nurse laughed.

Mr. Polansky recovered, I am happy to report, though not without a long and complicated convalescence. His bowel refused to function normally for two weeks and he became enormously distended. He was referred to at our nightly conferences as "Dr. Nolen's pregnant man." Each time the reference was made, it elicited a shudder from me.

During his convalescence I spent every spare moment I could at Mr. Polansky's bedside. My feelings of guilt and responsibility were overwhelming. If he had died I think I would have given up surgery for good.

3

Patients and Patience

Before coming to Bellevue, in the course of my medical school training, most of my meager experience had been with patients in private hospitals, well-to-do people who co-operated with us medical students at the request of their private doctor. It didn't take me long to see that there was an enormous sociological gap between Bellevue patients and private patients. Our Bellevue patients didn't think like private patients.

Take their attitude toward hospitalization. Most private patients have absolutely no desire to be hospitalized. They'd rather be in their nice, comfortable, warm homes, drinking martinis, eating steak, surrounded by their families. The most luxurious of hospitals can't offer the comforts of home.

But what if you have no home? What if you sleep in doorways in the warm weather and in a flophouse in the cold? What if you never know where your next meal is coming from and have no family to solace you? What, then, is your attitude toward hospitalization?

Probably like George Harrington's. The rich man goes to Miami for a few weeks every February; George came to Bellevue and had an operation. It wasn't difficult to arrange, if you knew the ropes. One year George complained of severe pain and a "lump" in the groin. He convinced an intern that he had a hernia and was admitted to have it repaired.

The next year it was a hemorrhoidectomy. Everyone has hemorrhoidal veins; they're a normal part of our anatomy. George claimed his bled and were painful. We removed them and he had three weeks in the hospital.

The following winter it was another hernia, the other side. By then I was on to his game and thought I'd see if he'd admit it. But George was no dope. When his hernia was healed and he was ready to be discharged, I made a big point of examining George's legs.

"George," I said, "you've got a few varicose veins here. Maybe we ought to fix them. What do you say?"

"No, thanks, Doc," he answered.

"Sure, George? It'll mean another couple of weeks in the hospital."

George smiled. "I'll tell you, Doc, I've had a pretty good rest for the last two weeks. Three meals a day and a warm bed. It's almost spring now and I can manage till next winter. Thanks, anyway, but I'm saving those veins for next February."

Sure enough, the next February George came back in and we operated on his veins.

The desire to be in the hospital led some of our patients to employ devious methods for gaining admission. On one occasion, for example, when I was working in the A.O. (admitting office), a fellow named Chad Davis came in looking to be admitted. Chad had a leg ulcer, which is as common as lice among the Bowery residents. These ulcerated sections on the lower leg develop when bruised areas go untreated. If the skin is dirty, as on our patients it always was, bacteria break through the bruised tissue and set up an inflammation which, if untreated, causes a complete breakdown of the skin. The broken-down area is even more susceptible to infection, and a vicious cycle is established.

Usually we treated these leg ulcers in the O.P.D. (outpatient department) with salves and bandages; it had to be an exceptionally severe wound to warrant hospitalization. If we weren't rigid about our admission requirements, we could have had a leg-ulcer patient occupying every bed in the hospital.

Chad knew the rules. He was a repeater, a guy who had been on our wards before with a variety of ailments, and he was aware of our leg-ulcer policy, but this leg ulcer—it involved the entire lower half of the inside of his leg—was a beauty and he knew it. He figured it would be enough to get him in.

I took him into an examining room and studied it. "It's a bad one, Chad," I admitted.

"Yeah, ain't it, Doc?" There was a note of pride in his voice. "It hurts like hell, too," he added with a smile.

If it had been down to bare bone I'd have sent him right in, but there was still some fat and muscle in the ulcer bed. As it was, I couldn't make up my mind. I decided I'd check his temperature. If it was up, I'd take him in. I had the nurse give him a basin of water to wash his leg, stuck a thermometer in his mouth and went off to see another patient. Five minutes later I came back and looked at the thermometer. His temperature was 104. "Pretty hot, Chad," I said.

"Am I, Doc? I been feeling kind of feverish."

I was about to send him on up when I had an idea. "Let me check it again. This thermometer may be broken." I got a new one, put it in his mouth and left. A few seconds later I tiptoed back and flung open the door. Sure enough, Chad was holding the thermometer in the pan of hot water. I caught him, literally, red-handed.

"Goddamn it, Doc," he said, "you're getting too smart."

"Sorry, Chad," I told him, "I guess I've been around too long."

He stood up and pulled on his pants. "No hard feelings, I hope."

"None, Chad. Here's a ticket for the Muny [the Municipal Lodging House]. Come back if it gets any worse." A week later he got in.

Money, more specifically the lack of it, affected our relationship with patients in another way. While private patients, who were paying their doctor to care for them, would often demand attention and get it, our patients couldn't do so. This had good and bad effects.

On the plus side was the fact that we could give patients attention solely according to their need. The sickest patients got the most attention; those who were only moderately ill got less. We weren't tempted to spend an extra hour of our time with a hemorrhoidectomy case simply because the man was wealthy—something I was to see happen not infrequently when I was working in a private hospital. But neither were we obliged to spend any time with any patient, and this was bad. Our patients knew that everything we did for them was done gratis; that they were, purely and simply, dependent on our good graces, and sometimes they resented this. Justly so, because occasionally it led us to behave in a manner we wouldn't have used with a paying patient.

One night, for example, when I was making rounds about eight o'clock, one of the aides from the admitting office wheeled in a new patient.

I always hated to get new patients at night and continually nurtured the hope that I'd be able to get caught up on my work and go to bed, so when I walked over to the stretcher to look at the admission sheet I was in a foul mood. The diagnosis was frostbite of the toes, another common derelict problem, and I said to the patient on the stretcher—a big man, at least two hundred pounds and six feet tall—"What's the matter, buster, the booze get you again?"

"What's it to you?" he answered.

"Listen, smart guy, you want me to take care of you, you

be nice. Otherwise you can get the hell out of here." Before
I could say another word I felt his hand close around my wrist
like a vise.

"Listen, Mr. Big-Shot," he said, "just because you've got
a nice white suit you think you can talk down your nose to
guys like me. We're just trash for you to practice on. Well,
I'm not going to take it. Get me my clothes—I'm getting out
of here."

The thing was, he was right. I had been looking at him
not as a patient who needed compassion and care, a human
being with a problem, but as just another bum who was going
to keep me from getting to bed that night. I picked myself
up, swallowed my pride, walked back to the stretcher and
apologized.

He stayed in the hospital, we treated and eventually sal-
vaged his toes, and I got along well with him for the rest of
his stay. When I got to know him I found he was really a
decent guy, just down on his luck.

Ambivalence toward patients was a constant characteristic
of the entire house staff, but particularly of the interns. We
were at Bellevue to learn, and we needed those patients just
as much as they needed us. But at the same time, we were
overworked and chronically tired. Sure, it was nice to have a
patient with a perforated ulcer under your care, but goddamn
it, why did he have to come in at two o'clock in the morning
and keep you up all night? We wouldn't have been human if
it hadn't bothered us. We tried not to give vent to our resentment, as I had on this occasion, but once in a while it was
inevitable and, I think, excusable.

The physical differences between Bellevue patients and
private paying patients were almost as marked as the social
and sociological differences. Take a simple case like a hernia.
A patient in a private hospital who undergoes a hernia repair
can ordinarily expect to be up and around on the first postoperative day, have his skin stitches out and be home on the
sixth or seventh day. Not a Bellevue patient. He might be up

and about on the first postoperative day, but he might not.
With our patients, complications were the rule rather than
the exception, and that might easily delay the patient's convalescence. Malnutrition, for example. Our patients had no
idea what a balanced diet was like. For many of them the bulk
of their calories came from alcohol. What they did eat was
usually starchy or fatty, since that's cheaper than protein-rich
food. Vitamins were a luxury with which they couldn't afford
to concern themselves. Their malnutrition would interfere
to a greater or lesser degree with wound healing. Take the
stitches out of one of our hernia patients on the sixth postoperative day and his wound edges might split wide open. Not
a pleasant event.

Malnutrition was almost omnipresent but there were
frequently other complicating ailments as well. For example,
tuberculosis, a disease rarely seen in a private hospital, always
had to be considered a possibility in Bellevue patients. Who
could tell whether our Puerto Rican patients had drunk un-
pasteurized milk before coming to the United States? No
one. Or spend a night in the Municipal Lodging House—the
Bowery flophouse—and there was an excellent chance that
someone in your dormitory would be coughing tubercle
bacilli at you. The possibility of latent, undiagnosed T.B. was
real, and afforded one reason why we never did any operation
without a preoperative chest x-ray. We didn't want to fix
a hernia only to have our patient die postoperatively of tuberculosis, disseminated under a general anesthetic.

Even without malnutrition or tuberculosis to complicate
things, we were often licked before we started. A disease we
were treating was apt to be quite advanced before we ever
got to see our patient—too far advanced to cure.

I remember Steve Wood, a Bowery resident in his fifties
who came to the clinic one morning complaining of weakness.
He was pale, his pulse was rapid and his clothes hung on him
as they might on a scarecrow. He was obviously very ill
and had been for some time. His blood level was half what

it should have been and I could feel a mass the size of a grapefruit in his abdomen.

"How long have you been sick, Steve?" I asked him.

"Not long."

"Come on now," I said, "you've lost at least thirty pounds and your blood is way down. This lump in your belly didn't begin yesterday. How long has it been?"

"Six months maybe." I guessed a year would have been closer to the truth.

"Why, Steve," I asked him, "why? You're no dope. You must have known something was wrong. Why didn't you come in earlier?"

"Listen, Doc," he said, "you ever been a patient here? Ever cool your heels for three hours waiting to see some pip-squeak who looks down his nose at you and then sends you off to get some damn blood test or x-ray and tells you to come back in two weeks? You bet your ass you haven't.

"Well, I have, and it's no fun. Go here . . . go there . . . come back later; nobody gives a goddamn about you. You want to know something? I did come in six months ago but I couldn't stand the run-around. I wouldn't be back now if I had the strength to keep going."

He was right, unfortunately; tragic as it was, at times patients did get the run-around. Not because we were intentionally inconsiderate, but because we were busy, and so were all the other doctors and departments of the hospital. It was one of the reasons our patients frequently had advanced diseases before we saw them.

Another reason, of course, was that our patients were too busy keeping body and soul together to concern themselves with things like "routine annual checkup." That's the prerogative of patients who can pay for their medical care. It isn't offered to the indigent, and if it were, he would rarely have the time or inclination to take advantage of it.

Anyone under the impression that our Bellevue patients were so used to their living conditions that they were "happy" despite the poverty, dirt and disease would be quickly disabused of that notion by working a week in the emergency room. There we saw the men and women who had been so beaten down that they could no longer take it. They gave up.

One afternoon while I was at card rounds I got a call from the E.W. The charge nurse said, "Dr. Nolen, Dr. Rantala asked me to call you. He's with a patient who has cut his neck open and he needs help immediately."

I raced down the five flights of stairs and got to the E.W. to find Mike Rantala, an intern, applying pressure to the neck of a man who was bleeding from a gash that ran the entire width of his neck.

"What happened?" I asked.

"He tried to commit suicide. Took a big knife and cut himself. It's a deep one. I'm sure he must have gotten both carotids"—the arteries on either side of the neck that carry most of the blood to the brain.

"Have you looked?"

"I've been afraid to. I thought if I let up on the pressure he'd shoot blood all over everything and bleed out."

I looked at the man. He was obviously alert, though he couldn't speak. He could only make gurgling noises.

"I'll tell you, Mike, I don't think he got his carotids. He's too wide awake to have cut off much circulation to his head. I imagine he's bleeding from some of the smaller vessels. And I think if we look under that sponge you're holding we'll find he has done a tracheotomy on himself. I'll get some clamps to grab bleeders with and then you let up on the pressure."

I was right. We were able to clamp the few small vessels he had cut, and put a tracheotomy tube into the hole he had made. We then took him to the O.R., and while he was under general anesthesia, cleaned up and sutured his wound.

After the case was over I spoke to Mike in the dressing room. "You haven't seen many suicide attempts, Mike," I said, "so let me give you a tip. If they use a knife they'll frequently be unsuccessful. Like this guy. When he throws his head back to make the cut, the carotid arteries get back in behind the muscle. The trachea comes forward and generally that's the only big structure they get.

"In the wrist the same sort of thing happens. The guy bends his wrist back to make the gash. When he does the artery disappears behind the edge of the bone. He cuts a few small veins. If he bent his wrist forward, it would be a different story."

Almost routinely, at some time or another during the night, a cop would come in with one or more addicts in tow. If they were willing to sign themselves into Lexington, the federal hospital for narcotic addicts, they would be taken to Bellevue for a shot of morphine to tide them over until they were hospitalized. This was a perfectly legal practice.

The A.O., on the ground floor of the building near the ambulance entrance, was the office through which every patient entering Bellevue had to pass. Whether they came in by ambulance, walked in off the street, were sent over from the outpatient department or were dragged in by the police, they had to get their stamp of approval here. It was a busy place.

Every service had to help staff the admitting office. Second Medicine always had an assistant resident assigned to the place, and so did we. There had to be three doctors on duty sixteen hours a day, and two doctors on duty the other eight hours. It took a lot of help to provide the necessary twenty-four-hour service.

There was one nice thing, and only one nice thing, about working there: you only had to work a forty-hour week. The midnight-to-eight shift would be extremely quiet, sometimes so quiet that the two of us who were on could split the shift and each get four hours' sleep on one of the examining-room tables, but at other times it was hectic. Of course what we all did right away was spoil our opportunity to rest by making switches and doubling up shifts so that we could get a "real" vacation. We'd trade around so that instead of working eight hours a day for five days and then having two days off, we'd work sixteen hours a day for two days, eight hours the next and take four days off. It was a mistake to do this, as I soon found out, because eight hours in that office was about all anyone should have to stand, but I did it anyway. On first appraisal it might seem that this assignment was a soft touch. What was there to it, really, except to say yes or no to people who were seeking admission? Nothing else indeed, but that was plenty.

There was never a problem when it came to admitting addicts to the hospital. You could be sure that any addict who showed up at the hospital asking for admission needed to be hospitalized, and probably should have been at least one week earlier.

The most frequent reason for addict admission was abscess formation. Anyone who uses the needle often enough is bound, at one time or another, to infect himself, and some addicts were on the needle two or three times a day. The infection couldn't be avoided indefinitely, no matter how careful they were to clean the skin and sterilize the needle. The heroin, which was what most addicts were on, was almost always adulterated with some other substance, frequently aspirin. Consequently, the addicts were partially dependent for protection on the peddlers, or pushers, who weren't the neatest people in the world. Sooner or later they would push some contaminated or infected drugs.

The skin-poppers were the ones most apt to develop abscesses. They are so called because they take their injection just beneath the skin; they pop it up with the needle and inject the drug into the fat. The first time I encountered a skin-popper at Bellevue was in the outpatient department. The man had come in with a small abscess on his arm. When I examined him I noticed round scars about the size of a nickel on all his extremities, and even on his abdomen.

"Take a look at this," I said to Riley, the head nurse on the O.P.D. "Mr. Stacy not only has an abscess on his arm but he also has ringworm all over his body. I've never seen such a bad case."

"Where the hell have you been, Nolen," Riley asked me. "Out in Squaresville, Ohio, all your life? Stacy here hasn't got ringworm any more than I've got wings. He's a skin-popper—aren't you, Stacy?"

" 'Fraid so, Miss Riley," Stacy said.

Riley explained the facts of life to me. Skin-poppers are almost all long-time addicts. As long as an addict can find a vein, he prefers to mainline the stuff, i.e., take it intravenously. He can get high faster traveling that route.

As I was to find out later, the addict becomes extremely skillful at this procedure—much more adept than most doctors. I've known addicts who could get a needle into a finger vein that I couldn't even see. But eventually all the veins disappear. Repeated injection with "irritating" substances—and heroin and aspirin are irritating—cause veins to thrombose, or clot, and from that time on they are useless for injection. It is only when all the accessible veins are thrombosed that the addict resorts to skin-popping.

Why addicts waited so long to come to the hospital when it was apparent that they were developing an abscess was never quite clear to me, but it was certain that they did. Ordinary patients can't tolerate an abscess bigger than a marble; the pain is too great. The addicts never came to the hospital until the abscess was at least the size of a baseball, and frequently not until it reached the size of a melon. They certainly didn't delay because they were afraid we wouldn't give them narcotics. We did, and most of them knew it. The addicts on our surgical ward weren't there to have their addiction treated, they were there to have the abscess drained. But I suppose they delayed coming in for the same reason they were so anxious to leave: because they preferred their heroin, even though it was adulterated, to the morphine we gave them. (We couldn't have given them heroin if we had wanted to. It can't be prescribed by a physician in the United States. It's too habit-forming.)

But any addict on our ward got all the morphine he needed to keep him from getting withdrawal symptoms. I remember Toni Larson, an addict we had on our female ward at one time. You could set your clock by her. She was on morphine every four hours, and every four hours, to the minute, she'd roll up to Jean's desk in her wheelchair—she had had a leg abscess drained—and say, "Miss Swanson, it's time for my shot."

Jean would look at her watch, smile and say, "Right on the nose Toni," and get the needle.

Toni wasn't a bad sort—she was actually very pleasant. There wasn't any point in trying to go into the history of how she had got hooked (the stories were never reliable), but I think she truly wished she could break the habit. She had gone to Lexington once and had got off the stuff, but as soon as she came back to New York she went right back to it. The heroin habit is damn tough to break.

Toni was, of course, a hooker. Every female addict I knew, at least any who had even a remote chance of finding a customer, was a prostitute. Heroin, even the adulterated stuff, is expensive. It took at least thirty dollars a day to feed even a moderate addiction. Where was a girl like Toni, uneducated and unskilled, going to earn thirty dollars a day except as a prostitute? And when her looks and figure went to pot so far that she could no longer hustle for a living, she'd turn shoplifter or petty thief. They all did.

Most addicts caused very little trouble on the wards. As long as they were getting their shots on time they weren't troublesome. But they were frustrating cases to manage. Unlike our other patients, who would stay in forever if we'd let them, addicts wanted to get out of the hospital as quickly as possible.

We'd take a patient to the O.R. (operating room) at eleven in the evening, lay the abscess on his arm or leg open with an incision eight or ten inches in length, and early the next day, with the packing still in his wound, he'd ask for his clothes and sign out of the hospital A.O.R.—assuming own responsibility. I'd plead with him to stay because I couldn't conceive of his managing this huge wound under the home conditions he undoubtedly had, but to no avail. He would want out, and that was that. So I'd give him a slip to the outpatient department, hoping he'd at least go there for an occasional dressing, and let him go. There was nothing else to do.

The skin-poppers, when they came in for admission, were almost invariably surgical cases. The mainliners, on the other hand, usually went to medicine, and frequently via the E.W. (emergency ward). Typical of the mainliner's special problem was Jimmy Bouman, a thirty-year-old Negro. Jimmy came to the admitting office one night complaining that his arms were stiff. "Can't seem to move them very easy, Doc," he said, "and sometimes I choke when I try to swallow. I think I got a fever too."

I checked him over. His temperature was only 100 and his throat was moderately red. Aside from these things (plus a higher degree of irritability than I could explain—he jumped when I touched him) he didn't seem acutely ill. But the case didn't smell quite right and I asked Tom Hawkins, a medical resident who happened to be working with me that night, to take a look at him. Tom spotted something I hadn't noticed—a small hemorrhage on the inside of one elbow.

"How'd you get that, Jimmy?" he asked.

"I dunno."

"Don't you? Are you sure you didn't stick a little needle in there?"

"Well, maybe I did. Okay, so once in a while I have a little. What's that got to do with my stiff arms?"

"Tell me, Jimmy," Tom continued, "is your mouth a little stiff? Are you having any trouble chewing your food?"

"Yeah, I am," he answered. "I'd forgotten about it. Just the last few hours."

Tom took me aside. "This guy's sick," he said. "I think he has tetanus. Better admit him. And I'd send him to the E.W. He's going to need care."

I admitted him immediately, but it was still too late. Jimmy Bouman died of tetanus—the mainlining addict's special disease—five days later.

The police would frequently bring in vagrants or petty criminals who had resisted arrest, and we'd sew up the scalp lacerations that the officers had given them. One of the rules at Bellevue was that anyone who had received a blow to the head and had been, even momentarily, unconscious, must be admitted to the hospital for observation. The Bowery denizens knew this, of course, so any time they got anything resembling a rap on the noggin, anything that left them with a lump or laceration that we couldn't deny existed, they showed up in the admitting office and claimed they had been knocked out, and the admitting physician would have to let them in.

These head injuries were, to put it mildly, a real pain in the neck. Usually the patient was drunk and most of the time he was belligerent. After a five-minute examination I'd know there really wasn't a hell of a lot the matter with him. Many of them were on the bum. When they weren't in the hospital they were living in the streets or in a Bowery flophouse, eating little, subsisting to a large extent on cheap muscatel. They were dirty, infested with lice, chronically undernourished and malingering. To them, admission to Bellevue was a godsend. True, they had to take a bath, which didn't appeal to them, but once that was over they'd have a warm, clean bed and three meals a day as long as they were in the hospital. Bellevue represented the height of luxury.

They'd do anything to stay in, particularly during the winter. I remember how on rounds one cold February morning we came to the bed of a Bowery bum named Ted Rosseter. We had repaired his hernia ten days earlier and it was now healed.

"Discharge Mr. Rosseter tomorrow," Ron Miller said to me.

"Gee, Doc," Ted said, dismay written all over his face, "do you really think I ought to go? You think this thing is really healed?"

"Sure it is, Ted," Ron said, looking at his wound, "those edges are nicely healed. It would take a lot of pulling to break that wound open."

The next day Ted came up to me bright and early and said, "Listen, Doc, I don't think I'd better go today. Look what happened." He pulled down his pajama bottoms and showed me his incision. The edges had separated. I knew damn well Ted had done it—he was all smiles—but what was I going to do? Anyone who works that hard to stay deserves an extra couple of days in the hospital.

We had to be very careful not to let some of these fellows talk us into unnecessary surgery, which, admittedly, was not difficult. One of my fellow interns made a diagnosis of early inguinal hernia—a physical finding which is often a matter of opinion, on every male patient admitted to the ward, no matter what his primary disease. Usually the patient was willing to accept the diagnosis, but of course the assistant resident, who wasn't as enamored of hernias as his intern, would usually nip the whole idea in the bud. We weren't hard to convince, but there had to be at least some pathology before we'd take a patient to the operating room.

There were, of course, two sides to this particular coin. We were so used to assuming that our patients exaggerated their complaints that we occasionally wrote off a legitimate problem as a sham. Larry Adson was a classic example. Larry, like Ted Rosseter, was in and out of the hospital all the time. He had terrible leg ulcers, due to a combination of poor circulation and constant exposure to dirt, and much as we hated to do so, we'd occasionally have to admit Larry to the ward for treatment.

One night during my hitch on the male ward, Dave Kelly, my assistant resident at the time, and I had just finished a tough case and were about to go to bed when an aide from the admitting office wheeled Larry Adson onto the ward. It was half past two in the morning.

"Goddamn you, Larry," I said, "what are you doing back here? Why the hell can't you take care of yourself?" I was really angry with him, and so was Dave.

"It's not my leg this time, Doc," Larry whimpered, "it's up here," and pointed to his groin.

"Don't give me that stuff, Larry," I said. "I know you."

We wheeled him into the side room so we could turn on a light to examine him without waking all the other patients. Sure enough, his leg ulcer was a mess. There were red streaks going up his leg, and swollen glands in the groin.

"Same old thing," I said to Dave. He agreed.

"It's not the same, Doc, honest," Larry insisted. "It hurts every time you move my leg."

"It's just worse than usual, Larry," I said. "You really let it go this time."

We stuck him in a bed in the corner, told the nurse to put wet packs on his leg and groin, and went to bed.

For the next three days, every time we made rounds Larry would moan about his groin. We ignored him, convinced that he was malingering. His leg ulcer was healing and he knew we'd soon be tossing him out. He didn't want to go.

Finally he wore us down. Ron said, "Bill, just for the hell of it, get an x-ray of his hip. Maybe that will shut him up."

Much to our chagrin the hip was broken. Larry had been

right all along. If he had been smarter, he would probably have sued the whole stubborn bunch of us. But fortunately no great harm had been done; we nailed his hip and eventually he recovered.

Such a legitimate case was only the exception. However, rules were rules, and once a man was admitted I had to examine him, write a complete history and physical, cart him down to X-ray for skull films and do the routine lab work, usually in the middle of the night. I'm certain that at least half the time that I was awakened at two or three in the morning I'd pick up the phone only to hear the nurse say, "Dr. Nolen, you have a head injury in the E.W."

I'd crawl out of bed, slip on my white coat over the scrub suit I always wore to bed, to avoid the necessity of dressing and undressing two or three times a night, and stumble my way to the E.W. This malingerer would cost me two hours of valuable sack time. He would, that is, until I learned the trick every intern eventually learned at Bellevue: how to get these guys to sign out A.O.R. It was really a simple matter. First, I'd examine the man, check his reflexes, listen to his heart, the whole ball of wax; then, when I was sure he was a faker I'd ask him, nicely, if he wouldn't like to sign a release and go home. The answer was almost always, "No!"

Then I'd go into phase two. "Well, in that case," I'd say, "I guess we'd better do a spinal tap." I'd take a spinal needle six inches long off the E.W. dressing cart and wave it under his nose. "I'm just going to jam this thing into your back for a minute. We'd better have a look at the spinal fluid." This usually convinced him that he might as well depart, but if it didn't work I'd grab the proctoscope, eighteen inches long and one and a half inches in diameter, and add, "After we check your back we'll stick this little number up your hind end and see if you've got any hemorrhoids." If that didn't make him reach for the pencil, we figured he was sick enough to stay.

The patients who came in with slips from the outpatient

department were no problem at all. The slip might say: "Please admit Mr. Williams to the Third Medical Service. Diagnosis—malignant hypertension. Ralph Shick, Resident, Third Medicine." All I'd have to do was hand the slip to Aggie Reardon, the boss nurse of the admitting office who, after checking the patient's identity, would get an aide to take him to the proper ward.

We were always careful about this identity check. Once a patient had been admitted to Bellevue, he "belonged" to whatever division had first taken him. If he came in in 1945 and Second Surgery took out his appendix, then for his heart attack in 1951 he'd be sent to Second Medicine. This policy allowed at least a semblance of continuity of care.

Though drug addicts and patients from the O.P.D. were no problem, every other kind of patient was.

Helen Johnson wandered into the admitting office at five o'clock one evening complaining of pain in the lower abdomen. If she had shown up at one o'clock, or even at two, I could have given her a note to the outpatient department and someone over there could have decided whether or not to admit her. But after three o'clock the O.P.D. referrals were out, so I had to decide whether she was to be admitted or discharged.

I had the nurse put Helen in an examining room and check her temperature. Then I asked her a few questions and examined her. I decided she might have appendicitis. I would have liked a blood count and a urinalysis to be certain, but I thought I'd better admit her to be on the safe side. Third Surgery was up for the next admission, so I sent her to the E.W. for them to see.

Half an hour later Charlie Dale, an intern on Third Surgery, came bursting into the admitting office. "Goddamn it, Nolen, why the hell didn't you admit this girl to GYN? Her white count is only eight thousand and her sed rate is eighty-five. Don't you know the clap when you see it?"

I took Charlie aside and explained to him that as an A.R.

(assistant resident) I naturally knew more about both the clap and appendicitis than he did, but that since I couldn't get all these fancy tests in the admitting office, I had to make the diagnosis on the strength of history, physical and intuition. So of course there were going to be errors. I calmed him down and sent him on his way.

This was typical of the difficulties which were encountered regularly. A patient comes in with a chest pain. What do you do, with no E.K.G. to guide you? Gamble that it's just a neuritis and let him go, or admit him and bring the wrath of the intern down on your head in the event it's a false alarm? If you were smart you admitted him.

Some of the boys weren't always smart. They worried too much about incurring the anger of their confreres, and consequently did a disservice to their patients. I remember one night when Hal Richards, an A.R. from medicine who was working with me, saw a four-year-old girl whose temperature was 103. She had been vomiting, and according to the mother, had been acting "strange."

Hal checked the child, found nothing, and since it was two o'clock in the morning and he didn't want to bother the intern on pediatrics, gave her a shot of penicillin. He told the mother, "Bring her back at ten tomorrow morning to the pediatric outpatient department," and gave her a referral slip.

At six that morning while Hal and I were taking a coffee break, a taxi roared up to the ambulance entrance. A woman stepped out, carrying a child who was convulsing wildly, and ran into our office in hysterics. It was the mother whom Hal had sent on her way only four hours earlier. It was now obvious that the child had acute meningitis. She barely survived. Hal never hesitated to disturb the pediatrician again.

The problems of admission were sociological as often as they were medical. Typical was the situation with

Mrs. D'Amato, ninety years old, feeble, unable to care for herself, but mentally alert. She came into the admitting office one morning via ambulance.

"What's the problem, Mrs. D'Amato?" I asked.

"Nothing, it's just my son. He can't take care of me no more. He fights with his wife all the time. They got only three-room apartment, two kids, no room for me. So he send me here."

What do you do in a case like that? And such cases weren't uncommon—"dump cases," we called them: families who for reasons good or bad could not or would not care for their elderly parents any longer. We couldn't send them home, they'd never make it. All we could do was admit them to Medicine and let the medical doctor set the social worker on to it. These were cruel situations.

Nerves ran thin in the A.O. The lines moved slowly and the long periods of waiting were trying on both the doctors and the patients. Some of the most difficult people to deal with were those who had nothing much wrong with them but who were lawsuit-conscious: patients who had had their cars tapped from the rear and knew about whiplash injuries; those who had stumbled off a curb and wanted to sue the city; the ones who had developed an ache while at work and wanted to establish the fact that the hernia was job-connected. These people came to Bellevue because they wanted to be sure they'd see a doctor that day. They didn't want to wait for an appointment with a private physician.

They weren't typical Bellevue patients. They had money, and at any other time they'd have gone to a private doctor and paid for their care. But they expected the same sort of prompt, considerate, thorough attention they would have had under those circumstances. When they didn't receive it they got angry.

My first approach under these circumstances was the rational one: "I understand, sir. I know your neck hurts. But as you can see, there are ten other patients ahead of you who also need care. You'll just have to wait your turn." If this approach didn't work I'd try the "unavailable" technique. I'd stay back in the examining rooms, doing my job where I couldn't be seen. The nurse would tell the griper I was tied up and he'd have no recourse but to sit there quietly.

Once I lost my temper and strayed from these two approaches. The patient, a Mr. Sidney Carlton, was a well-to-do businessman who had been riding in a cab when it was struck from behind by another car. He had sustained a whiplash injury, or at least so he thought, and the cabbie had taken him straight to Bellevue, the hospital nearest the accident, for a checkup.

On all cases of this type, whether the injury seemed real or imaginary, it was routine to take neck x-rays. There was no telling when a lawsuit might arise, and we needed protection. I examined Mr. Carlton, decided there was nothing much the matter and I told him we would need some films. I asked him to sit down and wait his turn; since there were three or four patients ahead of him, it might be an hour or more.

"Look, Doctor," he said, "I'm a busy man. I can't afford to sit around waiting. Can't you sneak me in a bit sooner?"

"I would if I could, Mr. Carlton, but it's impossible. It would be unfair to these other people. Your case really isn't any emergency."

"I know, I know," he said, "but take a look at the ones who are sitting here. Not one of them looks like a responsible member of society. What's an hour more or less to them?"

I was getting angry but I tried not to show it. "That may be so," I said, "but we have rules and one of them is 'first come, first served.' It's the only fair way to run this place."

He wouldn't take no for an answer. "Now look, Doctor," he said, "I'm trying to be nice. But if you don't get me into X-ray and out of here damn fast, I'm going to have your ass. Mr. Carter, the medical superintendent, is a very good friend of mine."

That did it. "Mr. Carlton," I said, "I couldn't care less what you do or who you call. As far as I can tell you're nothing but a pompous, phony ass who's planning to sue the poor cabbie who had the misfortune to have you for a fare. You can either sit on that bench and wait your turn like everyone else, or you can get out of here now. I've got sick people to take care of and the less I see of you the better." I practically ran away. I was afraid if I stayed there one more minute I'd hit him.

Mr. Carlton left, fuming, and ten minutes later I got a call from the administrator. "Nolen," he asked, "are you the one who told Mr. Carlton off?"

"Yes, sir."

"Look," he said, "I'm going to send this guy right through to X-ray. He's an influential guy—a bastard, yes—but a high-ranking one. If we don't take care of him, and fast, he'll get it in all the papers. We'll have a real stink on our hands.

"I don't like it any better than you do, but remember—this is a city hospital and politics is something we've got to live with.

"One more thing. If you hadn't lost your temper and told him off, I could have calmed him down a helluva lot easier. The next time you're tempted to blow up, do me a favor—send the guy to me. Handling situations like this is part of my job. It's what I get paid for."

Unfair? Preferential treatment? I suppose so. But it was one of the facts of life I had to live with, and as long as I could avoid taking sides it wasn't my worry. I didn't know Carter except remotely, but he seemed like a nice guy. There was no point in my making his job any harder than it already was, and I decided that I would try not to lose my temper again.

But I much preferred our regular clientele to these politicos.

4

To Err Is Human

It's sad that all through a book on surgery, mistakes and error should play such a prominent role.

Patients like to believe that doctors are infallible. They know they're not, of course, because they read about malpractice cases and lawsuits time and again in newspapers and magazines. Still, they like to think this can only happen to "other" doctors, not theirs.

Unfortunately, that's not the case. Not some, not most, but all doctors, at one time or another, make errors. This is the nature of medicine; it isn't an exact science. It's not simply a matter of adding up the symptoms, as you would a column of figures, and get the total, or diagnosis, then feed the result into a computer out of which comes the answer, the treatment. It's not at all like that.

There are too many variables. No two patients are alike, no two doctors are alike, and no two instances of a disease are alike. All the variables make medicine an inexact science. That's why doctors use what they call the "differential diagnosis." After talking to and examining a patient, the doctor generally writes down as his conclusion not just one possibility but two, three, four or even more. If the patient has pain in his abdomen, down in the right lower side where the appendix is, the number one diagnosis might be "appendicitis." But if the patient is a young woman who is suffering from diarrhea and weight loss, it might be a disease of the small intestine called "regional ileitis"; if the patient is a man in his seventies, the possibility of a cancer of the bowel would have to be entertained; and if the patient is a boy of eight, pneumonia, which may cause abdominal pain, cannot be ruled out. Even after getting the appropriate tests—blood count, x-rays, and the like—the best the doctor can say is "I think it is highly probable that the illness is acute appendicitis." He then proceeds with the operation and, hopefully, he was right. But perhaps he was not. He may have made a "mistake."

To stick with the appendicitis example, it's estimated that surgeons are wrong about 15 percent of the time even in their diagnoses of such a "simple" disease as appendicitis. That's what the figures show. A surgeon might be right more often if he only operated when he was almost absolutely certain of the diagnosis, but if he did that he would let some of the less certain cases go on to rupture. To avoid this catastrophe he errs on the side of early surgery. He accepts the fact that he will inevitably make some misjudgments. As one of my fellow residents used to say, "With pain in the belly it's appendicitis ten to one the field"; but as in horse racing, the long shot occasionally comes through.

Even if he makes the proper diagnosis the surgeon isn't home free. There are often two, three or more ways to treat a patient with a specific disease. You can operate or not operate; you can operate immediately or delay to get the patient in better condition; you can do one operation or another. Every step of the way you have to choose between options. Sometimes the choices are clear-cut; often they're not.

Even if we do make mistakes at times, why dwell on them? Because that's what surgeons do. Ask a surgeon to tell you about the last twenty gall bladder patients on whom he has operated. Chances are he won't remember anything at all about the nineteen who went through the operation and the postoperative course uneventfully. He probably won't even remember their names. But the one who got into trouble, the one who developed jaundice or an intra-abdominal abscess, about that patient the surgeon will remember, in great detail, every minute the patient was under his care. He has reviewed the case hundreds of times trying to see where, if at all, he erred; what he might have done to prevent the complication—or worse, the death—of the man or woman who was his responsibility. It's the trouble he gets into that sticks in the surgeon's mind.

If he did make a mistake, he doesn't want to make it again. If possible, he wants to learn something from this experience which may help him help his patients in the future.

That's why the surgeon dwells on errors.

At Bellevue we had what we called a "death and complication" conference where we'd go over the charts of all the patients who had died or experienced difficulties while under our care. Dr. Stevens was the only attending who came regularly to these meetings. This was dirty-linen day and there was nothing to be gained by turning it into a Roman holiday.

I sweated, as resident, over these conferences. Most of the deaths were acceptable, if death is ever acceptable. Ninety-year-old women with broken hips who died of pneumonia, patients with inoperable cancer, massive hemorrhages impossible to control—on these we wasted little time. On others, possibly preventable, we dwelt for as long as Dr. Stevens thought it productive.

I remember one such case, a woman in her seventies with an obstructing ulcer. When the obstruction failed to relent after medical therapy, I removed her stomach. The operation was too much for her and she died.

"Why did you remove her stomach, Bill?"

"She couldn't keep anything down, Dr. Stevens. We had a tube down for five days trying to get her to open up; when we tried refeeding her she wasn't any better. She couldn't even tolerate clear liquids."

"I'm not questioning the need to operate on her, Bill. I'm

just wondering if you couldn't have done a lesser operation—
a gastroenterostomy, for example?" This is a by-pass procedure in which the stomach and bowel are sewn together,
but the stomach is not removed. "I realize it isn't as good an
ulcer operation and that the recurrence rate is high," he continued, "but after all, this woman was seventy-six. She couldn't
have been in very good shape after not eating for two weeks.
It might have been better judgment to relieve her immediate
problem and not worry about curing her ulcer."

Perhaps she wouldn't have tolerated the simpler operation,
either. Who could say? But it wasn't a question worth raising.
What was clear was that the operation I had done had resulted
in her death. All Dr. Stevens wanted to do was point out
an alternative that I might consider when I next encountered
a similar problem, as I undoubtedly would sometime in the
future.

The point of "death and complication" conferences was to
try to discover how we might have done things differently,
hopefully with a better result. It's true that surgeons bury their
mistakes, but we never buried ours without asking ourselves,
"Could we have avoided this tragedy?"

There was one sort of death we rarely had to discuss:
death that occurred on the operating table. To the uninformed
our impeccable record must have seemed almost miraculous.
Operating on critical patients, as we so often did, it was only
logical that occasionally one would die before the surgery had
been completed.

The explanation for our cheerful record was a simple one:
we refused to allow patients to die on the operating table. If a
patient died on the table there were stacks of complicated
forms that had to be filled out, explaining why we had
operated on such a sick patient, and we wanted no part of
these forms. We looked upon them as a waste of our valuable
time. So when a patient's heart stopped and his pulse and
blood pressure disappeared, the anesthetist would continue to
administer oxygen and aerate the lungs just as if everything

were all right and we'd close our incision as quickly as we could, usually with a single layer of stitches through all the tissues of the abdomen, chest or wherever we were operating. As soon as the incision was closed we'd move the patient onto a stretcher and then, and only then, one of us would put a stethoscope to the chest and say, "I'm afraid Mrs. So-and-so has died." We'd check the O.R. clock and note the time of death. It must have seemed odd to whoever checked the deaths that so many patients made it through surgery, only to die a few seconds later.

Since, in comparison with our attending surgeons, we were all relatively inexperienced, we had a rule that no patient could be taken to the operating room without first getting the approval of an attending surgeon. This policy was designed to keep the incidence of mistakes in judgment to a minimum. For example, on a routine appendicitis case that came in one night, I first called Jack Lesperance, who was the chief resident, and then Dean Voss, the attending on call.

"Dean," I said, "we've got a fifty-year-old man in here with pain in the belly and a tender right lower quadrant. His temp is a hundred and his white count is fifteen thousand. Otherwise he's in good shape. I think he's got a hot appendix and we'd like to take it out."

"Go to it, Bill," Dean replied. That was all there was to it.

It wasn't always that simple. Some of the cases were complex, and we learned to pick and choose among the attendings so we could call one who would let us do what we wanted to do. One night, for example, a patient came in who was bleeding massively from a giant ulcer of the stomach. We washed out the clots and poured blood into him; still, after four hours, his blood pressure was borderline and he was still bleeding actively. I called Jack and told him the story.

"We'd better crack him," Jack said—"crack" is Bellevuese for "operate on." "Who's on call?"

I looked at the schedule. "Bob Lacey."

"Jee-sus," Jack moaned, "you know how Bob is about bleeders. He'll want us to give this guy six more pints before we do him. Tell you what—why don't you give Frank Jenkins a buzz? He'll let us get at it now."

I called Frank and he gave us an immediate go-ahead. Jack came in and did the case—he hadn't done many acute bleeders yet—and I helped him. It went beautifully and the patient made an uneventful recovery.

On elective surgery we were stuck. There was an attending assigned to each ward, a different one every two months, and we had to clear cases on the wards with whoever was on service at the time. There was no other choice. Usually it didn't make much difference. Most of the attendings were nice fellows, and after all these years we knew them, and they us, very well. We rarely locked horns. But they had their idiosyncrasies, as did we, and there were occasional disputes. Sometimes we gave in, sometimes they did. In the process we all became wiser.

I remember one case very well. We had a patient on the male ward with a cancer of the bowel located about seven inches from the anus. We had him ready to go, but before I called Bill Starr, the attending, I asked Jack if he planned to do a colostomy. This is a procedure in which the surgeon, after removing the tumor and sewing the two ends of the bowel together, brings out a segment of colon on the near side of the suture line onto the abdomen. For about three weeks the patient moves his bowels through the colostomy, giving the suture line time to heal. After three weeks the colostomy can be closed. The tumor in question was in an area in which the suturing would be technically difficult. Some surgeons might use a colostomy to protect the suture line; others might not. It was a matter of judgment.

Jack was feeling his oats about this time. He had been doing a lot of major surgery, with good results, and he didn't think any technical problem was too great for him to handle.

"Hell, no," he replied, "I'm not going to do a colostomy. Why give this guy two operations when I can fix him up with one?"

I called Bill and described the case to him.

"Go ahead," he said, and added as an afterthought, "You'll do a colostomy, won't you?"

"Jack wasn't planning to," I answered. "He thought he'd have enough room to do a safe anastomosis [suturing]."

There was a pause. "Well, I haven't seen the patient so I don't like to tell you boys what to do, but tell Jack this: If I were he I'd do a colostomy."

"Okay," Dr. Starr," I said, "I'll tell him."

Jack did the case the next day and didn't bother with the colostomy. The suture line broke down, the patient got peritonitis, and a week later we had to take him back and do the colostomy we should have done as the first operation. As a result the patient had the colostomy for six months instead of the three weeks that would have sufficed earlier.

Jack learned a lesson. For the next few months he did colostomies on patients when even I thought they were unnecessary. But Jack had been burned and it takes a while for a burn to heal.

The worst mistake a resident could make was falling into the trap of overconfidence. It could be disastrous. But everyone, at one time or another, got caught.

It happened to me shortly after I had become a first assistant resident. By that time I had done several gall bladders on my own, and had recently helped two A.R's through their first ones. So when Jack Lesperance told me I could do the common duct exploration on a Mr. Salvatore and asked if I wanted him to help, I told him, "No, I can handle it alone."

It turned out to be a bitch. Salvatore's gall bladder had been removed some years before, and from the condition of the gall bladder bed, I would have guessed that whoever did it must have been using a Bowie knife. Everything was plastered together.

Russ Smith was helping me on the case. He was a pretty fair assistant, but the dissection was tedious and it took me almost two hours to get the duct exposed to the point where I could work on it. I opened it, fished out a stone and stuck a probe into the duct to make certain it was now clear. I couldn't get the probe into the bowel.

"Damn it," I said to Russ, "he must have another stone stuck in the lower end."

At this point Jack looked into the O.R. "How's it going, Bill?" he asked.

"Tough one," I answered. "There's a stone stuck down below."

"Want me to scrub in?"

I was stubborn. "No, don't bother. I'm sure we can get it."

"Fine. Then I think I'll sneak out and get a haircut. Betty's been after me. See you at card rounds."

I worked on that duct for another hour, but I couldn't get the stone. Finally I said to Russ, "I think we'd better open the duodenum. Maybe I can get it from the other end." Opening the duodenum, the portion of the small intestine into which the bile duct empties, is a formidable procedure even under the best of circumstances. With all the adhesions in this patient, it was terrifying.

It took me two more hours to get the job done and when I closed the duodenum I wasn't happy. I was afraid I was narrowing the opening. But Mr. Salvatore's blood pressure was dropping, he had been on the table for almost five hours and the anesthetist was anxious to get him off. So I closed.

Mr. Salvatore barely made it. I had indeed narrowed his duodenum. We had to keep him on intravenous feedings for three weeks and then go back in and do another operation to by-pass the bowel I had fouled up. I sweated blood during his entire convalescence. I was never happier than the day we were able to send him home well.

All, I'm sure, because of my pigheadedness. It was my stupid false pride that had made me turn down Jack's offer of help. I swore I'd never be such an ass again.

So we made errors. We operated when we shouldn't have, didn't operate when we should have; sometimes we performed the wrong operation; occasionally we chose the right operation but did it poorly. We made all these errors. But, to keep the proper perspective, not often. We did our damnedest to avoid mistakes—we took every precaution we could to eliminate errors and struggled to keep them down to the absolute minimum. And for every patient we hurt by one of our mistakes, we did, I hope, help hundreds.

Which is, in this all-too-human profession, all any surgeon can hope to achieve.

5

All About Nurses

I got clobbered just once at Bellevue—the night in June when we gave Jack Lesperance his farewell party.

The party for the resident was a tradition on each division. The hospital administrator co-operated by closing the division wards for the evening—no new admissions. The interns and residents from the Columbia Division looked after our patients the night of our party; we returned the favor when they had theirs.

The party was held in the eighth floor recreation room in the doctors' residence wing. There was always plenty of liquor and food, paid for by the attendings, and occasionally we had a band. Usually, however, there were only records. It was one of the few occasions when the wives of the house staff members met—those that chose to come. All the nurses on our division were invited as well as the attendings and their wives. Even Dr. Stevens usually came, though he never stayed long. He was afraid he'd put a damper on the party.

About seven Walt and I wandered down to Walsh's just to prime the pump for the later festivities. On this night instead of beer we drank Scotch. We got to talking about the next year; I was to be resident and Walt my first A.R. and we were looking forward to a great twelve months. What, with one thing and another, by the time we reached the party, about quarter to nine, we were both moderately loaded.

"Where you guys been," one of the A.R.'s greeted us. "You look half gassed."

"None of that now," I said, "rank has its privileges. Get smart and I'll farm you out to a dog lab for the next six months."

I found the bar—the booze was free—and in another hour I was completely bombed. I was dancing, singing and generally raising hell. I hardly looked like a man about to take the responsibility of supervising, for the next twelve months, a hundred surgical beds.

Unfortunately one of my duties that evening was to present to Jack the captain's chair, which was given to each outgoing resident. About eleven o'clock Russ Smith caught me and said, "Bill, have some coffee. You've got to make a speech in half an hour."

"Come now, Smith," I reportedly said, "are you implying that your chief resident-to-be can't hold his liquor? I'll have you in Podunk Hospital before you know it." I was far out of reach.

At eleven-thirty, as I began my presentation speech holding on to the captain's chair for support, who should make his appearance but Dr. Stevens. Even this didn't stop me.

When I get loaded, there is one thing I can do and that is talk. Make sense, no; but talk, yes. I spoke for forty-five minutes on every conceivable topic, none of which had anything to do with Jack Lesperance or Bellevue. When I had finished I pushed the chair in Jack's direction saying simply, "Here's your chair, Jack." This was greeted by thunderous applause—solely, I'm sure, because I had finally shut up.

Sharon Avery told me the next day, as I nursed the daddy of all hangovers over coffee in the kitchen off the ward, that Dr. Stevens, who had been standing next to Sharon during my speech, whispered in her ear after my first half-hour, "Bill isn't ill is he?" "Ill" of course meant "drunk."

"Oh, no," Sharon replied, "he's just a little nervous."
Thank God for nurses like Sharon.

We had, generally, high-quality nurses at Bellevue
—better nurses than are found in most private hospitals.

The explanation was a simple one. The rule that applied
to interns and residents also applied to nurses—"take all the
responsibility you're capable of assuming." A capable nurse
at Bellevue could utilize her talents to the fullest. No one was
going to say to her, "Don't do that, Miss Jones, that's a doctor's job." If she could do it—change a dressing, pass a catheter, draw some blood—more power to her. No one worried
about her title; it was her talent that counted. So Bellevue
appealed to nurses who thrived on responsibility. And these
nurses would rise to positions commensurate with their talent;
they became head nurses on the wards or ran one of the many
other hospital departments.

The nurse in charge of Second Surgery's outpatient department was the ruddy-faced little Irishwoman known to
everyone simply as "Riley," who had set me straight on addicts in general and skin-poppers in particular. She's the only
nurse I've ever known who never wore a nurse's cap. I don't
know to this day why she didn't. I'd have been afraid to ask
her. I knew what her answer would have been: "None of
your goddamn business, Nolen." She used language that was
as strong as any of the patients'. She was tough as nails. It was
Riley, not we doctors, who really ran the outpatient department, and it was she who made the place bearable.

When I arrived there the first morning, I walked into the
big examining room and introduced myself. "I'm Dr. Nolen,
and I'll be working here from now on."

"The name's Riley," she said, sticking out her hand. "Nice
to see an Irishman for a change. All I'm going to tell you is
—be tough. If you aren't, these lugs here"—and she swept

her hand around the examining room to indicate the patients who were listening to every word—"will crap all over you. Let's get to work."

Riley had put three patients in one examining room. Each had his pants rolled up to reveal a large ulcerated sore on the leg.

"This is Darby," she said, introducing the first man. "I've been putting a clean gelocast on him every week. He lies around in the dirt so much that he rubs off any other kind of bandage. Isn't that right, Darby?" Darby nodded his assent.

"Jonesy," she continued, pointing to the big Negro who was in the next chair, "he's not so bad. I have him come in three times a week. He keeps clean, and we wash it off and put on bacitracin ointment. It's getting better, isn't it, Jonesy?"

"Yes, it is, Miss Riley," he agreed.

We moved to the last patient. Riley bent down and examined the angry red ulcer. "Samson's getting worse. He tries hard, but his veins are shot. We're going to have to get him off his feet for a while if we're going to clear this thing up. I think you'll have to admit him." She straightened up. "That is, of course, if you agree." She looked at me.

"I agree," I said quickly. "Where do you keep the admission slips?"

If Riley hadn't been there to guide me on that first day I'd have admitted all three patients. But she'd seen thousands of leg ulcers; I'd seen thirty or forty. Thank heaven I at least knew enough to take her advice.

While I was examining a patient with a sore abdomen in another room Riley dressed the legs and got these patients on their way. When I returned to the examining room she had replaced them with three others and was unwrapping the bandage from a burly individual wearing the dirtiest pants I'd ever seen. As she took away the last layer of gauze I saw, crawling around on three inches of bare bone, a swarm of maggots. I almost vomited, but not Riley. Without batting an eyelash she reached up to the treatment cart, took the ether can and poured ether on the leg. The maggots rolled off onto the dressing.

"Those maggots sure keep an ulcer clean," she said. "Not much to look at, but they do the job."

She was right. The maggots had eaten the dead tissue, and the ulcer looked red and healthy. I was to see maggots on many more occasions during my sojourn at Bellevue, but this was my first exposure to them. While Riley dressed the wound I went out for some fresh air.

The last patient I saw that day was a nice old man of seventy who had lost about twenty pounds. He told me that for the last three months he had been vomiting off and on, and that sometimes he vomited blood. He looked sick, but I couldn't find anything specifically wrong when I examined him. I left him in the examining room while I went out to the desk. "This guy's sick," I said to Riley. "I can't be sure, but it's possible that he has a cancer of the stomach. Where are the lab and x-ray requisitions? I'm going to order some studies."

Riley handed me the slips. "Look, Nolen," she said as I wrote, "I don't want to tell you your business, but you're new here, so I'm going to make a suggestion. You can kick me in the ass if you don't like it.

"Admit this old geezer. If you order stomach x-rays out here, it will take at least two weeks to get them. God only knows when you'll get the blood chemistries done. By the time everything gets back here, this old man is going to be so goddamn sick of walking around this nutty hospital looking for the right elevators that he's apt to just give up. Admit him. So if he doesn't have anything, what are you out? Nothing. If you don't admit him you'll lose him."

I admitted him.

Riley knew from her experience what I later learned from

mine. At Bellevue you sometimes had to let patients get into the hospital for studies that could, under better circumstances, be done on an outpatient basis. A private patient who had gone to his personal doctor with the complaints of this old man would have had his x-rays and all his blood studies done the next day. At Bellevue there were waiting lists for everything. Nor, in the Bellevue outpatient department, was there the continuity of care that is so essential to good practice. I might not have been there the next time the old man came back; I might have been tied up in the operating room. The doctor that saw him might not have had my concern for him. He might easily have been lost in the shuffle.

We did the best we could, but there's no doubt that the charity patient who came to the Bellevue O.P.D. received care of lower quality than that which a private patient would have received from his personal physician.

Even at Bellevue, with its numerous and eager house staff, many hours of each day and most hours of every night there were no doctors on the wards. At such times we relied on the nurses to keep our patients alive, well and happy.

This could be a difficult job. One nurse might have the responsibility, from eleven at night to seven in the morning, for a thirty-bed ward, many of the beds occupied by acutely ill patients. She would have to dispense medication, check blood pressure and watch intravenous solutions on these critical patients, while at the same time seeing to the routine needs of all those who were less acutely ill. There wasn't much time to rest.

To make things a bit easier, the usual practice was to put the sickest patients—recent postoperatives and others who needed particular attention—at the front of the ward. The nurse on duty could then keep an eye on them from the desk at the nurses' station up front, because, even with all the running around her job entailed, she had to spend a considerable amount of time sitting at her desk "charting." This simply means recording on each patient's chart the medications he has been given, as well as notations regarding any significant change in the patient's course. It might seem like a waste of important time, but it is of course necessary to have a complete record, otherwise a medication might be repeated too quickly with disastrous consequences for the patient.

The nurses varied in personality and ability just as widely as did the doctors. We had efficient nurses and inefficient nurses; pleasant and nasty nurses; fast and slow nurses. The trick was to discover what each was like, and treat her and her ward accordingly.

In charge on our female surgical ward, for example, was Jean Swanson, the wonderful nurse I had met on my very first day at Bellevue. She was intelligent, pleasant and a hard worker—an invaluable combination of qualities in any individual, but particularly in a Bellevue nurse. This ward was almost always filled to capacity, usually with very sick patients. It often got me down, particularly in the morning when I couldn't see how I would possibly be able to get through all the work I had to do that day. Then Jean would step in.

"Dr. Nolen," she'd say, "if you want, I'll take care of the dressings on Mrs. Chalmer and Mrs. Pica. We've got a few new students and I'd like to teach them about dressing technique."

"That would be great, Jean, if you wouldn't mind. As long as you can manage those dressings, I'll run down to X-ray and see if I can find Perez's films."

"If you can wait an hour," Jean might say, "I'll pick them up for you. I'll have to stop down at the nursing office before nine o'clock, anyway." Thus Jean would relieve me of a big share of the work for which I was responsible. She didn't have to do these things, but she did them.

No matter how hectic things got Jean always remained calm and pleasant. One day while taking care of a patient, a Mrs. Ramos with a bleeding ulcer, I lost my temper. I wanted to put a cutdown in her ankle—her arm veins weren't suitable for a transfusion—and she refused to let me. She was afraid it would hurt too much.

I had been up most of the previous night and was operating on a short fuse. "Damn it," I shouted at her, "if you won't let me do this job you can bleed to death! I'm sick of your bellyaching." This, quite naturally, only made matters worse. Mrs. Ramos started to cry and became completely unco-operative.

Jean had been watching me from the nurses' station. Now she got up and walked over to the bed. "Dr. Nolen," she said, "there's some fresh coffee in the kitchen. Would you like a cup?"

"Thanks," I said, "I guess I will." I left the dressing cart where it was, walked back to the kitchen and sat down. Jean joined me a few minutes later and we chatted over our coffee about a movie we'd both seen. After a while I went back to Mrs. Ramos' bed, accompanied by Jean. It was obvious that she had spoken to Mrs. Ramos while I was in the kitchen. Jean held her hand while I did the cutdown and there was no rebellion of any kind. When I finished Mrs. Ramos said, "I'm sorry, Doctor—I was just so scared."

"I'm sorry too," I said. "I shouldn't have lost my temper."

"I understand," Mrs. Ramos said. "Miss Swanson explained how hard you work." Jean made no comment.

Eileen Gomez, who ran one of our male surgical wards, was as pleasant as Jean, but that was the sole point of resemblance between the two: Eileen was completely and utterly inefficient. She meant well, but she was totally unreliable.

On one occasion I remember asking her if she would please see to it that Mr. Raskin, a preoperative varicose-vein patient, be given a tub bath that day. I wanted his legs well cleaned before surgery. She promised it would be done.

It wasn't. When I asked her why, as she was getting ready

to leave for the day, she replied, "It completely slipped my mind. I'm so sorry. It's been one of those busy days." Which didn't do me, or Mr. Raskin, any good.

The trick was to learn to identify who of the ancillary help on each ward were reliable. On Eileen's ward, for example, Miss Martin, the ward clerk, was intelligent, efficient and reliable. Her job, according to the civil service job description, was purely clerical; all she was required to do was fill out x-ray requisition forms, paste reports onto the charts and see that the charts got to the record room. In actual fact, she ran the ward. She'd find x-rays . . . run up to Central Supply for syringes . . . locate aides who could wheel patients to the operating room—all the things Eileen should have been doing.

Unfortunately, she couldn't perform the pure nursing chores—make beds, change dressings, and the like. But she would see to it that these things were done. Instead of asking Eileen to get a tub bath for Mr. Raskin, I soon learned to ask Miss Martin to see to it that Eileen arrange for the bath. Then it would be done.

On female surgery, when Jean was away, Lena was the one we turned to. The head nurse who worked on Jean's day off was both lazy and dense. We would have been better off having no one. Lena, on the other hand, though she was only an aide, was both a good worker and a reliable one. She was a Puerto Rican—many of the menial jobs in the hospital were done by Puerto Ricans—and she could barely speak English, but she knew how to work.

"Lena, would you run up to the fracture room and get me the cast cutter?" . . . "Lena, could you take Mrs. Tarson to X-ray?" "Lena, would you get me a cutdown tray from Central Supply?" Lena never said no. She'd do any job we asked her to do, although if she had wanted to make an issue of it, she could have. She hadn't been hired to do these things, but she did them cheerfully and well. Without any training, and for the minimum wage, she contributed twice as much to the running of the ward as did some of our nurses—or, for that matter, some of our doctors.

The aides on the male wards were men. I'd say 90 percent, conservatively, were homosexuals. Almost everyone was a damn good worker. They had a rough job. They emptied bedpans, ran errands, shaved patients prior to surgery (not their faces but the preoperative area, which usually included the genitalia), dressed the dead, did any heavy work that had to be done, (e.g., moving oxygen cylinders). Again, for the minimum wage.

Why did these men, most of whom seemed to be of at least average intelligence, choose such a job? Because it satisfied their homosexual tendencies? Possibly, in part, but in the five years I was at Bellevue, I never heard of an aide making a "pass" at a patient. I prefer to think that at least some, and probably most of them, took the job out of compassion. They themselves, because of their deviation, were ostracized from society in general. They were pariahs. Their homosexuality kept them from finding work in the "straight" world, so they turned to places like Bellevue where they could find work; and work that was of benefit to other outcasts of the "civilized" world. Whatever the reason, the male aides were invaluable. The hospital would have foundered without them.

All things considered, the quality of the ancillary help at Bellevue was excellent. When we were short-handed, which was most of the time, you could count on those who were there—nurses or aides—to pitch in. They'd give medicines to sixty patients instead of thirty; run to Central Supply twenty times instead of ten; prepare eight patients for surgery instead of four. They'd do it cheerfully, without a complaint, and for a pittance of a salary.

The ancillary help—when you stop to think that they weren't in training and that these difficult jobs were their permanent livelihood—was even more dedicated to Bellevue than we doctors. All of them deserved a lot of credit; they never got it.

On the other male ward the head nurse was Sharon Avery.
Jean and she were as different as night and day. Jean was
gentle, Sharon was tough; Jean was always pleasant, Sharon
was usually sarcastic; Jean was feminine, Sharon was not. They
had nothing in common except the fact that they were both
excellent head nurses.

The reason why two women with such diverse character-
istics could both do their job so well stemmed, of course,
from the fact that Jean's patients were women, Sharon's men.
Jean's approach would have been fatal, to her, on a male ward;
Sharon's would have been disastrous, for the patients, on a
female ward.

I remember very well one of the first days on the male
ward. I walked in just as the patients were finishing breakfast.
Sharon was standing next to the bed of a big husky patient
who, I learned later, had had a hernia repair. "Don't give me
that nonsense, Simmons," she was shouting at him, "I wasn't
born yesterday. You're no sicker than I am. Get off your
butt and start picking up those breakfast trays. This isn't any
hotel." Simmons lumbered out of bed and did as he was told.

This was the way she ran her ward, with an iron hand.
The patients—most of them tough guys from the slums of
New York—quickly learned that Sharon wasn't afraid of
any of them, and that as long as they were on her ward, she
was the boss. Any funny stuff and she'd make life miserable
for them. Which she could, of course, do quite easily. There
was no law that said any one patient had to be fed first, or
with the best piece of meat; no law that said the pain medicine
had to be given as soon as the patient asked for it; no law
that said a soiled sheet must be changed immediately. Sharon
could control all these things, if she so desired. Any guy who
crossed her learned immediately how much power she had.

With the interns and residents the relationship was similar.
Play ball with Sharon, and your hitch on her ward was as
pleasant as time on any Bellevue ward could be; cross Sharon,
and she'd make your life miserable. Sometimes this wasn't

obvious initially to new interns, but it was quickly pointed out to them.

Phil Rogers, whose first assignment was to male surgery, complained to Ron Miller at card rounds. "Damn it, Ron," he said, "she refuses to do what I tell her to. I've told her a dozen times how I want the blood-drawing trays set up in the morning, and every day she has them set up her way. I'm getting tired of it."

"Is that so?" Ron said. "That's too bad. Tell me, Phil, how long have you been on male surgery?"

"Ten days."

"How long has Sharon been there?"

"I don't know."

"Well, I'll tell you. Ten years. And for all those ten years she's run a damn good ward. Now, if you don't like the way she sets up your blood trays, just keep bitching about it. I'll tell you what will happen—she won't set them up at all. She doesn't have to, you know; she does it to make life easier for you. If she gets tired of listening to you she'll tell you to shove it, and she'll be right."

Phil stopped complaining.

Sharon was a severe judge of interns. If she liked the way you worked, fine; if she didn't, she'd drive you nuts. Charlie Robbins, for example, was sort of a goof-off. He did just what he had to do to get by. He'd tell the nurses to do his work for him, then he'd go over to his room and sack out.

On Sharon's ward it didn't work. If Charlie wasn't on the ward, Sharon would track him down. She'd call his room, and if he didn't answer, she'd let the phone ring until he couldn't stand it any more. She'd call and ask questions about every little thing, and when he'd ask her to do some task for him, she'd answer, "Oh no, Dr. Robbins, I can't do that; that's a doctor's job," and he'd have to do it.

On the other hand, if she saw you were working hard and doing a good job, she'd do all she could to help you. "You look tired, Dr. Nolen," she'd say. "Why don't you go on over to your room and lie down? I'll keep an eye on Perez. If his blood pressure drops I'll call you. Otherwise I'll call you at half past three so you won't be late for card rounds."

That's the sort of nurse Sharon was. She'd seen interns come and go, and she was sharp; she could size them up pretty quickly. Which brings me to the high spot of my year as an intern. I was on Sharon's ward at the time and I was making dressing rounds—going from patient to patient taking off old bandages and putting on new. Sharon was helping me. We came to Pedro Diaz, who had a circular bandage on his leg that had to be cut off. I asked Sharon, for the hundredth time that month, "Can I borrow your scissors?"

"No," she answered, "you can't."

I thought she was kidding me. True, scissors were like diamonds at Bellevue—there were never enough to go around —and for a nurse to lend you her scissors was tantamount to admitting she was madly in love with you. But I wasn't trying to borrow Sharon's scissors; I just wanted to use them while she was there to guard them.

"Come on now, Sharon," I said, "be nice. I'm not going to steal your scissors. I'll give them right back to you."

"No," she said, "you can't use them." Then she reached into her pocket, took out a brand-new pair of bandage scissors and handed them to me. Engraved on the blade was, simply, "Dr. Nolen."

"Here," she said, "keep them—you've been a good intern."

I damn near cried.

6

Broken Bones

The first time I went without sleep for more than forty-eight consecutive hours, from seven o'clock Thursday morning until eight o'clock Saturday morning, was while I was an intern on the fracture service.

Fracture patients are tedious management problems. Many of them are in the hospital for weeks or even months. They need x-rays, cast changes, adjustments in their traction, dozens of little things that are time-consuming, annoying and not very interesting. Together with the A.R. on Fractures I plugged away steadily, trying to keep our patients and our schedule under control. It wasn't always possible.

There wasn't any outstanding event that kept me up. Just one thing after another—an ankle and a hip to operate on, several casts to change, two or three minor fractures—enough to keep me going all of both days, and then, both nights, emergency surgery at odd hours coupled with the usual run of head injuries and lacerations in the E.W. I got to my room three times, but not once was I able to get more than just into bed before the phone rang.

After forty continuous hours, I was all but out on my feet. I can remember sitting at the nurses' station drinking coffee and filling out a chart, and when the phone rang I just knew it would be the emergency room looking for me. When

I hung up I began to laugh, almost hysterically—the whole situation was becoming so ridiculous. Dave Kelly—the A.R. on nights with me—was almost as tired as I was. He'd only had about three hours' sleep himself, and he started to laugh too. The night nurse gave us a puzzled look as we giggled our way off the ward toward the elevator.

And this is what I remember most distinctly of those long hours—the emotional instability that they brought. By Saturday morning at eight, I was on the verge of hysteria. I didn't even feel tired any more, just hyper. I thought I was functioning beautifully, though I'm certain, in retrospect, that I couldn't have been. I'm sure I was a mess.

Ron showed up on the wards at eight o'clock, chipper and raring to go. He took one look at me and said, "Bill, hit the sack. Anything that's left to be done we'll get someone else to do. You've had it."

He was right. I went back to my room, collapsed on the bed and slept until four in the afternoon. And by ten o'clock that night I was ready for bed again.

The fracture service was always hectic, but Tuesday, the day we held fracture clinic, was a three-ring circus. At nine o'clock all the fracture patients who had been discharged in casts or on crutches but who were still in need of supervision would begin to congregate in the hall outside our fracture room. There were usually between twenty and thirty with arms and legs in plaster or on crutches. "Smiley" Kent, one of the two secretaries on the Second Surgical Division, would pull her typewriter into the fracture room, get out the patients' records and we'd go to work. Any assistant resident or intern who wasn't tied up in the operating room or on the ward was supposed to come to the fracture room and help, but basically it was the responsibility of the fracture A.R. and intern to see that the patients were given care.

For three hours, or longer if there were more patients than usual, we'd take x-rays, cut off old casts and put on new ones if necessary. Most of the decisions were routine—after six weeks we'd take the cast off a man with a simple fracture of an ankle; after three months the woman with the broken hip would be allowed to bear weight when she walked—and Dave and I would do as we saw fit. If there were questionable cases —problems as to whether the fracture was healed sufficiently to allow the cast to be removed, or whether a reduction was adequate—we'd hold the patient back until later in the morning. Then we'd find Ron or an attending surgeon—usually one or two would drop in for fracture clinic—and get their opinion. Fracture clinic was a lot of work but it was a great opportunity to learn the practical management of fractures.

One thing I learned as an intern was to trust the patient's reaction more than my own immature judgment. This particular lesson I learned while removing a cast from the leg of a Mr. Swanson.

I didn't think it would be difficult. We had our own fracture room, with a cast cutter, plaster and a portable x-ray machine. All I'd have to do would be to find a stretcher or a wheelchair for Mr. Swanson, take him to the fracture room, remove the cast, take the x-rays, develop them, and apply another cast. Really, not too bad a job, once you knew how to do it. The trouble was that as an intern, I didn't know how to do it. Not any of it.

The cast cutter we used was an electric one. The blade didn't rotate; it simply vibrated rapidly. Theoretically, it should be nearly impossible to cut anyone with it.

"Mr. Swanson," I said in my most reassuring voice, "this won't hurt you a bit. You might feel a little heat from the blade as I cut through the plaster, but this blade doesn't spin, it shakes; it can't cut you."

Mr. Swanson still seemed dubious, but he lay back on the stretcher and I went to work. He had on a long leg cast.

I applied the blade to the plaster and pushed the switch. The blade bit into the cast and suddenly I was through it.

"Stop," Mr. Swanson screamed, pulling his leg out of my grasp, "you're cutting me!"

"Nonsense, Mr. Swanson," I replied, "this saw doesn't spin, it shakes. You're just feeling the heat."

"Goddamn it, it feels like a cut to me," he said. "Take it easy."

I went back to work, cautiously and still, every second or third cut, Mr. Swanson would let out a scream. I was beginning to wonder myself whether the saw was actually cutting him.

When I finally got the plaster off, there was no doubt. It had. On both sides of his legs were beautiful incisions. Not deep, thank the Lord, but awfully long. It took some talking but I managed to convince Mr. Swanson that the cuts were his doing; he had jumped too much. I washed his wounds, took the films, and got him back to bed. I had a lot of respect for that saw in the future.

We learned in fracture clinic many things that weren't in the textbooks. One day, for example, I was about to cut the cast off a patient when Dean Voss sauntered up to me and asked what I was doing.

"Just about to cut this cast off, Dr. Voss," I answered, "Mr. Stanhowcy here broke his lateral malleolus six weeks ago. I figure it's time to get him into an Ace bandage."

"What makes you figure that?" Dr. Voss asked.

"That's what it says in the book. Six weeks ought to be enough."

"Take a look at that cast before you cut it off, Bill," he said. "Kind of battered, isn't it?" By now we were far enough away from Mr. Stanhowcy so he couldn't hear us.

"It sure is."

"Why?"

"I don't know. I suppose it's because Mr. Stanhowcy is on the bum. He lives at the Muny."

"Right. Now, what do you think Mr. Stanhowcy is going to do after you take that cast off? He's going back to the Bowery. And what will he do with the Ace bandage you put around his ankle? He'll take it off and try to trade it for a bottle of muscatel. And what will happen to that ankle of his? It will take all the battering that has made such a shambles of that cast.

"If I were you," Dr. Voss continued, "instead of taking off that cast I'd get a couple more rolls of plaster and fix it up. Make it stronger and leave it on him for three more weeks. That book you read tells you how to treat a fracture in some guy who has the money and brains to follow your directions; it hasn't got anything to do with how to treat a patient on the skids."

I put two more rolls of plaster on Mr. Stanhowcy and sent him on his way.

The tip Dr. Voss had given me was one I learned to apply as a matter of policy from that time on. Consider the kind of patient and not just the kind of fracture. If the man was from skid row I made his cast heavy—it was going to take a lot of punishment—and I'd leave it on longer than would ordinarily be necessary.

I always padded casts very well. I might tell the patient to stay in bed and keep his foot elevated for a few days so that his ankle wouldn't swell, but was he going to do as I said? Could he, even if he wanted to, if he was kicked out of his flophouse at seven in the morning? Of course not. Better to put a lot of soft compressible wadding under the plaster and leave room for the swelling; better to take a chance that the bones might slip out of position a little way than to let his foot lose circulation in a cast that has become too tight.

As far as the old women were concerned—sure, I could send them home after two or three weeks in the hospital with a fractured hip. The nail was in place, the wound was healed, they could be up on crutches as long as they didn't put any weight on their leg. But watch them walk. Hell, they might as well leave their crutches in the closet. They were fine when there was a physiotherapist to guide them, but put them out on their own, and they couldn't manage. All the weight went right on the injured hip. Far safer to keep them in the hospital an extra three weeks if I didn't want the good of the operation undone.

We had one fracture patient who interested us more than the others. The fracture itself wasn't much, a run-of-the-mill break of the collarbone. The only treatment needed was the arm in a sling for a few weeks. But the patient was something else—a dancer in a Village night club with a shape that was simply stupendous. And she delighted in showing it off.

She came into the fracture room on clinic day wearing a fur coat. I happened to get her card, so I brought her in and said, "Let's take a look at the arm."

"Could you unbutton my coat?" she asked. "I'm helpless with my arm tied up." I obliged. Lo and behold, she had nothing on underneath except her sling! I guess she noticed my double take because she said, "It's so difficult getting into a blouse that I've decided to go without till this thing heals."

Word got around, and when she came back for her next visit, rank took over. George Mattson, one of the attendings, watched that fracture like a hawk. You'd have thought it was the most complicated problem he'd ever seen.

Doctors are human too.

As a matter of fact, this case illustrates very well a point that laymen sometimes find difficult to comprehend—that from the sexual point of view, the circumstances are most important.

If this girl had come to the clinic as a regular patient for a breast examination, I—or George Mattson—would have palpated and examined her breasts without the slightest erotic interest. True I might have mentioned to one of my buddies the "nice pair I saw this morning," but I wouldn't have been sexually stimulated by the experience. And yet, because these breasts were unnecessarily on display I, as well as every other doctor on the staff, enjoyed the sight of them in a purely non-professional way. I had all I could do not to take a grab at them when I was examining the fracture. I damn near did.

"Unnecessarily" is, I think, the key word. When we have to examine a woman visually or in any other way, our professional sense dominates us to the extent that we become purely doctors and not really men. But let the examination be accidental or unnecessary and we respond just like any other normal man. Thank heaven!

When fracture cases went bad they really went bad. Bone infections are always difficult to treat. Bones don't have as rich a blood supply as most soft tissue organs, so antibiotics, which do their work by attacking bacteria by way of the blood stream, aren't always effective in bone infections. And when there's hardware involved, a metal rod or screw for example, the problem is even worse. The body will tolerate metal as long as there's no infection around it. Once infection sets in it can't be cleared until the metal—the foreign body—is removed.

One of the most distressing cases we had in fractures was a patient named Rafe Johnson. He was a husky Negro, twenty-seven years old, who had been hit by a truck in midtown Manhattan. He had originally been taken to a hospital near the site of the accident, because he had sustained a head injury which needed immediate attention. Ten days later, with his initial problem under control, he was transferred to Bellevue.

His main problem now was a fracture of the femur, the thighbone. It had been shattered in the accident, but probably because his head injury was of paramount importance, had been more or less ignored while he was in the private hospital. At the time of his admission to L4 the x-rays showed that the two ends of the femur were still widely separated.

We put Rafe in traction and for the next five days did our

best to reduce the fracture. We weren't anxious to operate on the injury this long after it had occurred. Rafe, however, was big and muscular—he weighed about two hundred and twenty pounds—and we couldn't get the bones into an acceptable alignment. Reluctantly we decided we had better do an open reduction.

Jack didn't like fracture work very much, so he turned the job over to me. "It'll be a tough one, Bill," he said. "Why don't you get Dean to help you?" So I called Dean Voss, who was particularly interested in fracture work, and he agreed to scrub.

I scheduled the case for eight in the morning; as usual Dean was late. By the time he arrived I had made the incision and was down to the bone. He scrubbed, and with a great deal of tugging and pulling, we managed to get the fracture into an acceptable position.

Our plan was to insert the Kuntschner nail, a long metal rod, into the marrow cavity of the bone. We would thread the two ends of the bone onto this nail and thus maintain the reduction. With the fracture reduced I took the biggest nail we had and prepared to drive it home. Dean stopped me.

"That nail's too narrow," he said.

"It's small for this guy," I conceded, "but it's the biggest we've got. Let's use it."

"No, let's use nested nails"—two nails inserted side by side, to fill out the marrow cavity.

"They'll be too wide, Dean," I objected.

"Let's try them."

I took the two nails, locked them together and tried them for size. "It won't work," I told him. "They just barely fit here, and this is the widest part of the bone. We'll never be able to drive them all the way."

"I think we can," Dean said. "Let's try."

So we tried. We got those nails jammed in the bone and then couldn't drive them all the way without running the risk of splitting the bone wide open. Dean finally agreed it wouldn't work. We'd have to use one nail. But when we tried to pull out the nested nails they wouldn't budge. It was as if they were caught in a vise. We worked with a hammer and pliers for more than an hour before we were finally able to back them out and slip in the single nail.

In a bone case it is dangerous to keep the wound open for a long time. Infection is the Achilles heel of fracture work, and it always means a prolonged hospitalization, and frequently permanent disability. The chances of infection increase in almost direct proportion to the length of time an incision is open.

Rafe Johnson got it. He ran a temperature of 103 degrees every day. We opened his incision and let the pus out, hoping against hope that we could lick the infection without removing the nail. But it was no go. Three weeks after the original operation we took Rafe back to the O.R., removed the nail, and put him back in traction. We had him on the ward for the next six months, a constant reminder that we had screwed him up.

Of all the operations that were done on the fracture service, hip nailings were by far the most common and the most tedious, particularly from the intern's point of view. On a morning when we were doing a hip I'd get up early, pick the blood up in the blood bank, and then stop by the emergency room, take the portable x-ray machine that was kept there and wheel it to the operating room. We needed two x-ray machines so that we could get two views of the hip as we operated.

Then I'd go down to the ward, take the patient out of traction and put him in a Thomas splint, an apparatus that could be applied to the hip to keep it from wiggling, for his trip to surgery.

I'd run back to the operating room in time to help unload the patient and put him on the special table we used when we were operating on hips. It was a table with adjustable leg holders. These enabled us to apply traction to the leg and pull the hip into proper anatomical position. It took ten or fifteen minutes to get the patient strapped into it. Then the anesthetist would put the patient to sleep, and we'd be ready to start the operation.

On hips the intern didn't even scrub. He had to be available to run and develop the x-rays. Most hip operations consist of putting a nail, about three fourths of an inch in diameter, across the fracture, to hold the bone ends together; then, depending on the specific kind of fracture that it is, a metal plate may or may not be attached to the nail and the side of the bone. At various stages of the operation it is necessary to take x-rays, front and side views, to be certain that the fracture is adequately reduced and that the nail is in the proper position. This was the intern's job.

I'll never forget the hip nailing we did on Frank Marlowe. Frank was an old friend of ours at Bellevue, one of those patients who came in as often as he could to dry out and build up his strength for a return to the Bowery. I had only been at Bellevue eight months, and I had already met him on two previous occasions. This time he had fallen down a flight of stairs at the Municipal Lodging House and smashed his hip. And I mean smashed it. Not a nice neat break, but a fracture that left the hip in three big fragments with several smaller chips. A real mess.

When we got Frank on the table Dave Kelly, who was doing the operation, cranked the hip into what he assumed would be the reduced position and then, as he and George Walters scrubbed, I took the films and ran off with them to the developing room. When I got back to the O.R. with them, ten minutes later, they showed that the hip wasn't adequately reduced. Three more turns on the crank, two more x-rays, another dash for the developing room, and fifteen minutes later I was back with the new films. The position was still not perfect, but in view of the fragmentation of the bones, George decided to go ahead with the nailing.

Things went steadily from bad to worse. The first pins weren't in a satisfactory position. Neither were the second. The nail, when Dave finally drove it in, split the shaft of the bone and was too loose to do any good. When he tried to drive another at a different angle it kept slipping into the tract of the old nail. By this time George had taken over, hoping his luck would be better. It wasn't. Finally, in desperation, George sent for Ron. It was then seven o'clock. We had been operating for five hours. I had made at least twenty runs to the developing room. We were all soaked with perspiration.

Ron sauntered up to the O.R. and stuck his head in. "What's up, boys?" he asked. "Running into a little trouble?"

"Ron," George answered, "this goddamn hip is a mess. Every time we try a new angle the nail slips into the old tract. We can't get a decent position."

"Let's see your last films," Ron said.

I held them up. Ron studied them. "Leave it the way it is," he said. "If you don't get out of this O.R. soon, the damn thing will be healed before you can get the wound closed. Frank's tough. He'll be all right."

So we quit. We left the hip not much better than when we had started, but Ron was right. Frank never turned a hair, the hip healed beautifully, and he was back on the bum three months later. It was amazing what some of these Bowery boys could take.

If I were to sum up what I learned during my two months on Fractures, I'd put it this way: textbooks are fine guides to fracture management—for the average patient. But it's important to remember that the average patient is a rare bird; at Bellevue he was all but extinct. So when the doctor stands there looking at an x-ray, he has to remember that the arm or the leg or whatever it is that's shown on the film is attached to a human being, and it's the human being he has to treat.

7

Strange Problems

When it comes to rare diseases, Bellevue is a gold mine. We saw patients with every conceivable problem, many of which rate only a footnote in the standard text; diseases so rare that they're hardly worth mentioning to a class of medical students. Most of the class will never see a case.

Many of these oddities came to the G.U.—genitourinary —service, where I spent eight weeks of my internship. Most of our G.U. patients had prostate, bladder or kidney trouble, which can be painful but is seldom acutely life threatening, so when the nurse in the admitting office woke me on one of my nights on duty to tell me she was sending a patient up to the ward, I was only slightly interested when I mumbled over the phone, "What's his problem?"

"You'll see for yourself soon enough, Doctor," she answered—and giggled. I put the phone down, wondering what this could be all about and, yawning, walked over to the ward.

When I arrived I found a man about fifty sitting in a wheelchair. He was reasonably well dressed and was cleaner than most of our patients. He didn't seem to be in pain, but he looked frightened. I took the admission slip from him and looked at his name.

"What's the problem, Mr. Brooke?" I asked. "Can't you pass your urine?"

"No problem there, Doc," he replied. "I don't even have to go."

"Then what's bothering you?"

He looked around to be certain no one else was listening, then leaned toward me and whispered, "I got a hard-on, Doc, and the damn thing won't go down."

I did a quick double take, and promptly wheeled him into an examining room. He wasn't lying; his penis was turgid and erect.

"What happened?" I asked him. "And tell me the truth."

"I will, Doc—don't worry. You've got to get me better." He was ready to cry. "I got paid today. I'm a longshoreman. After work I went home and washed up and then I stopped off at the Red Owl bar down on the East Side to have a couple of belts.

"After I'd been there an hour I met this broad who was on the make. One thing led to another and about nine o'clock we went up to her place. The deal was the whole night for fifty bucks.

"I'm not a bad man in the saddle, Doc, and this broad was stacked. I knocked her off three times before midnight and then went to sleep. When I woke up at two, I decided to have another.

"It took about half an hour to get it up, but I made it. I stuck it in and went to town, but the goddamn thing wouldn't come. I worked at it for an hour and finally decided to quit. But now the sonuvabitch won't go down. And it's beginning to hurt."

Mr. Brooke, though he didn't know it at the time, was in real trouble. He had what is known as "priapism." I won't go into the anatomy or physiology of the disease, but it's a problem with the blood and blood vessels in the penis and it's difficult to treat. Unfortunately, once it has been cured it's almost impossible to have an erection again.

I didn't tell Mr. Brooke this, of course. As a matter of fact, I didn't know it myself at the time. Instead I went to the phone and called Keith Lang, the G.U. resident on duty with me that night. He came down and we started treatment with anticoagulants and sedation. Eventually we got it down. But, sad to say, Mr. Brooke never got it up again.

Priapism wasn't common, but bizarre sexual problems were. It's amazing what devices men and women will put either into the orifices of their bodies or around the genitalia. We kept a "trophy board" on the second G.U. service on which were displayed a variety of metal rings or tubes into which men had stuck their penises to find later that in the swollen condition, they couldn't be pulled out. The contraptions had to be sawed off the turgid organ.

One of our most interesting cases occurred when a man, rather heavily inebriated, found a willing partner in a woman who was equally drunk. But alcohol, to paraphrase Shakespeare, often "increases the desire but decreases the performance," and to the great disappointment of his lady friend, this man was unable to achieve an erection. Being a resourceful girl, however, she decided to remedy the situation. She took a plastic stirring rod, the type you're likely to find in a Tom Collins, and jammed it into her partner's penis to serve as a "backbone." The sudden pain which he experienced not only erased any libido he might have had, but to his dismay, when he tried to remove this weapon it wouldn't budge. He had to come to the hospital, where, under sedation, we were able to extract it. There was no permanent damage to our patient, but the romance between him and his girl friend was over.

While I was on G.U. there was some interesting experimental work being done on the construction of an artificial penis. Most amputations of the penis are elective surgical procedures done for cancer, and most are done in men of the older age group for whom the loss of the penis is not of great consequence. But once in a while a young man loses his penis, either through an accident or via attack by an enraged individual, and the loss of the organ is disheartening, to say the least. Frank Reilly, our patient with the missing penis, had lost his appendage to the knife of an angry husband. Frank had used his penis with a vengeance and missed it terribly.

When I arrived he had been on the ward for six months, and the chief of surgery and the resident had done several operations in preparation for the fashioning of a new organ. The plan was to create a tube of skin and fat in the lower abdomen, six or eight inches in length, and to insert into it one of Frank's ribs, which could be fastened to the brim of his pelvis. This would, hopefully, give him an organ that might be serviceable.

The problem, of course, was sensation. The penis is an extremely sensitive organ and this new construction would not have anywhere near the number of sense receptors that a normal penis had. But it was expected that simply being able to indulge in sexual relations would make Frank a happier man.

Preparing the tube and implanting the rib required not one but several operations, all of which had been completed before my arrival on the ward. The case was an unusual one, and Dr. Rostad, the chief of surgery on G.U., was reluctant to discharge Frank before he was certain everything was healed. He was also afraid that once Frank was released he would never come back, a course that many Bellevue patients followed.

Finally it was decided to let Frank go out on a forty-eight-hour pass to try out the new organ, if the opportunity presented itself. Frank assured us it would, and he promised to come back and report. We waited anxiously for Frank to reappear on Sunday night. He was supposed to be in by seven, but eight, nine and ten o'clock came and he never showed up. Reluctantly we decided we had lost him, he had let us down, and we prepared to make our late night rounds and head for bed.

As we stepped out of the x-ray reviewing room, where we—the chief resident, assistant resident and I—had been sitting, we saw Frank stumbling down the hallway, drunk as a lord. We ran up to him and helped him into a seat, and the resident asked, "Frank, tell us—what happened? How did it work?"

Frank looked up at us, a broad grin on his face, and said, "Doc, if I were you I'd get rid of the one you got. This baby never goes down. I wish I'd had it twenty years ago. My wife would never have run away with the milkman." As far as Frank was concerned, the operation had been an unqualified success.

Since there were few emergencies on our genitourinary service, the tempo was much more relaxed than on the general surgical wards. This was all right with me. I'd eat breakfast, get to the wards about eight and do my work, which wasn't much different from what it had been on general surgery: draw blood . . . change dressings . . . order x-rays. The only added feature was the necessity of toying with the catheters that weren't functioning well or had become infected. I'd irrigate them until they started functioning again, and if this couldn't be done I'd take them out and insert a new one. Either way the job was more of an exercise than a challenge.

There were exceptions, of course. Passing a catheter into a bladder blocked by a huge prostate can be difficult. There are tricks to it. Phil Bernard, the chief resident, and the assistant residents could usually manage it when I failed, but at times even their skills fell short. When that happened we'd take the patient to the operating room, open into his distended bladder directly through an incision just above the front rim of the pelvis, and sew the catheter in. This would decompress him until we could remove his enlarged prostate. And, great as the discomfort of an inserted catheter might be, there were no patients more grateful than those who had been relieved of a blocked bladder.

Prostate disease, which was what brought at least two thirds of our G.U. patients to the hospital, is a disease of older men. The majority of our patients were in the sixty to eighty age group, and many of them had problems other than their prostate impediment. A fair number were senile, and if we didn't watch them they would wander off the wards and get lost in some other wing of the hospital. It wasn't uncommon to see, taped to the back of a bathrobe, a sign reading "MY NAME IS MICHAEL FINCH. I BELONG TO WARD K4." It was the only way to be certain the old boy wouldn't be permanently lost.

Like all the other wards, G.U. had its equipment problems. But besides the usual lack of needles, syringes and gloves, G.U. suffered constantly from a lack of bottles into which the patients' catheters could be drained. This problem was solved, in typical Bellevue style, by using empty milk cartons as receptacles. The cartons were tied loosely around the waist of the patient, and with his catheter inserted into it, he was then free to stroll around the wards. Not very fancy, but it worked.

Although I had no desire to specialize in G.U., I was anxious to learn as much as I could about the specialty, so I watched and worked diligently while I was there. Mornings when Phil or the assistant residents did cystoscopies, I would work with them. A cystoscope is like a miniature telescope with a light; when it has been passed through the urethra and the bladder is filled with water, it is possible to look through the eyepiece and visualize the inner lining of the bladder. You can spot tumors and other abnormalities which need treatment. I became reasonably adept at cystoscopy. But aside from the techniques of genitourinary practice I learned something of even greater value during my eight-week hitch. I learned that much as I disliked the discipline that Ron Miller imposed on us when we were on the general surgical wards, it was the only way to run the service.

G.U., with its more leisurely pace, attracts a different kind of doctor than does general surgery. Its chief resident was a typical example. Phil Bernard was an easy-going fellow who didn't believe in worrying much about anything. Never wore a necktie to conferences, though it was an unspoken rule that we should; didn't get too concerned if the intern slept an extra hour occasionally; made rounds at whatever time of day he felt like it. He wasn't a slave to routine. But Phil, with his relaxed, happy-go-lucky style, was not a good resident. There was no guiding force, no organizer, no iron-handed supervisor snapping a whip behind us underlings. At times, through negligence or oversight, important tasks would not be done, and the patient would suffer. One case in particular comes to mind—that of Charles Hale, a patient with a cancer of the bladder.

Bladder cancer of a certain type, when it is located in an accessible area, is sometimes treated by removal of the entire bladder and reconstruction of an artificial bladder from an isolated segment of bowel. This is a big operation, and frequently a bloody one. It is only performed on patients who are relatively young and in otherwise good condition.

The key to getting patients through any major operation is to have them in the best possible condition prior to surgery. This means making certain that their heart, lungs and kidneys are all working as well as can be expected and that their nutrition is good. Sometimes this means delaying surgery for a week or two, possibly longer, with the expectation that the time spent in preparing the patient adequately will pay off in an increased chance of survival and a relatively smooth convalescence.

This was, of course, what was planned for Charlie Hale. We kept him on the ward for three weeks, saw to it that he ate well and drank plenty of fluids, had the appropriate x-rays taken and the proper consultations. Then we put him on the schedule.

There was only one oversight. No one bothered to check his latest lab tests before we took him to the operating room. After an hour of surgery he went into shock, though he hadn't lost a great deal of blood, and it was only then that we noticed that his blood level that morning had been only ten grams—two thirds of normal. We poured three pints into him on the operating table and he made the grade, but it was a near miss.

On general surgery, with old compulsive Ron directing the show, Charlie Hale's hemoglobin level would have been checked and double-checked before he left the ward. There would have been no chance for a slip-up. Oversights in surgery can be lethal.

8

Blood

I don't think anyone who isn't a doctor can really appreciate just how important blood is. You have to try to salvage some man who is bleeding like the devil from a peptic ulcer, or work to save some young woman in shock with a ruptured ectopic pregnancy, or treat a child who has just fallen out of a tree and ruptured his spleen, to realize how disastrous blood loss can be. One minute this man, woman or child is pink, warm, dry, calm and collected; the next he's pale, cold, sweaty and irrational. It's enough to scare you out of your wits.

I'll never forget the first patient I ever saw who was bled out. I was an intern at the time, covering the female emergency ward at night, and I was called down to see a young Negro girl who had just been admitted via ambulance from another hospital which had had "no beds." She had gone there complaining of pain in her belly and had been transferred to Bellevue.

By the time they wheeled her into our emergency room, maybe fifteen minutes after she had left the other hospital, she wasn't complaining of anything. She was just writhing wildly around in the bed holding on to her belly and talking irrationally, "Jesus save me!" she'd shout, and then, "Watch out, you bastard, don't hurt me!" at some imaginary assailant.

My initial guess was that she was either drunk or crazy, so I immediately grabbed her head between my hands and held her still long enough to get a sniff of her breath. No booze—and if you worked at Bellevue you knew what booze smelled like.

So I assumed she was out of her mind, hysterical for one reason or another. I had the nurse hold her arms and I slapped her face to try to snap her out of it. How else was I going to find out what was bothering her?

No go. I couldn't get her to talk sense or to stop jumping around. I said to the nurse, "That jackass in the emergency room has pulled a lulu. He admits a nut to surgery. Why the hell didn't he bug her? Better get Dr. Walters down here. Maybe he can get her transferred."

We strapped the patient down, and while the nurse went to call my senior resident, I made a start at examining this wild woman. Before I was half through, mumbling to myself about what a waste of time it was for me, a surgeon, to be taking care of a psycho patient, George Walters arrived. He felt her forehead, took her pulse, pushed once on her adbomen and said, "Bill, this woman's no nut. She's in shock, and I'll bet she's got a ruptured ectopic. Let's get her to the operating room."

And of course he was right. She had all the classic signs of shock—sweaty, cold, faint and rapid pulse—but I'd missed them. I'd been too impressed by her wild behavior, which arose not from any mental disease, but from the fact that she just didn't have enough blood to pump through her brain. We poured two pints of blood into her as rapidly as we could, took her to the operating room and opened her up. She had a ruptured extrauterine pregnancy, with blood pouring out of one of the arteries to the fallopian tube, and about four pints of blood lying free in her belly. The next morning, with her blood level back where it belonged, her mind was clear as a bell.

Needless to say, I had learned a great lesson.

With crises like this a daily occurrence in a place like Bellevue, it's easy to understand why so much emphasis is put on the necessity for keeping the supply high in the blood bank. If we hadn't had two pints of A+ on hand at the time this young woman came in, the most astute diagnosis in the world wouldn't have saved her. She would have been gone in another hour.

But the filled bottles just didn't appear on the shelves of the blood-bank icebox; it had to be put there either through donations or by purchase. At Bellevue there just wasn't enough money to buy blood. We relied on donors. It was the job of each division of the house staff to keep its blood-bank credit good. Records were kept, and if an intern on Second Surgery found a donor, the pint contributed was credited to the Second Surgical account. If we used two pints, they were deducted from our credit.

It was imperative that we maintain a positive balance. Once a division got into the red, all elective surgery was canceled. Only cancer and emergency surgery could be scheduled, no hemorrhoids, hernias, veins or even gall bladders. A terrible situation, particularly from the intern's point of view, because elective surgery was just about the only kind he got to do. If this was canceled, his days and weeks were nothing but work without even the occasional reward of a hernia to repair, hemorrhoids to remove or a vein to strip. A fate, from his point of view, too horrible to contemplate. So, inevitably, it became another of the intern's many responsibilities to keep the blood flowing.

There were very few restrictions on how to approach the problem. You could use your ingenuity any way you wanted in getting donors, and the administration would either condone your methods or look the other way. On our division we had an incentive plan—a fifth of liquor and an afternoon off for the intern who brought in the most donors each month. The competition was terrific.

The key to the problem was to get the people to give blood for a patient *before* he needed it, and even if he would probably never need it. Once a patient had had blood—once the transfusion was given—families and friends were much more difficult to persuade. They knew very well that you couldn't take the blood back. But beforehand it was a different story. Then you could say, "Look, your mama needs blood—at least three pints—or she may bleed to death when we operate on her. You'd better go right down to the blood bank and donate, and take your friends with you." This figure, three, was given for cases such as hernia repairs, hemorrhoids and veins, when you would almost never need to transfuse the patient—a fact with which most laymen aren't acquainted. If there was a chance that the patient might actually need a pint or two—say, for a gall bladder, a stomach or a breast—then six or ten pints were demanded.

When a patient was young and healthy, it was even possible to get him to donate blood to himself. If, for example, we ran across such a man in the outpatient department and he happened to have a hernia, we might say, "Go over to the blood bank and donate a pint of blood to the credit of the Second Surgical Division. Then come back in two weeks and we'll fix your hernia." Two weeks would be enough to get his blood level back to normal.

Sometimes we'd get the patients to donate after their operation. Usually we'd be unable to talk them into it, but once in a while it worked. It could be dangerous. One intern talked a hernia patient into donating on the day he left the hospital, advising him to keep the fact of his recent surgery to himself. When the man got off the table after giving up his blood he fainted, fell to the floor and fractured his skull. He spent the next three weeks in the hospital. (The intern who recruited this donor was asked to please use more discretion in the future, but he won the bottle of booze that month.)

The best time to find potential donors was on Sunday

afternoon during visiting hours. The intern on duty was expected to make "blood rounds" on Sunday and to cajole, threaten or even bludgeon families and friends into giving blood. No holds were barred.

There were some very original and devious tales told. "Your father must have blood immediately," one of my co-interns once said to a big family. "If you don't all donate we'll just have to give him dog blood, and that doesn't always work well." Needless to say, the family moved en masse to the blood bank.

A more subtle approach was to simply stand at the foot of the bed, shaking one's head in dismay, watching the clear sugar-water infusion running into the patient's veins and muttering, "If only it were blood!"—just loud enough for the family to hear. Usually the discussion that resulted from this approach was good for at least one pint.

Occasionally some member of a family which had donated ten pints for Mama's hemorrhoidectomy would learn from her that she had never had a transfusion. He would then accost the intern, as belligerent as a man who has been "taken" is apt to be, demanding that Mama be transfused. The standard approach was to explain that Mama had received her blood while under anesthesia, so naturally she wouldn't know anything about the transfusion. This would usually suffice, but I know one intern who, when up against a real tiger, surreptitiously added a vial of congo red—an innocuous vegetable dye—to a bottle of 5 percent dextrose in water and transfused Mama with the red water in full view of the family, satisfying them immediately. He didn't *say* it was blood; they simply assumed it.

The obstetrics and gynecology division had by far the easiest time getting blood donors. When our surgical patients bled, it was usually into the bowel or during surgery, so the blood wasn't visible and the family had to take our word for it, but when the obstetrical or gynecological patients bled, the blood was there for everyone to see. The gynecology resident could hold up a blood-soaked pad—if necessary, he would do just that—and the husband would run for the blood bank, dragging his friends with him.

To make things even sweeter, in most of their patients the bleeding was more apparent than real. Ninety percent never lost enough blood to warrant even a one-pint transfusion. It just looked like a lot of blood. So they'd get six pints donated for a woman who hadn't lost more than a few ounces. For the gynecology service it was routine to have a hundred or more pints of blood to their credit in the blood bank.

But for the rest of us, using every trick we could think of, it was a constant battle. Just when we'd get twenty or thirty pints ahead and think we were on easy street, *bang!* A derelict from the Bowery would come in—no family, no friends, no money—and proceed to bleed out fifteen pints from his esophageal varices, the dilated veins in the esophagus resulting from cirrhosis of the liver. We'd be right back where we started from.

There were instances when we had to schedule a patient for surgery on whom we didn't want to operate just because we were running out of blood. We might have wished that we could keep transfusing a bleeder, because he might stop, and his chances of surviving surgery were extremely poor, but when the blood was almost gone our hand would be forced. Sometimes disastrously.

When we had two or three big bleeders in a row and were in desperate straits, the resident would fire his last gun. He'd pick up a few dollars from the party fund of the division, buy some bottles of muscatel and head for the Bowery. For a bottle of wine it was usually possible to get a denizen of the Bowery to come up to the hospital and donate. We'd round up enough of these cheap donors to get us back in the black. (Eventually about half the pints so purchased were rejected because the donor would have a positive Wassermann, but by the time the serology test came back we'd have re-established our credit by more conventional methods.)

The medical services had it even tougher than we did on surgery. Many of their patients required blood for medical anemias of one kind or another, and there was often nothing dramatic enough about their diseases to persuade potential donors that blood was a critical necessity. They had a very tough time staying in the black. Which led, on occasion, to some real battles between our medical and surgical services. A typical instance was one which concerned an ulcer patient.

I was a senior resident at the time, and one of my jobs was to do consultations for the medical division. I'd see their patients when they developed surgical complications, just as the medical resident would see one of our patients if, for example, one of them had a coronary—the general rule being to keep the patient on the ward that best suited his major illness. In other words, if a patient who had come in to have his hernia repaired had a massive heart attack, the medical consultant would take the patient in transfer to the medical ward, just as we would accept a patient from the medical ward who developed a perforated ulcer while undergoing treatment for virus pneumonia.

The battle I remember particularly well concerned a patient with a duodenal ulcer. He had been on the medical ward for two weeks when he suddenly started to bleed. The medical resident asked me to examine him to see if I thought we should operate on him as an emergency. I saw the patient and agreed he ought to have surgery. But at that point he needed about three more pints of blood before we could take him to the operating room. So I wrote on the order sheet: "Give this patient three more units of blood before transferring to surgery." Then I left the ward.

When the medical resident read my consultation he blew his stack. He called me, over the phone, every name under the sun. He would like hell transfuse this patient—we could do that. We were going to operate on him; we could use our blood getting him ready.

I was as mad as he was by this time. Why the hell should we use our blood to bail their patient out of the mess they'd gotten him into by temporizing with their cockeyed medical treatment? Why hadn't they called me as soon as he started to bleed? If they wanted to let their patients bleed down, that was their business, but I'd be damned if I was going to use up three pints of our blood to get them out of the hole. As it was, it would probably take two more of our pints just to get him through the operation.

I won the battle. There was nothing the medical resident could do. The patient was theirs until I accepted him in transfer, and I wouldn't take him until they had given him the blood. They finally transfused him and sent him over, but the resident stayed sore at me for a week.

This sort of exchange worked both ways, of course. They'd refuse to take our patients in transfer until we had tranfused them, if they needed blood; it was just a matter of protecting one's blood supply. And so the battle for blood went on constantly. With the patients, the families, the other services and the administration. If you let up, if you stopped hustling, you'd get so far behind that you could never catch up—but we never did let up.

Once you've worked in a hospital where blood is in short supply, you never lose your respect for it. Even now, with a local Red Cross program that keeps our hospital refrigerator well stocked, I never order a transfusion without momentarily wondering where the pint's coming from and what the transfusing is going to do to our credit. You can bet none of my patients get any blood unless I'm damn sure they need it.

Which is, of course, as it should be.

9

Pathology: Six Months In the Death House

"Nolen," Dr. Williams said, giving me a look of disgust, "you've botched this heart up completely.

A first-year medical student could do a better job of opening a heart. Didn't anyone show you how to do it properly?"

"No, sir. I didn't ask. It didn't seem that complicated."

"Didn't it?" The sarcasm was inches thick. "Well, it is. And don't you do another autopsy till you've learned to do the job right."

All of us on pathology who had done autopsies the previous day were assembled at eight-thirty in Williams' office for a ritual known as "the organ recital." We'd place our tray laden with segments of organs, or even entire organs if it seemed necessary, before Williams much as a waiter at the Four Seasons might present a pressed duck. Williams received our offerings with undisguised pleasure.

Thumbing through the clinical chart of the deceased patient, I had presented the pertinent information, ending with the clinical diagnosis (acute myocardial infarction) while Williams handled and examined the organs. "Take a look at this liver." Williams said, picking up the slab from the tray. "See the congestion?" He squeezed it and blood ran out. "This man had chronic passive congestion, probably due to his heart failure."

After examining the lungs and kidneys, he came to the *pièce de résistance*—the heart. He turned it over and over in his hands, and with a puzzled look on his face made that scathing remark about a first-year med student, which was particularly humiliating since I had just graduated from intern to assistant resident on the pathology section. He then made several more cuts in the heart—showed us the fresh hemorrhage, the old scars, the arteriosclerotic plaques in the organ—and said, "This is one of the rare times when those damn fools on Medicine were right. The man died of an acute infarction. Next case."

After the conference I asked Harry Dennis, the chief resident, what Williams meant about the heart.

"I should have warned you," Harry said. "That's one of his pet peeves. He can't stand it when someone opens a heart any way other than his. Bring it over here and I'll show you how he wants it done."

The technique was simple, and I could see that it made it easier to examine the heart without missing any pathology in the valves or the muscle.

Autopsies took up a lot of time. I hated them. I still do. There is something about working on a dead body that repels most doctors. I suppose it's just that we're human and can't help but realize that this is how we too will wind up some day. We're all aware of this anyway, I know, but subconsciously. Spending three hours examining a corpse drives the point home with brutal intensity. It's also true that autopsies remind us of our fallibility. Doctors are supposed to keep patients alive. Every time we let a patient die we've failed to do our job. Inevitable, no doubt, but still hard to take.

But autopsies are a necessity. Medicine, despite all its elaborate diagnostic techniques, remains an inexact science, and if we did not discover mistakes before we buried them, we'd never realize where we went wrong or even if we had. The purpose of post-mortem examinations was not solely to make us aware of our errors. Most of the time there were no errors to be noted, except in the sense that any death represents a failure, an error for the responsible physician.

Autopsies gave us the opportunity to see and study the end result of disease. Just where had the cancer spread? What effect had the infection had on the various organs of the body? How did the scar in the heart correlate with the changes in the electrocardiogram? Hopefully, by studying what had happened to our patients who had died, we'd be able to learn something of value that we could use in treating our patients of the future.

An entire autopsy took me about two hours to perform, sometimes a little longer if the findings were unusual. When I was done, I'd have the entire heart and representative slices of all the other organs on a tray. These fresh tissues were kept in the refrigerator overnight covered with a damp cloth, to undergo "gross" examination—examination with the naked eye—the next morning. In a jar, "fixed" in formalin, would be small parts of all the internal organs—liver, pancreas, adrenal gland, etc.—and many pieces, known as "sections," of any diseased organs. These preserved pieces had been cut in thin slices and stained with dyes by technicians for subsequent microscopic examination, and were "fixed" immediately for that purpose only; otherwise autolysis, a sort of self-digestion, would occur and make microscopic interpretation impossible.

Two or three times a week an intern would walk into my office and hand me an autopsy permit. The first thing I'd do was check the signature because pathologists live in constant dread that they'll perform an autopsy on someone whose next of kin has denied permission. People are awfully touchy about what happens to the deceased. They'll sign a permit allowing you to do a huge operation on their ninety-year-old mother without batting an eye, but when it comes to an autopsy it usually takes a family conference before the responsible member will give permission.

Sometimes there are no relatives—no one to claim the body. The corpse then becomes a "five-day case." The body is put in the morgue in a refrigerated drawer, and if no one shows up to claim it in five days, then the autopsy can be done. Afterward the city will bury the remains in potter's field. Frequently, however, one or the other of the medical schools will claim five-day cases for their anatomy classes. Bodies for dissection aren't in great supply and these unclaimed corpses provide the bulk of them. If a part was missing—if, for example, a major abdominal operation had been done and several organs removed—then the body was of no value to the school and we'd do the autopsy. Otherwise, if the case had been a puzzler and the clinicians wanted the autopsy badly, they would have to fight it out with the medical school. The medical school usually won.

The only circumstances under which a permit was unnecessary was when the case belonged to an M.E. (medical examiner). Any death which resulted from an accident, or where the circumstances suggested foul play, or in which the patient hadn't been under a doctor's care—e.g., a patient who passed out on the street and was brought to the hospital D.O.A. (dead on arrival)—was an M.E. case. It was the medical examiner who had to sign the patient's death certificate, and he could elect to do an autopsy or not.

The M.E.'s were the only doctors I knew who didn't seem to mind autopsies. I suppose it was because they did so many; since Bellevue was the chief city morgue, all the accidents, murders and suicides in Manhattan wound up on a slab in our autopsy room.

Most pathologists wear rubber gloves, not only for esthetic reasons but for protection against acquiring infectious diseases, tuberculosis in particular. If a pathologist should inadvertently cut himself while handling a diseased organ, he might acquire whatever infection the organ harbored. But Dr. Williams and his assistant always worked barehanded; they insisted that rubber gloves interfered with the sense of touch and hence the accurate interpretation of the pathology. One of the M.E.'s even smoked a cigar when he worked, resting it occasionally on the slab and then nonchalantly popping it back into his mouth. I could hardly bear to watch him.

The worst cases of all were the "floaters"—the bodies that were fished out of the East River when they surfaced weeks or months after immersion. As soon as you stepped into the building in the morning you knew if a floater was being autopsied. The stench spread through all five floors of the building. You couldn't escape it. How an M.E. could go close enough to one of those bodies to do his autopsy was beyond me. But I guess some people can get used to anything.

Each of the four medical schools—Columbia, New York University, Postgraduate and Cornell—ran its own pathology division, but the entire department was under the direction of one full-time chief. Ralph Williams was the boss when I arrived; Leo Benson was his assistant. To the Cornell pathology section were assigned one resident in surgery and one intern in medicine from our Cornell Surgical and Medical Divisions. I was the assistant resident in surgery; Sam Hanson was the intern from the Cornell Medical Division. Sam took care of the pathology interests of his medical confreres; I watched out for those of our surgeons.

With few exceptions, like the early-morning organ re-cital in Dr. Williams' office, the days on pathology were mostly routine. The next interruption was apt to come from the operating room. One of the interns would phone to tell me that the resident had just removed a breast. I'd go over to the operating room and get it fresh, rather than having them put it in formalin, because it is easier to find the lymph nodes—the bean-sized glands that are excised with the breast in a cancer operation—when the specimen is fresh. It's important to find as many of these glands as possible and to note their relationship to the breast proper. After picking out the glands, we would put them, with the rest of the specimen, into formalin to await fixing.

Frozen sections also interfered with the routine progress of the day. These are slides made by instantly freezing and staining a fresh, as opposed to a formalin-preserved, piece of tissue. The quality of the color on the slide is not as good, nor are the microscopic details as fine, as when "fixed" tissue is used, but the frozen-section technique has the advantage of allowing a diagnosis to be made while the surgeon is still operating.

Emergency frozen sections weren't common but elective frozen sections were frequent. With breast lumps for example, frozen sections were always done. The surgeon would remove the lump, and while waiting for the result of the biopsy, would close the incision. If it indicated malignancy he would change his gown and gloves, and using fresh instruments to avoid introducing any cancer cells, proceed with the radical removal of the breast. If the lump was benign the operation was over.

In many hospitals there's a laboratory in the operating suite where frozen section can be done. At Bellevue the assistant resident on pathology got a lot of exercise tearing from the operating room to the pathology building.

My day began, after breakfast in the doctors' dining room, with a trip to pick up the specimens from the surgery done the previous day. There might be a gall bladder, an appendix and a prostate, each one in its own individual bottle of formalin, on the Second Division shelf in the specimen room off the operating suite. I'd carry the bottles in a small basket to our room in the pathology building. There were two ways of getting there from the main hospital building. One route required a trip outdoors through a small courtyard that separated the buildings. The other was via a tunnel which ran between the two buildings. Although the trip through the courtyard took a few extra minutes and necessitated a climb up a long flight of stairs, I chose the long way around, even when a blizzard was raging. Why? Because the trip through the tunnel was a veritable nightmare. Bellevue, because of its age and its clientele, was a dirty hospital even in its cleanest areas. In its subterranean passages it was, to put it midly, frightening. The tunnel to the pathology building and morgue was poorly lit. It was damp and dirty, and one could hear rats scurrying around in the areas where the light didn't penetrate. Nor was it unusual to encounter a stray cat wandering around looking for these rodents. And where did the tunnel enter the pathology building? In the basement morgue, where death was in the very air we breathed. So maybe I wasn't frightened of the tunnel, really, but neither was I fond of it. Cold ears and wet feet were a small price to pay for avoiding that route.

On arrival in our second-floor office, a big room with three desks, a sink and specimen bottles on every shelf, I'd take my collection of tissues over to the cutting board and go to work. If there were no interruptions, and depending on how many specimens I had to examine, I'd usually finish this job about ten-thirty. The rest of the morning I'd devote to examining under the microscope the slides made from the surgical tissues which I had cut the previous day.

To say that during the first few weeks my interpretations of the microscopic slides were worthless would be a gross understatement. I had studied pathology in medical school—it's a standard required course—but that was three years before. Even at my best I had never been very adept at recognizing what I was looking at, nor, if I may say so, had any other sophomore medical student of my acquaintance. You can't acquire that skill by reading *Anderson's Pathology* any more than you can learn to take out an appendix by browsing through *Cutler's Atlas of Surgical Technique.*

But I had to begin sometime and at Bellevue the philosophy was, as usual, "Throw him in; he'll learn to swim." I'd sit down at the microscope and look at the tissues, thumb through the pathology atlases trying to match what I saw, and then write a description and a microscopic diagnosis. If I didn't know the slides were taken from a thyroid I might study them for fifteen minutes and then make a diagnosis of "prostate cancer," but it was assumed that after enough stumbling around and thumbing through the books, perhaps I'd at least acquire a nodding acquaintance with the microscopic manifestations of surgical disease.

An assignment I had to take care of during my occasional nights on duty was that of performing emergency laboratory work. It was a farce. I had no more business doing blood chemistries than a night watchman. But there were no lab technicians on call at night, so it fell on the pathologist—and I use the term loosely—to do the job.

One night I got a call from a resident on medicine named Charles Floyd. I didn't know the fellow very well but I had heard he was the compulsive sort. He needed three pages of lab work before he'd diagnose a hangnail.

"Dr. Nolen," he said to me, quite formally, "I have a patient here that I think may have pancreatitis. I'd like to have you do a serum amylase on him stat." "Stat." means "immediately."

"Gee, Dr. Floyd," I said, adopting his formal approach, "I've never done an amylase. Can't it wait till morning?"

"No, it can't," he said emphatically. "I want it, and I want it now. I'll send the blood right over."

When it arrived I took the blood to the laboratory, got out the books, and finally found the tubes and reagents I needed for the test. The thing was awfully complicated. It required two determinations, made separately, the second of which was to be subtracted from the first to give the final answer. A normal serum amylase runs between sixty and eighty. In pancreatitis it often gets well into the hundreds.

After laboring mightily for two hours I finally came up with the figures. I called Dr. Floyd and told him, "I've finally got your answer."

"It's about time," he snapped. "What is it?"

"Minus forty," I said.

There was a silence at the other end. Then: "What's this, Nolen—your idea of a joke? There's no such thing as a minus amylase—"

"I don't give a goddamn whether there is or isn't," I interrupted. "That's the way it comes out for me, and that's the way it's going to stay. If you don't like it you can shove it up your ass." I hung up.

Word got around, and I was never asked to do an amylase again.

The final variant in my established daily routine was provided by the "sign-out" conference, the belt the pathologists wore to go with their suspenders. At this conference we'd all sit around a big table, each with his own microscope, and the tissue slides which we had reviewed, described and diagnosed earlier would be passed around the table for one final general perusal before the diagnosis was sent to the clinical ward. It was my job to present the Second Surgical Division slides, one by one, to the chief pathologist, who would take responsibility for signing the pathology slip.

I was also expected to run periodic pathology conferences with our surgical division. I'll never forget one such conference which took place near the end of my stay on pathology. The projector we used to show these slides was powered by a carbon arc. It took an intense light to bring out the details of a microscopic slide projected in a conference room.

I was proud of my ability to run this projector. It required a certain amount of finesse and I had mastered it. I had gotten so good at using it that I was continually being called upon to show slides at conferences, not only in general surgery but even on the subspecialties. I enjoyed doing it. I didn't know a hell of a lot about pathology, but I usually knew more than anyone else at the conference, and it made me feel like a professor to flash the microscopic picture on the screen, take my pointer and say, "Here's the point of transition from normal mucosa to malignant mucosa—can you all see that?" I reveled in the appreciative nods.

On this particular day I was really rolling, carried away by the sound of my own voice. I was discussing kidney and prostate pathology for the G.U. service, and there were half a dozen attending surgeons in the crowd. I knew most of them, from my stay on G.U. as an intern, but there was one I didn't recognize. I assumed he was a new addition to the staff.

I had just shown a kidney slide, so now I thought I'd show a case of benign prostatic enlargement. I chose the slide from my box and projected it onto the screen.

"Would anyone care to tell me what this slide shows?" I asked. I really enjoyed playing teacher.

Bud Levi, who was the resident on genitourinary surgery at that time, said, "It looks like a cancer of the prostate to me."

"Sorry, Bud," I corrected him, "that prostate is benign. Take a close look at those glands—see how regular they are? If that were malignant you'd see more variation in the size of the cells, and a greater pleomorphism." This was one of my favorite new words; it meant only "many shapes," but it sounded good. "Now I'll show you a real cancer." As I reached for my slide box, a voice from the corner said quietly, "That is a cancer."

I looked up. It was the attending I hadn't recognized.

"Look again at those glands," he said gently. "See the bizarre pattern? That only occurs in cancer."

Instead of looking at the slide I sneaked a look into my

box. He was right. I had picked up the cancer slide rather than the benign slide. Fortunately the room was dark; my red face didn't show.

"I think you're right, at that, sir," I said quickly. "I hadn't noticed that before. In fact, I'm certain you're right. Thank you for correcting me."

For the rest of the conference I was considerably less authoritative in my tone. I found out later that the unidentified attending was a visiting pathologist whose specialty was genitourinary diseases. It was hardly fair.

But, even considering this incident, I found that as the end of my six-month assignment approached. I had learned a fair amount of pathology, and in the autopsy room I was reasonably adept. I could do a post-mortem examination neatly and efficiently, and I rarely overlooked any significant pathology. I might still have to call someone with more experience to tell me what that lump in the kidney was, but at least I wouldn't overlook the lump. I would still never dare rely on my interpretation of a frozen section—I knew I wasn't that good—but I hadn't expected to reach that point in a six-month hitch, so I wasn't disappointed.

As an aspiring surgeon, perhaps the most important thing I had learned in these six months was that pathologists are fallible too. Before I had any experience in their field I was under the impression, common to most clinicians, that pathology is an exact science. When a pathologist said, "Cancer" —by God, it was cancer, and when he said, "This man died of a cerebral hemorrhage"—why, that too was gospel. Now I knew this just wasn't true. Sure, pathologists could recognize cancer and find the cause of death most of the time, but not always.

I also learned that they are a very cautious breed; they have to be. If they make an error in the interpretation of a slide, it may mean the difference between life and death for a patient. When a pathologist says a breast lump is malignant, the surgeon will do a radical mastectomy—a major operation which is occasionally fatal. If he calls the lump benign, then no big operation is necessary. Either way, he had better be right.

Sometimes, even after consultation, doubt would remain. "Better dig out that stomach and take a few more cuts. The ulcer looks peculiar. You may be on the edge of a cancer. Send a few more pieces through." The next day at sign-out conference we'd go over the slides again.

In my six months on pathology I decided that a lack of self-confidence was an endemic disease among pathologists. Instead of exercising the reasonable caution the pathologists ought to apply, they would become unreasonably irresolute and indecisive, unable to make up their minds even in clear-cut cases. The lack of pressure for immediate decisions was probably what attracted some of them into the speciality in the first place. Surgeons were used to making weighty decisions immediately; you couldn't sit and think about a possible perforated ulcer for twenty-four hours. You weighed the pros and cons, made a decision, and for better or worse, took action. Doctors who couldn't take this sort of pressure gravitated to specialties like pathology.

With exceptions, of course—and Drs. Benson and Williams were among them. They could take pressure—they were willing to sign slides out—and it was partly because they had guts that they headed the department. When Williams was absent Dr. Benson took the responsibility for signing out the slides. But if Benson too was away, lecturing or at an autopsy, then we were in trouble. The next man in seniority was Jeff Brown. He had his boards and was well trained, but he lacked guts.

If the specimen was an obviously inflamed gall bladder, he wouldn't mind signing his name to "acute cholecystitis." It didn't really matter much whether the gall bladder was inflamed or not; it was out and that was that. The surgeon wasn't going to do something wild, no matter what Jeff Brown called it. But when it was a weighty decision, one that might mean radical surgery for the patient instead of conservative management, Jeff Brown would turn chicken.

"This breast lump looks malignant," he'd say, "but it's kind of an odd one. Better save it for Dr. Williams." "This lymph node might be an early leukemia, but I really can't be certain. Why don't you get some more sections, and we'll show it to Dr. Benson tomorrow?" When Jeff ran the conference, only the most obvious things were ever signed out.

I knew now that in my future career as a surgeon I'd look upon the pathologist as just another guy trying to help in the total care of the patient. I knew that the more information I gave him about my case, the easier it would be for him to help me manage my problems, and that, distasteful as the autopsy room might be, it was a place I'd have to make myself visit on occasion if I was to learn from my mistakes.

10

Assistant Resident: One Step Up

Early in my career as an assistant resident on general surgery, Bob Knudson, the intern who worked with me nights, called me out of card rounds about four o'clock one afternoon to come to the E.W. He had a patient, admitted earlier in the day, who he thought was getting into respiratory difficulties and he wanted me to see him.

Mr. Anders was in trouble, all right. He had six broken ribs on the left side, and four were cracked on the right. He had so much pain that he couldn't take a deep breath, and his lungs weren't expanding fully. Mucus was beginning to collect and he bubbled when he breathed.

"I think we'd better trache him, don't you?" Bob asked me. (There's no such word as "trache"—the *a* is long—but a verb we had created out of "tracheotomy"; more Bellevuese.)

"Yeah, I guess so," I replied. I wasn't dead certain that the man couldn't pull through without it, but there's a rule in medicine which says, "Whenever you think about doing a tracheotomy, do it." If you follow the rule you avoid letting bad situations get worse because of a natural reluctance to make a hole in a man's neck. A tracheotomy allows you to suck out mucus and makes breathing much easier for the patient.

I'd done a half dozen tracheotomies as an intern, but I'd always had help from the assistant resident. Now I was the A.R., so I was supposed to lead my intern through the case. He was happy as a lark at the thought of operating. I was scared to death of the whole thing.

Tracheotomies usually aren't all that hard. In a pinch I think anyone with guts, layman or doctor, could do one if he had read the directions. But this guy looked like he might be an exception to the rule. He was bull-necked, which is to say he had almost no neck at all, and even with his head bent way back, his shoulders up on a pillow, I had difficulty feeling his trachea. But it had to be done, so, with the tracheotomy set arranged on the table, I washed his neck with an antiseptic, and Bob and I put on gloves.

"Go ahead," I said.

He put in the novocaine, took his knife and cut through the skin.

"Give me a clamp." He handed one to me.

"I'll spread in one direction, you spread in the other," I said. After several attempts we managed to spread the muscles, and at the bottom of the hole, which was perhaps two inches deep, we could see the trachea. So far so good.

"You're hurting me," Mr. Anders said. Bob put in more novocaine.

"All right," I said, "give me the tracheotomy tube. You cut a hole in the trachea, and I'll put in the tube."

I'd better explain what the instrument looks like. It's a hollow metal tube, the curve of which makes a quarter of a circle, and it comes in a variety of sizes. (the average tube measures about three quarters of an inch in diameter). The curve is such that one end of the tube can rest at skin level while the other is in the trachea.

Down at the bottom of the hole I could see the glistening white trachea sliding up and down as Mr. Anders breathed.

"Ready?"

Bob nodded.

"Okay—cut."

Bob shoved his knife into the trachea, and air immediately began bubbling up into the wound. He made another stab at right angles to the first. Mr. Anders was now coughing and spitting into the wound.

I took the tube and jammed it into the wound. "There," I said. "Not a bad job." But Mr. Anders was still coughing and sputtering, and his color was none too good.

I took the rubber catheter of the suction machine and put it into the tracheotomy tube to suck out the mucus. The catheter wouldn't go past the end of the tube.

"This damn thing is plugged," I shouted. I was beginning to perspire.

"Gee, Bill," Bob said, "look at his neck. It's getting bigger." Sure enough, Mr. Anders' neck was increasing in size by the minute.

"He's blowing air into his neck, goddamn it!" I was in a state of panic. "Let me see that tube."

I looked down into the hole in the neck. The lower end of the tracheotomy tube was resting on top of the trachea. It hadn't gone into the hole Bob had cut. All it was doing was blocking the opening in the skin so that the air from the trachea blew into the tissues of the neck.

"Hold that light," I said. All pretense that Bob was doing this case was now gone. I had got us into this mess and it was my job to get us out.

I pulled out the tube, grasped the trachea in a clamp and this time managed to put the tube into the trachea. Mucus and blood spurted out of the open end but so did air, and Mr. Anders went from blue to pink.

I sat down and wiped my brow. The towels which we had draped near our incision had long ago fallen by the wayside. Sterile technique had vanished.

I looked over at Bob. He was as wet as I was.

"How you doing, Mr. Anders?" I asked.

He gurgled his reply. I'd forgotten he couldn't talk with his tracheotomy. I plugged it momentarily. "Okay now," he said, "but I thought for a while there I was a goner."

"Now, now, Mr. Anders," I said. "No need to worry. We have everything under control." It was true at that moment, but it certainly hadn't been two minutes before.

From all the air that had leaked into his neck, Mr. Anders looked like a chipmunk with a mouth full of nuts, but that wasn't going to hurt him and it didn't worry us. It would be absorbed in the next few days.

We tied his tracheotomy tube in place and went back to card rounds.

"What have you been up to?" Ernie Gallow asked as we joined the group.

"We had to trache Anders, the one with the fractured ribs," I answered.

"Any problems?"

I looked at Bob. "No," I said, "everything went just fine." I had to give Bob credit; he didn't crack a smile.

What goes on in the operating room is important, even critical, to a patient's survival and well-being. But faulty preoperative preparation or careless postoperative management can ruin even the finest of surgical procedures and spell disaster for the patient. It was now my job to be certain that this didn't occur.

My career as an A.R. in general surgery began on New Year's Day. This, even at Bellevue, is a holiday. We were open for business, naturally, but with the weekend crew— one intern and one A.R.—to cover both male wards and the female emergency ward. There was no elective surgical schedule, so, after breakfast, I sat down at the nurses' station and went through the charts of the patients on the ward.

The assistant resident's job differs from that of the intern in many particulars, all of which grow out of the increased responsibility that the A.R. assumes. As an A.R., I was held responsible for running the ward. The intern had to draw the blood and take out the stitches, but it was my job to tell him what blood studies should be done, which patients were to have their stitches removed, and equally important, to make certain that he did as I told him.

It was also my job to supervise the "work-up" of the patient. Take, for example, René Goudin, who was on the surgical ward when I arrived. René was sixty-three years old. According to the history written on his chart, he had been admitted because of "occasional blood in his stool." He also suffered from increasing constipation and had lost ten pounds in the three weeks before he was admitted. His physical examination, aside from evidence of weight loss, was unremarkable.

There was much more information on the chart, but these were the essentials. The diagnosis on admission was "? Cancer of the colon." It was my job to pin this down. It meant ordering all the studies which might be necessary to show whether René's constipation and bloody stool were due to hemorrhoids, colitis, cancer or perhaps some other, completely unsuspected disease.

René had been admitted just the evening before and nothing had yet been done to establish the diagnosis, so I took the scut book and started to write some work orders for my intern—things to be done the next day:

> *Mr. Goudin—*
> 1. *Check stool guaiac* [*chemical test for blood*]
> 2. *Proctoscope* [*examination of his lower bowel might reveal the source of his bleeding*]
> 3. *Hemoglobin* [*this test of his blood level would tell us whether he had been bleeding significantly or only to a minor degree*]

After writing these orders for the intern, I took out an x-ray card and made out a requisition for a barium enema, an x-ray study of the lower bowel. These were all the things that needed to be done on René at the moment. Further orders would depend on what these studies revealed.

Let's assume—and this proved to be the case—that the barium enema showed a cancer of the lower bowel. What next? It was then my responsibility to see that René was prepared for surgery.

I ordered a blood-urea nitrogen to check his kidney function. Then I looked at his chest x-ray to make certain that he had no lung disease which would have to be taken into account by the anesthetist. This was routine. There was a rule at Bellevue that no patient could be given a general anesthetic until he had had a chest x-ray taken. Tuberculosis and other lung diseases are easier to diagnose by x-ray than by physical examination.

Next I ordered the bowel preparation. This meant a restricted diet, as well as laxatives, enemas and antibiotics to be given for a few days before surgery to make certain that the bowel would be as empty and clean as possible for the operation. When the operation was scheduled I told my intern to reserve and cross-match three pints of blood for that day. I told him to be sure and pass a levin tube through the nose into René's stomach on the morning of surgery, to keep him from vomiting and becoming distended during, and for a few days after, the operation. Finally I wrote orders for the necessary sedation to be given before the operation, and for the preoperative shaving of the abdomen.

I got to the operating room ten minutes before René's operation was scheduled. I didn't arrive as early as Bob Kofstad, the intern, but I was there before Eddie Quist, who was going to do the case. Colon cancers were not for the A.R.

In the O.R. I checked to make certain that Bob had passed the levin tube. I took a final look at the chart to see that everything was in order. Then I scrubbed in.

My job as an A.R. in the operating room was now much more interesting and demanding than it had been when I was an intern. Surgery is a team affair. The operator is the boss, and he's the guy who does the sweating, but his first assistant can make a hero or a bum out of him. I was now the first assistant.

While the intern tugged on the retractors and cut sutures, as I had done six short months ago, I was engaged in giving Eddie the exposure and countertraction he needed to work. Exposure is the secret of success in surgery. If you can see the tumor, if you can get it up and out, or even if you can pack the other organs away from it, then it's much easier to cut and tie and sew.

On this particular case I wasn't much help to Eddie.

"Look, Bill," he said as the small intestine spilled into the pelvis for the tenth time, "you've just got to keep that bowel out of there. This tumor is stuck. I've got to see what I'm doing, or I may nick the ureter." Then, patiently, he pushed the small intestine back into the upper reaches of the abdomen, laid a wet laparotomy pad—a small towel—on it, and placed my left hand over the whole mass.

"There, now try not to let it slip." And he went back to his dissection. When the tumor was out and the first layer of the abdominal wall, the peritoneum, was closed, Eddie dropped out for a cigarette and I closed the remaining layers. With half a dozen appendectomies under my belt, I could handle the rest of the closure with aplomb.

Now it was my job to supervise René's postoperative management. For the next few days, while the tube was in his stomach and he was on intravenous feedings, I made certain that the fluids he was given were the proper ones. The stomach secretions contain, among other things, sodium, potassium and chloride. The fluids we gave intravenously had to replace these constituents and also supply the sugar René needed to recover from his operation. Every day I listened to his abdomen with my stethoscope to determine when peristalsis, the propulsive motion of the small intestine, had returned. On the third day he had bowel sounds, so I told Bob to remove the levin tube. Each day we gave him more to eat, from clear liquids through soft food to a regular diet.

And, of course, I watched his wound. Bob did the dressings, but I had had one big year of experience more than he had so it was my job to check the wound for any early signs of inflammation which he might miss. Finally I told Bob when the time had come to remove the stitches. Then I discharged the patient and arranged for his follow-up care. From the moment he arrived on the ward until the day he walked out of the hospital he was my responsibility.

After two months on the male wards I switched to the female ward. I didn't mind moving. There are more women with gall bladder disease than there are men. I would have been much less enthusiastic about the change if I had realized what Art Thompson was going to be like. Art was my new intern. When I first met him he seemed great—jumped to attention when Ernie Gallow arrived, wrote down every suggestion made on rounds, and as I'd leave for the outpatient department, he'd be rolling up his sleeves ready to get to work. However, when I got back to the ward in the afternoon, I found that nothing, or next to nothing, had been done.

"How about the proctoscopy on Lorenz?" I asked him the second day on the ward. "What did you find?"

"Couldn't do it, Bill. The proctoscope light was burned out."

"Why didn't you get another from Central Supply?"

"Is that where they keep them? I didn't know. I'll get to it tomorrow."

"What about Mrs. Ryan's skin graft? Did we get a good take?"

"You know, I couldn't find the cast cutter anywhere," he

answered. "So I couldn't get at the graft. I wonder if First Division borrowed it again?"

On and on and on it went. It was impossible to pin him down. He always had an explanation for why something hadn't been done.

I asked Ernie about him. "There's nothing we can do, Bill," he said. "That's Thompson. I've chewed his ass out so many times I can't count them, but it doesn't register. He shapes up for a few days, then he's off again. You've got to ride herd on him all the time. Dr. Stevens knows about him. He's all through after this year. But we'll have to let him finish. Do the best you can."

Which, unfortunately, was all I could do. When the emergency-room nurse couldn't find him, I had to take his call. When the blood hadn't been drawn, I had to do it. I would have liked to say, "To hell with it. Get Thompson." But you can't do this in medicine. The job has to be done. If one guy goofs off, someone else has to pitch in. If you've got any conscience at all, you won't let a patient pay for the sins of a fellow doctor. Fortunately, guys like Thompson are rare birds.

As usual, Jean was a big help. She changed dressings, ran to Central Supply, set up the I.V. fluids. More than that, she pestered Thompson until he had to do something. Whenever he disappeared from the ward and she suspected he had gone to his room to sleep, she'd call his number and just let the phone ring. Although he might refuse to answer it, at least he wouldn't get any rest, and half the time she'd drive him back to the ward. She made him work despite himself.

Even with Thompson as my intern, my two months on female surgery went smoothly. I did two more gall bladders, a few big hernias, three sympathectomies (removing part of the involuntary nervous system) and half a dozen skin grafts. I also assisted Ernie and Eddie on several bowel and stomach cases. I still wasn't a smooth operator, but I knew I was improving. Ernie acknowledged it, in a backhanded way, when he said to me after one gall bladder case, "You know, Bill, this is the first time you haven't stabbed me at least once in the course of an operation. You must be improving."

The only bad time I remember came right after we operated on Bridey Shannon. Bridey was the cleaningwoman on the female ward, a big, hearty, good-natured Irishwoman. She was one of the many menials at Bellevue who did their work in truly dedicated fashion.

Bridey had had leg trouble for years. Her ankles were almost always swollen, and every time she bruised one or the other she'd develop an open sore which would lay her up for weeks. I examined her on the ward one day and told her, "Bridey, you've got to have those veins operated on. They're no good. Why don't you let me admit you and we'll do it next week?"

"All right, Dr. Nolen," she said, "I guess I'd better. I've been having too much trouble lately."

Ordinarily the intern would have done the operation, but since Thompson was the intern and Bridey was a friend, I did it, with Eddie helping me. I wanted to do a superb job for Bridey, so I spent extra time dissecting out the vein in her groin. When I finally tied it off where it joined the big deep vein of the leg, I left practically no stump.

"Getting kind of reckless, aren't you, Bill?" Eddie observed.

"I don't think so," I answered. "I don't want any recurrences."

That night, at midnight, I got a call from the ward. "Dr. Nolen, you'd better get right over here. Mrs. Shannon's in shock."

I ran to the ward. Bridey's blood pressure was down to eighty over forty. She was sweating, and her pulse was racing. I lifted the dressing from the incision in her groin, and the blood literally ran out of the wound. My tie had come off the vein. While I compressed the wound to control the bleeding, the student nurse called Eddie and Russ Smith, who was working nights as my intern. I sent Russ off to cross-match two pints of blood.

Eddie knew immediately what had happened and made a quick decision.

"Don't worry, Bridey," I said. "We're going to take you back to the operating room and fix a little leak in one of your veins."

"Fine," Bridey said. "You do whatever's best."

Fortunately we managed to close the stump without sacrificing her deep circulation. She made an uneventful recovery, but it had been a close one. I should never have cut that vein so close to its junction. In my desire to do a good job I had done too much, and too much surgery can be as dangerous as too little.

I had damn near killed Bridey with improvements.

11

Life on
the Outside

The wife of an intern or resident could make or break him. Without ever setting foot in the hospital, and some of the wives never did, she could influence her husband so that he couldn't do his job worth a damn; or she could help him make a real success of his training. It was up to her.

The philosophy of the senior men was that house-staff members should not be married. They argued that while the young surgeons were in training they had more than enough to do caring for the patients and had no business worrying about a wife and children. Theoretically, this was good advice. Unfortunately, it was unrealistic.

We were all in the age group between twenty-five and thirty-five, and we were ready for marriage. Most of us had had enough of the single swinging life in medical school, and we were ready to settle down. Once we began interning, the desire to marry usually increased. Why? My own opinion is that we felt if we were going to run ourselves ragged for five years it would be nice to do it not only for ourselves but for a wife and family. We also wanted a life away from the hospital. Bellevue was all right when we were working, but it was no place to live when we were off duty. We needed a change. We needed a home.

We needed wives—and we got them. At least most of us did. There were seven interns in my group. We were all single, none of us so much as engaged, when we began our internship. Before the year ended, five of us were married.

This was a nice arrangement for us when we were on the house staff, but it wasn't a very attractive job for the wives. We were in the hospital much more than we were at home. Every other night and every other weekend we were on duty. Half of Saturday and all day Sunday we were free every two weeks. Even on the nights when we were off call, we rarely got out of the hospital before six o'clock. At least one night a week we'd go to a medical meeting or an anatomy lecture and wouldn't get home until nine or ten. And then we were often exhausted. All we wanted to do was eat and go to bed. I say "we" because I know that all of us on the house staff followed more or less the same schedule. How we managed as individuals depended entirely on how our wives adapted to this sort of routine.

We didn't do much drinking at Bellevue. It would have been too dangerous, not only for the patients but for ourselves. But every few weeks, when we'd hit a slow afternoon, we'd dig out a couple of bottles, mix up some daquiris, and have a "party" in the library. Usually these affairs began about four and lasted only a couple of hours.

The nurses who were getting off the 8-to-4 shift would drop in, some of our friends from medicine and G.U. might come over if they heard about it, but generally it was just our own house staff. Someone would dig up a phonograph, so we'd have music, but there was rarely any dancing. Generally all we did was sit around getting smashed. It doesn't take much booze to do the job when you're as chronically tired as we always were.

The junior staff on night duty usually held themselves to one drink. The senior men might take two. No more than that. Occasionally, of course, someone would slip and get plastered. We'd cover for him—once. There was never a second time.

There was no problem about seeing a patient after one drink. You might smell slightly of liquor but at Bellevue the odds were that your patient would reek of the stuff.

Monday nights were also, on occasion, drinking nights. Dr. Lampe, a senior attending on our division and one of the nicest men I've ever met, gave an anatomy course at the New York Hospital. Every Monday evening he would either lecture on surgical anatomy or dissect a cadaver and demonstrate the anatomy. Sometimes he'd bring a blackboard into the dissecting room and do both. Those of us who were off duty would attend (not always; after being away Saturday and Sunday nights, and with another night on call Tuesday, it was hardly fair to your family not to get home at a decent hour on Monday).

When the lecture ended we'd head for Walsh's, a steak house and tavern about four blocks from Bellevue, and drink beer for a few hours. The bartenders always set up every third beer for the boys at Bellevue. It doesn't sound much like a wild night on the town, but after spending the previous seventy-two hours in Bellevue we were generally beat and this was the ideal sort of evening for us.

Most of us made sacrifices of one sort or another to keep our wives content. For example, during my last three years at Bellevue I lived in Eastchester, about twenty-five miles north of New York. Walt Kleiss lived on Staten Island, Russ Smith in Queens. The only ones who lived in Manhattan were those who had either a lot of money or no children.

I didn't like living twenty-five miles from Manhattan. It meant an hour of commuting each way, but by the time I was in my second year as an assistant resident—having spent two years in the Army—Joan and I had three children and our Army life had given us a taste for the wide open spaces.

Those two years were spent in a place called, believe it or not, Igloo.

Igloo was an ordnance depot built on the plains of southwestern South Dakota. (The "was" is intentional. Igloo was shut down completely in 1968.) To reach it you drove straight west from Edgemont, South Dakota, a ranch town with a population of fifteen hundred. After ten miles of barren countryside you reached the cluster of barracks, shops and homes known as the Black Hills Ordnance Depot, or Igloo.

There were about two thousand people in Igloo: twelve officers, three enlisted men, and one thousand nine hundred and eighty-five civilians. Most of the civilians worked for the government, storing, shipping and occasionally detonating the ammunition of various kinds which was stored in concrete buildings ("igloos") on the many barren acres outside the town limits.

Igloo was designated as an "isolated post in the zone of the interior," which meant, in essence, that the government assumed an obligation to provide in the town itself all the ordinary essentials and conveniences of life. There was a nine-hole golf course, with buffalo-grass fairways and sand greens, a movie theater, a barber shop, and grocery, drug and clothing stores.

There was also a fifteen-bed hospital to which I, one other doctor and the three enlisted men were assigned. The enlisted men were tech sergeants who ran the pharmacy, the lab, and x-ray machine, and took care of the purchasing of supplies. My co-worker, a general practitioner with ten years' experience, and I provided all the medical care, within the limits of our abilities and facilities.

So for two years I did general practice. I delivered babies, took care of kids with runny noses and listened to the complaints of women with backaches. I also did some surgery—a few hernia repairs, appendectomies, tonsillectomies, and whatever acute emergencies presented themselves. I kept busy. I learned two things from the experience:

(1) I might not know much about surgery, but I knew a helluva lot less about the rest of medicine. If I hadn't had as a co-worker a G.P. with a lot of experience and common sense to whom I could turn whenever I was uncertain about what I was doing, I'd have been completely lost. As an example, I once followed a woman for seven months, examining her every month, on the assumption that she was pregnant. I had even written notes on her chart saying "The fetal heart tones are regular" and "Baby very active today." In my absence one afternoon my associate saw her, examined her and took an x-ray which confirmed his immediate impression —she wasn't the least bit pregnant.

(2) I really wanted to be a surgeon. I enjoyed doing the tonsillectomies, the hernias and the appendectomies. I didn't enjoy delivering babies, treating measles or listening to patients with neurotic symptoms. I acquired enormous respect for the G.P. who could do a little of everything and do it well, but it just was not for me.

It would have been cruel and inhuman treatment, after two years in the most open of spaces, to squeeze my family into a Manhattan apartment. We had to live in a place where the kids could run around a little without Joan riding herd on them all the time. I commuted to Eastchester for the sake of my wife and kids.

Being married to a guy in surgical training is no picnic. After the wedding, in November of my internship year, Joan and I had lived in a railroad flat on Eighty-second Street. It was on the East Side, and cost us sixty-five dollars a month. The living room was so narrow that when we opened up the day couch that doubled as bed, you couldn't get through the room without climbing over it. We didn't mind the cramped space, though. I wasn't home much and Joan was free to get out whenever she wanted. We ate and slept there, and that was all.

But when our first child was born we started to look for another place. The building on Eighty-second Street was old and loaded with cockroaches—I can still remember them running out of the refrigerator—and it just wasn't a suitable place for an infant. We stuck it out for a few months, but when Joan became pregnant again, we moved. We sublet an apartment in Greenwich Village which cost more than I could afford, but since I knew I'd be going into the Army in another eight months, we took it. It made the difference between peace of mind and anxiety for me because when Joan was upset it affected my work. On East Eighty-second Street there were often drunks on the sidewalk and punks in the street—not a place conducive to a feeling of safety for a woman whose husband was not home. It was no good being stuck in Bellevue at night, working my tail off, and finding, when I called her sometime in the evening during a lull in the action, that she was depressed or distraught. When I had to worry about her, I wasn't able to concentrate on the care of my patients. It was well worth the extra money to know that when Joan was home alone she was, if not happy with the situation, at least content.

In Eastchester, where we settled down after I returned from the Army, we lived in a housing development with lawns, picnic tables and even a lake where the kids could swim. It was a pleasant place and most of our neighbors were in my age group: men in advertising, young lawyers and engineers—all, hopefully, on their way up. The housing development was the kind of place where you lived, if you could afford it, until you had the money to buy a home.

Joan loved it. There were kids all over the place, so ours had lots of playmates, and Joan had made friends with many of the other young wives. And in Eastchester, Joan never worried about spending nights alone.

The commuting problem notwithstanding, I enjoyed Eastchester too. On my nights and weekends off, when the weather was pleasant, we'd sit around outside drinking beer or gin and tonic while the kids played. Once they were put to bed, we'd grill hamburgers, or if we were flush, chuck steak saturated with Adolph's tenderizer. Then we'd talk or play bridge until ten or eleven.

Neither I nor any of the other interns or residents at Bellevue lived what could be called, by any stretch of the imagination, a swinging social life. None of us had much money—the salary of the chief resident was only one hundred and ninety dollars a month—and we were all in debt or getting by with the help of handouts from parents or in-laws. We weren't in any position to dine at Luchow's, to say nothing of Le Pavillon. Nor did we have the energy to live a fast life. Even on our nights off we often didn't get home till seven, after having worked at Bellevue for at least the previous forty-eight hours. A drink or two, dinner and maybe a movie or bridge were about all any of us were interested in.

Weekends we might do more. Joan and I both enjoyed the theater, so occasionally we'd go to a Broadway show (the rear of the second balcony isn't really too bad), but more often we'd have dinner at some local restaurant, take in a movie or go to a house party at the home of one of our friends. I preferred to spend my leisure time with people who were not doctors. I got enough of medical conversation during the week.

Many of my fellow residents and interns had wife problems. More so, I suspect, than men of comparable age in any other profession. Working at Bellevue took most of the time and energy of the husband; many wives weren't content with what little of each was left. Charlie Greer, for example. How he ever made it through the residency is beyond me. His wife, Louise, bitched all the time. This wasn't Charlie's story—he rarely complained—but I met her socially two or three times, and even under what were probably optimum conditions, she nagged him constantly. "Why couldn't you get home earlier last night? You knew I wanted to go to the movies"; "You've certainly got it easy. Sitting around the hospital while I struggle to raise two kids. What a life"; "Why can't you take an afternoon off? Every other man does." It was embarrassing to hear her.

Once in a while Charlie gave in. Louise would call—and she did this at least once a day—and after he hung up, he'd wander over and say, "Bill, would you cover for me for a couple of hours? Louise wants to do some shopping and she couldn't find a sitter. The ward's quiet and I don't think you'll be bothered." He didn't ask often, so I was happy to oblige. With a wife like Louise he needed every friend he could find.

I think the unappealing life which most of us offered our wives was one of the reasons there was damn little fooling around with the nurses. No self-respecting man could bring himself to carry on an affair with another woman when he knew that his wife was home alone, taking care of his children, managing on her own the family life to which he should have been contributing. Some men did, though. Tom Reeves, even on his nights off, would occasionally stay at the hospital, sneaking a nurse into his room. But no one on the staff respected Tom and he was dropped from the program after two years. It's not that we were prudes. When Ron caught Monty Larson developing student nurses as well as x-rays in the darkroom, we all had a laugh about it at card rounds. But Monty was single, and as far as we were concerned that made it different. He was on his own, and more power to him. In fact, we kind of admired him. He was a real stud. For a while it got so we were knocking on the doors of the linen closets before we entered, for fear of embarrassing some sweet young thing. Monty wasn't even adverse to trying a little something in the side room of the ward when the bed happened to be unoccupied. We almost hated to see Monty get married, as he did in his second year. Some of the vicarious thrill of his adventures melted out of our lives.

Some of the staff lived better than I did; others weren't as well off. At the time I started at Bellevue, interns were paid sixty-five dollars a month, plus room and board in the hospital. As chief resident my salary had, roughly, tripled. No one—at least no one with a family—could get by on these wages.

There were several methods for increasing income. You could borrow money, put your wife to work, ask for help from your, or her, family. Which approach you used depended on your circumstances and philosophy.

Mike Rantala's wife was a dancer in the chorus line at the Copacabana. Russ Smith's wife worked as a model. George Walters' wife took jobs as a private nurse on the evenings when George was on duty. I got help from my family and borrowed money as well. I had also saved money during my two years in the Army and that helped a little.

Most of us preferred going into debt to the alternative of submitting our wives to years of marginal existence, but there were exceptions. Steve Drew, for example, refused to borrow the money it would have taken to get his wife and children out of the slums. The apartment in which he lived was in the shabbiest section of the Lower East Side. His wife didn't dare let her children so much as step out the door unless she was with them. He bought day-old bread at the bakery and even refused to buy a newspaper; instead he'd pick one out of a trash can on First Avenue on his way home from the hospital. It was a mistake. His wife couldn't take this kind of life. He came home one evening to find her in hysterics. She was lying on the bed sobbing wildly, completely irrational, while her children, unable to understand what was going on, sobbed on the floor beside her. She had to be hospitalized, in a sanitarium, for three months. When she got out, Steve quit Bellevue. He went to a private hospital where he could earn a living wage. He should have made the move earlier.

It was tougher for our wives to accept Bellevue than it was for us. Even Joan sometimes wondered why in the world I hadn't picked a place to train where the money was better and the pace more leisurely. She couldn't see why I insisted on Bellevue. It was impossible to explain. You had to be there —sensing the challenge of the place, being part of the constant battle against overwhelming odds—to understand why we didn't want to leave. It couldn't be put into words.

I can only thank the Lord that my wife was willing to take the five years as part of the total package of our marriage. Some guys weren't as lucky.

12

Surgical Research?

We weren't very "long" on research at Bellevue. Most city hospitals don't have the money that it takes to do basic, or laboratory, surgical research. The taxpayers, who foot the bill for municipal hospitals, would be up in arms if someone slipped in a request for an extra million for a complete dog lab with all the personnel and equipment needed.

On our division we didn't do any basic research at all, and that was fine with me. Some of my friends had chosen to train in research-oriented hospital centers without realizing what they were getting into, and most of them hated what they were doing. One of them, Jack Stent, said to me when I met him at a medical meeting, "Bill, I'm desperate. I've been down in the dog lab for eighteen months and I'm afraid I'm going out of my mind. I'm beginning to think like a dog. Last week I found myself wondering if I couldn't make a little time with a pretty Irish setter in the last pen. I'd give my left nut to get back to some real human patients."

He was stuck. He had picked a training program headed by a "pioneer"—a professor of surgery who published an article almost every month in one or another of the many surgical journals. Dr. Ramsey was famous, and his name alone annually drew a full quota of interns to the surgical department in the hospital he headed. Once the professor had the house staff, he used them—exploited them, really—for his research scut work. After one year as an intern on the ward, off would go the would-be surgeon to the dog lab, there to carry out some study that the professor wanted done.

Jack, for example, was working on a problem that had to do with the function of the stomach. Twice a week he and another assistant resident would operate on dogs, hooking up the stomach to the bowel in a way that hadn't been tried previously. Then they'd spend hours draining off fluids from the organs for analysis in the fancy lab that Dr. Ramsey had at his disposal for research work. Every Friday afternoon Jack would go to Dr. Ramsey's office and present him with a summary of the week's work. Other residents, from other corners of the lab, would meet with the professor at their appointed times and report on the projects they were doing under his supervision.

After six months of this sort of thing the resident would write a paper on what he had learned, or not learned, from his research. Dr. Ramsey's name would go on the paper as a co-author and it would be published in one of the surgical journals; then back to the dog lab the resident would go for another six months.

This sort of thing was fine if you liked it, but it was not for me. I had no desire to spend a year or two of my training period in a dog lab. Admittedly, some of the information acquired in this way was significant and important to surgical progress, but the bulk of it resulted in garbage that wasn't worth the paper it was printed on. It wouldn't have gotten into print, either, if Ramsey's name hadn't been listed as an author. But the "publish or perish" philosophy is just as true in academic surgery as it is in any other field of academic endeavor, and Dr. Ramsey kept his house staff busy maintaining him at the forefront of the academic ranks.

Dr. Stevens wasn't that kind of a surgeon—thank the Lord. He had published a number of papers in the course of his career but never for the sake of publishing, and he never encouraged us to do research for that purpose. He told me once, when I suggested that perhaps it would be nice to write a paper on an unusual case we had recently had on the wards, "Go ahead, Bill, if you think you really have something to say. If you think that reporting this case will be of any benefit to the surgeons who read the report, and to the patients for whom they care, by all means write it. But don't do it, please, just for the sake of seeing your name in print. The journals are already much too full of that sort of nonsense." I thought about it, decided the case report really wouldn't be of any particular benefit and dropped the idea.

Despite the fact that we didn't have a dog lab and couldn't do basic surgical research, we did have a heavy load of patients, and this gave us ample material for clinical research, which is done on patients. Often it consists of reviewing a case or a group of cases in the hope that the surgeon will learn, from an appraisal of his results, something of value about methods of treatment. What he learns is sometimes useful only to the surgeon or service that does the research. At other times the clinical research may be universal, of value to every surgeon who cares for patients of this particular type.

For example, during my second year as an assistant resident we seemed to be having an extremely large number of eviscerations. An evisceration is the catastrophe that occurs when a surgical wound breaks open and the contents of the abdominal cavity spill out onto the abdominal wall. It is associated with a high mortality. Typically it occurs on about the seventh postoperative day. In the usual sequence of events the intern takes the skin stitches out of a wound that looks perfectly normal; the patient gets out of bed, coughs or strains in some other way, and suddenly the skin edges separate. If the patient is lucky the deeper layers will hold together long enough for the nurse or doctor to put a dressing and abdominal binder—a girdlelike wrapping—over the wound. With bad luck, all the layers will separate instantly, and the intestine spill out. In either case the patient must be taken to the operating room immediately for reclosure of the wound.

Jack Lesperance was the one who first noticed our increased incidence of these catastrophes. He went over the records of the previous year, and discovering that his impression was accurate, he showed the figures to Dr. Stevens. They reviewed our closure technique, decided it needed to be modified and made some changes. The incidence of eviscerations declined to an acceptable level.

This was a piece of clinical research that was valuable, but only to us. Jack hadn't discovered anything new; he had simply found a defect in our surgical practice. It wasn't worth publishing because it wouldn't have helped surgeons or patients elsewhere, but it certainly saved the lives of some of our patients.

I was glad that we weren't forced to do research, unless we were so inclined, but there was one drawback to this attitude. When we finished our training there were certain hospitals, like those under Dr. Ramsey's direction, where it was virtually impossible to obtain an appointment to the staff unless you had a bibliography as long as your arm. I had no desire to practice in that sort of institution but Al Johnson did. Al came from Chicago, where Dr. Ramsey's hospital was located, and he wanted to go back to the Midwest to live. When he neared the end of his training he applied at the hospital where Dr. Ramsey reigned supreme, but was not accepted. Dr. Stevens, who considered Al a fine surgeon, looked into the matter and learned that Al had been turned down because he wasn't "well rounded"; i.e., he had no academic record. He hadn't done any research or written any papers.

Al was determined to get the appointment and asked Dr. Stevens to intervene in his behalf. "What it boils down to, Al, is this," Dr. Stevens told him after talking with Dr. Ramsey. "If you're willing to spend some time doing research, and if you can come up with two or three papers that are publishable, Dr. Ramsey will reconsider your application. It's another year or so out of your life, but if you want the job you'll have to make the sacrifice. I'll try to arrange a grant from some foundation, and you can do your work here at Bellevue if you can find a suitable project."

My reaction to this proposition would have been an immediate and emphatic "No"; there were plenty of other hospitals as good as the one Dr. Ramsey headed. The appointment certainly wouldn't have been worth a year of my life. But Al felt differently. He accepted the deal, and after a few weeks of mulling it over, decided he'd devote his research time to solving the problem of leg ulcers. He couldn't have chosen a problem better suited to investigation at Bellevue, since there were always half a dozen such patients in the ward.

Al went to work. Healing was the problem. Leg ulcers are a result of poor circulation, infection and injury. They may, and frequently do, extend from the ankle halfway up the leg. In our patients, with their poor hygiene and substandard living conditions, it was virtually impossible to get these sores to heal without several weeks in bed and, eventually, a skin graft. Even when we finally did get them healed, it was 2 to 1 that within six months the patient would be back with a recurrence.

At the time when Al embarked on his research project there were reports in the surgical journals of an enzyme, a chemical substance, that had been used successfully to expedite healing in dogs, but the work hadn't yet been done on humans. After reading all the literature on the subject, Al decided to try the drug on some of our patients.

Jack Lesperance agreed to admit six leg-ulcer patients from the outpatient department for Al's purposes. We brought them in on a Monday morning. There was no problem from the legal point of view. These gentlemen would have sold their mothers into slavery just to spend two nights in a warm hospital away from the Bowery. They signed the releases authorizing Al's research without a moment's hesitation.

All day long Al could be seen running back and forth from the intern's lab to the small room into which we had jammed the six beds for his vagrants. He had to complete some base-line (preliminary) blood studies before he could give them the intravenous solutions which he hoped would hasten the healing of their leg ulcers. It was five-thirty in the evening before he really had things under way and all six of his patients had fluids running into their arms.

Everything went smoothly for the first fifteen minutes. He might as well have been giving them sugar water for all the effect it had. Then one of them, Russ Peters, an old friend of ours, called Al over. "Say, Doc," he said, "I feel kind of hot. Could I be getting a fever?"

"I wouldn't think so," Al answered, "but let me check."

Russ's temperature was 103; by the time Al had finished checking the others, all five of them were perspiring profusely and shouting for help. Al was beside himself. He ran out onto the ward looking for an intern and bumped into our entire house staff. We were just escorting Dr. Stevens onto the ward for his Monday-night rounds.

"Can we help you, Al?" Dr. Stevens asked.

Al couldn't stand still. "I'd just like to borrow an intern or two, if I may, Dr. Stevens," he answered. "I need a little help."

"Certainly, Al. Who would you like to send, Jack?"

Jack gave him two interns. Al all but ran off with them down the hall. He wrapped the patients in alcohol-soaked sheets, threw ice water on them, turned fans on each one. All during rounds, each time Dr. Stevens looked up he could see Al or one of his co-workers running through the hall with ice or some other cooling medium. "Al's certainly taking a vigorous approach to his research project, isn't he?" Dr. Stevens commented.

It was a near disaster. Even though he had shut off the

I.V.'s as soon as temperatures started to climb, every patient hit 106 and five of them went temporarily off their rocker from the fever. The new chemical just wasn't ready for human use. Of course, Dr. Stevens got a full report on the fiasco. The next day he called Al and "suggested" he drop this particular project. Al was glad to oblige.

Some doctors just aren't cut out for research. They don't have the meticulous, painstaking, patient temperament that a good investigator must have. They want results and fast; they don't think things through. This was the kind of guy Al was.

But he did have one quality that can be of value to a research man—he was stubborn. The ordinary fellow would have given up after this and told Dr. Ramsey what he could do with his appointment. Not Al. He wouldn't quit.

After his near miss with the intravenous treatment of leg ulcers he decided to approach the problem from another direction.

Al had noted, as we all had, that maggots, repulsive though they are, did a remarkable job of cleaning up dead tissue, leaving the ulcer bed healthy. There was little known about this phenomenon. Did the maggots literally eat the tissue, or did they do their work via some digestive secretion? Al decided to study the problem.

When you want maggots, it's amazing how difficult they are to find. Al finally heard of some place in the South where they were available and ordered a supply of blowfly maggots, a vigorous species, for his studies. He was now doing his experimental work away from Bellevue. Dr. Stevens had lost his enthusiasm for Al's research after the previous fiasco and had encouraged Al to find more congenial surroundings. He had been granted space in a laboratory uptown which he shared with other research-oriented surgeons.

The maggots arrived—as hideous a boxful as one could imagine—and Al stuck them away in a corner of the laboratory while he formulated his plans. The maggots had arrived on a Wednesday, and by Friday he was ready to go. But with the weekend coming up he decided to wait and begin, instead, on Monday.

Lo and behold, when the lab door was opened on Monday, the maggots were gone from their box. But not, unfortunately, from the room. It literally swarmed with blowflies buzzing here, there and everywhere. Al had forgotten, if he had ever known, that maggots, like caterpillars, mature. His had done just that over the weekend and were now not only useless as ulcer eaters but were a positive menace to everyone in the area. The entire lab had to be shut down until the fumigators had erased the blowflies. When the room was once again ready for occupancy, Al's corner was no longer available to him. The hospital authorities had assigned it to another, less adventurous investigator, at the request of Al's fellow researchers. And the leg-ulcer problem remains unsolved.

The fundamental weakness in Al's research lay in his motivation. He had no burning desire to make a major contribution to the science of surgery, nor had he come up with a brilliant new idea that was worth the time and energy it would take to prove its value. He was doing research solely so he could get his name on a paper and win an appointment to a "prestige" hospital. He was the wrong sort of surgeon working at research for the wrong reasons. Unfortunately, for every single dedicated, capable research surgeon there are dozens like Al. They clutter up the literature, burn up government and foundation funds that could be spent for a better purpose and waste their own talents, energy and time. In the year and a half Al spent messing around in a laboratory, to no avail, he might have cured a couple of hundred patients with tumors, appendicitis, gall stones or any of a myriad other ailments which he had the knowledge and training to treat.

An old attending surgeon, Dr. Lewis, used to say when I'd come up with some kooky diagnosis, "Nolen, learn all you can about appendicitis and leave the Dumdum fever to the experts."

It was damn good advice.

13
T.B.

Debra Shane was in trouble. The tube that ran from her chest into the bottle at the side of her bed had plugged with blood and the pressure inside her rib cage was rising. Her one remaining lung had begun to collapse. She was gasping for breath.

I worked on the tube for a few seconds, milking it with my fingers trying to work the plug loose, but I couldn't clear it. Debra was getting rapidly worse—she was all but unconscious now, time was running out.

I gave up on the tube and grabbed a syringe and needle from Miss Geramo, the nurse who had called me to Debra's room. I stuck the needle into Debra's chest. She winced, but she was too far gone to feel much pain. With the syringe I sucked out all the air under pressure that had accumulated. In less than a minute Debra's color had gone from blue to pink and she was breathing easily.

"How do you feel, Debra?" I asked.

"Better," she said, "much better. For a minute I thought this was the end."

"Your chest tube plugged, Debra. I'll put a new one in now and you'll be okay."

Chest tubes meant the difference between life and death to our postoperative chest patients. Crises like this one were not uncommon. After operations on the lung there were usually small leaks of air and blood. If these things weren't drained out of the chest they would accumulate, and pressure inside the chest would eventually cause the collapse of the lung on the unoperated side. It required constant vigilance to be certain that this didn't happen. A few minutes with a blocked tube could mean death for a patient with borderline lung function.

Debra Shane, whom I had just treated, was one of our patients at Triboro, a hospital for chest diseases in Jamaica, Long Island, where we went to learn chest surgery.

Many surgical programs utilize the facilities of other hospitals to help train their residents. This policy serves three functions. First, it enables the resident to get specialized training that might not be available in his "home" hospital; second, it gives the resident a chance to compare surgical procedures elsewhere with the practices in his "home" hospital; third, it often benefits the secondary hospital by providing a house staff that it might otherwise not be able to attract. There are always more positions available than there are interns and residents to fill them. Specialized and private hospitals often have difficulty attracting a house staff.

Besides Triboro, our division at Bellevue co-operated with North Shore, a private hospital in Manhasset, Long Island. As an assistant resident I spent six months in each.

I went to Triboro immediately after returning from the Army, into which I had been called after my first year as an assistant resident at Bellevue. Triboro is a city hospital with a patient load that runs at about the 300 level. Tuberculosis was the disease that most often brought patients to our wards. It's a difficult disease to cure. Even with the best of drugs, months of treatment are necessary. Because it's contagious, patients have to remain in the hospital while they are under treatment, to protect their families in particular, and the public in general.

Much of the time that the patient is receiving treatment he doesn't feel, nor does he look, very ill. He can wander around the ward, go out into the day room and watch television, play cards with his fellow patients. He takes his medicine two or three times a day, the frequency depending on what drug he is on, and every week or two a sputum specimen is sent to the lab, where it is stained and cultured for the tubercle bacilli. As soon as he has three successive negative sputum tests, and his chest x-ray no longer shows active tuberculosis, he is pronounced "cured" and is discharged.

If the patient is fortunate, if the diagnosis has been made early and if the bug he harbors is sensitive to one of the drugs, he may be in and out of the hospital in six months. But, unfortunately, all patients don't follow this ideal course. In some, the tubercle bacilli may develop resistance to the drug, with subsequent complications. These patients then need surgery.

That's how Debra came to us. She had had tuberculosis for two years and had been in the hospital all that time. A year earlier, part of her right lung had been removed, in the belief that it was the only residual focus in her body. Two months after surgery her sputum remained positive and x-rays had revealed a dark area in the upper portion of her left lung. When this spot failed to respond to drugs the decision to reoperate was made.

Tuberculosis surgery is almost always difficult. The inflammatory response to the infection causes the lung to stick to the chest wall, and postoperative bleeding and air leaks are common. This had been the situation in Debra's case— and it was the persistent, heavy leak of air that had almost caused her death.

I was at Triboro for six months, not to become a chest surgeon—that required two years of special training after completing the four years of general surgical residency—but to learn enough about this specialty to be comfortable managing chest injuries. I also expected to get enough operative experience to feel at home when I was performing any general surgical procedure that required opening the chest.

I was one of the low men on the totem pole at Triboro. There weren't any interns—an intern simply wouldn't have enough experience to safely manage these patients—so I and two assistant residents from other hospitals served as interns. It wasn't as bad as it had been at Bellevue—we didn't run an emergency room and only rarely got up at night—but it was no picnic.

When chest cases went sour they really went sour, but when they went smoothly they were easy to manage. The patients could eat on the first or second postoperative day. This meant there were fewer blood studies needed, and not much in the way of intravenous feeding to worry about. But the dressings, which I'd usually do in the morning, were another matter. On a chest service, one with T.B. patients, sterile precautions had to be rigidly maintained. I didn't want to carry tubercle bacilli from one patient to another of course, and this was one reason I was extremely careful; the other reason, a more selfish one, was that I certainly didn't want to acquire active T.B. myself.

So dressing changes were time-consuming. I always wore a mask and gloves, disposing of them, along with the dirty dressings, after visiting each patient. It might take me an hour or more to change three dressings. The most pitiful patients, with the messiest dressings, were those with long-standing bronchopleural fistulae.

A bronchopleural fistula is a chronic lung leak through which both air and pus drain to the outside. They occur occasionally after surgery for tuberculosis when the bronchial stump fails to heal properly, usually because of infection.

Tom Walsh had one. He had been on the surgical service for three years when I arrived. He harbored a strain of tubercle bacillus that was resistant to all drugs. Two years earlier a partial removal of his right lung had failed to cure him. His bronchial stump had broken down and he had had a chronic air leak since that time. When he coughed, or even took a deep breath, air and mucus would leak out through his right armpit, where the fistula had established itself.

"What's new, Doc?" Tom would ask me as I redressed his wound. "What did my last culture show?"

"I hate to tell you, Tom, but it's still positive."

"Sensitive to anything?" he asked.

"Don't know yet, Tom. We're going to switch you over to I.N.H.—an anti-T.B. medication. Maybe that will do the trick."

"God, I hope so," he said. "I dunno how much longer I can stand it, Doc. I'm getting stir-crazy. I may have to get out of here."

This is one of the perennial problems on a T.B. service. Patients become discouraged at the slow response of medication and sign themselves out of the hospital. I have to admit that if I were in Tom's shoes I'd have been tempted to sign out myself. T.B. is always a discouraging disease; for some, it's unbearable.

Sometimes, simply because the patient was desperate, we'd gamble on surgery that might or might not work. Pete Waring was a case in point. Pete was fifty-two. He had been in the hospital almost three years. He harbored a resistant bug and had a chronic fistula that opened onto the side of his chest. Pete was desperate to get out. He was so desperate that we were afraid he might commit suicide if he weren't cured soon. Suicide is not a rare occurrence among long-time tuberculosis patients.

We had evaluated Pete for surgery, and the pulmonary function studies were borderline. If we operated on him we'd have to remove his entire left lung to have any chance at a cure, and it was doubtful that his right lung was healthy enough to keep him going.

"What's the verdict, Doc?" he asked me the day after we had done his studies. "Can I take it?"

"I'll level with you, Pete," I said. "It's not good. You

might make it, but it would be close. I don't think Kevin's going to risk it." Kevin Jonas was the chief resident at Triboro.

"Listen, Doc," Pete said, "I want it done. I'll sign any papers you want signed so you guys won't be blamed if I don't come through, but I want to take the chance. I won't stay here any more. This isn't a life—it's an existence. I'd rather be dead." He meant it.

The attending staff went along, reluctantly, and two weeks later, after intensive preparation with drugs and exercises designed to give his right lung optimum function, we operated.

For three days after the operation it was touch and go. If we cut the oxygen off for more than five minutes Pete would get restless, dusky and mentally disoriented—typical signs of oxygen deprivation. It didn't look as if he'd make it. Abruptly, on the fourth day, he came out of it. It was impossible to say why—but, as occasionally happens, his lung efficiency had spontaneously improved. We were able to shut off the oxygen without any ill effects. It was another week before he was able to take more than a few steps without running out of breath, but after a month he could get around without any trouble. We wanted him to stay longer but he refused and went home. He had won his gamble.

This desire to get out as quickly as possible once you were cured was universal—and very reasonable. Who, once he was "clean" would want to pal around with someone who was still infected? The "clean" patients avoided the "dirty" patients almost as if they were lepers. (In point of fact, T.B. is much more contagious than leprosy.) I couldn't really blame them for demanding a prompt discharge.

14

Heart Surgery: The Early Days

Patients with heart disease were the other main source of surgical material at Triboro. Heart surgery was then, a dozen years ago, still in its infancy in most hospitals. At Triboro it was practically a newborn. We didn't have a heart-lung machine, so we couldn't do any open-heart surgery, but since the bulk of cardiac surgery was still being done by closed techniques, we weren't too far behind the leaders.

Kevin Jonas was, naturally, eager to do some heart cases. He would gladly have paid a thousand dollars apiece for potential patients even if he'd have had to steal to get the money, but of course there weren't any for sale. He had to depend on the medical men and they weren't eager to have their patients operated upon. Internists don't take kindly to new surgical procedures; they're from Missouri when it comes to surgical pioneering—as, I suppose, they should be.

The cases Kevin got were usually those who were on their last legs—patients so far gone in congestive failure that they bubbled when they so much as walked to the bathroom. It was difficult even to anesthetize some of them. They turned blue if they were laid flat. The anesthetist would have to pass his tube into the trachea with the patient in a semi-upright position.

The patients who were candidates for surgery were admitted to the ground-floor cardiac ward, which was under the direction of Victor Dellesandro, a medical resident. Victor was a good fellow, a smart internist and a diplomat. He managed Kevin beautifully.

"What do you say, Victor," Kevin would ask him on rounds, "do you think we can do Mrs. Radunz next week?"

"I don't think so, Kevin. It's a little too soon. She's still ten pounds overweight, and most of it is fluid. Her blood chemistries aren't bad, but I don't think she can stand it yet. Give her two more weeks and I think we'll have her ready."

"How about Russell? He doesn't look too bad."

"Not too bad; but not too good either. I don't like the looks of his heart tracing. He may be getting a little digitalis toxicity. I'm going to cut back for a while and see if his E.K.G. won't straighten out. Let's give him another week. What do you say?"

"Okay, Victor, sounds reasonable. Let me know when you think he's ready."

Victor no more had to ask Kevin's permission than he had to ask mine. But he kept Kevin happy by letting him think he was helping to make the decision. Victor ruled the ward with an iron hand, but gently.

It was thanks to Victor that our mortality was no worse than it was. It wasn't good, but it was better than it was in a lot of other hospitals at that time. Victor wasn't the guy who opened the heart and stuck his finger in to crack the scarred-down valve—Kevin did that job—but Victor was the fellow who got the patient into shape so he could stand this meddling.

It was to Kevin's credit that he recognized Victor's value. After the operation, with the patient back on the ward and then technically a surgical patient, Kevin still deferred to Victor's judgment regarding intravenous fluids and medicines.

"How much saline do you think we ought to give him,

Victor? How about his quinidine? Should we stop it? Do you think it's safe to discontinue his dicumarol?"

Kevin would ask the questions—Victor would answer—and Kevin would do as he said. It takes a smart surgeon to realize that a medical man, a good one, can sometimes manage a postoperative patient better than he, the surgeon, can. It was never truer than after heart surgery.

We sweated more over the good-risk patients than we did over the bad risks. No one blames the surgeon if a bad-risk patient dies—it's accepted that the odds are against success—but let a good risk die and the surgeon takes the bulk of the blame. Which is fair enough. To make the shoe even tighter, our good-risk heart patients were mostly kids, children of six or eight, with congenital problems. One I remember particularly well was a little Negro boy named Rick Anthony.

Rick had a coarctation of the aorta. This is a congenital condition in which the aorta, the main arterial trunk of the body, has a narrow area in it about six inches from the point where the aorta arises from the heart. Sometimes the opening in the aorta at this point isn't much bigger than a lead pencil. The pressure in the vessels to the head, which come off the aorta before the narrow area, rises to dangerous levels; there is practically no pressure in the lower part of the body.

The operation to relieve this obstruction is, in theory, a simple one: clamp the aorta above and below the narrow spot, cut out the narrow portion and sew the two wide ends together. Unfortunately, it is not as easy as it sounds. The operator has to work high in the chest, a difficult area to expose. There are a number of vessels near the constricted spot which are extraordinarily dilated as a result of the disease and cause troublesome bleeding if they are nicked. And the operation has to be done quickly once the aorta is clamped; if the kidneys and the spinal cord are deprived of blood supply for too long they may sustain irreversible damage.

Kevin wanted to do this case so badly he could taste it. He knew that if he didn't do this one he wouldn't have another chance until he got into practice. Naturally, he had some qualms. He'd never done a coarctation—he'd never even seen one done—they aren't common. He'd read up on the technique but he had been around long enough to know that reading about how to do an operation is a far cry from actually doing it. Things are never as neat and clean in the body as they seem in the illustrations in a book.

"What do you think, Bill," he asked me one day, "do you think I ought to ask the boss to do it?" The boss was Dick Ames, the director of surgery.

"I just don't know, Kevin. I see your problem. I'd surer than hell want to do it if I were you, but I'd be scared. It would be great if you could get a little practice before you tackled it."

Kevin looked up. "You know," he said, "that's not a bad idea. There's a dog lab back in the morgue. We did some heart-valve cases last year. I think I'll do a few dogs."

In my innocence, in my desire to be helpful, I had launched Sirry and Oscar, my two co-assistant residents, and myself into a veritable nightmare—the dog lab. For the next three weeks, while Victor prepared Rick for surgery, Kevin practiced. At least twice a week Kevin would say to one of us, "Nothing much doing this afternoon—let's do a dog."

I remember one afternoon particularly well. It was my turn to be the errand boy so, at Kevin's command, I went down to the ambulance headquarters to look for Mike, the most congenial of the drivers.

"Not another goddamn dog!" he said to me by way of greeting.

"I'm afraid so, Mike. Will you take me?"

"What the hell can I say? No? I'd be fired. All right, get

in. Not in that one, for Christ's sake. That's clean. Get into that heap over there." Off we went in the most rattletrap of the ambulances to the pound in downtown Queens.

"Back again," the pound attendant greeted me. "What'll it be this time?"

I looked over the stock, and against my better judgment, chose the biggest animal available. I'd come back with a beagle once and Kevin had blown his stack. "What the hell do you think I'm planning," he'd asked, "an operation on a dwarf?" On this particular trip I chose a dog that looked like a cross between an Irish setter and a wolf. The attendant muzzled him, I tied my rope around his neck, and together the dog and I got into the back of the ambulance. The dog, not unreasonably, was frightened. I tried to calm him, hoping against hope the inevitable wouldn't happen, but as always, it did. The dog defecated, not once but thrice, at various sites in the back of the ambulance.

After a fifteen-minute trip—Mike drove as fast as he could on these dog runs—Mike opened the back door to let me out. Then he stuck his head into the ambulance. "Jee-sus," he said, "he shit three times! I'm going to shoot the next bastard that asks me to drive a dog."

My troubles weren't yet over. As I led the dog toward the morgue I tripped, and in regaining my balance, I dropped the leash. The dog ran and me after him.

Fortunately there was a fence around the hospital complex, so he couldn't get out into the streets, but there was a lot of territory within the fences and that dog led me all over the place.

To make matters worse, one of the patients on the third floor spotted me, in my white suit, chasing this mongrel, and soon the windows were full of patients enjoying the pursuit. "Get a bicycle, Doc"; "My money's on the mutt"; "Watch out Doc, he may bite"—the comments were shouted down from every window.

Finally I had to go into the kitchen and beg a bone from

one of the cooks. With this as a lure I was able to get close enough to grab the rope. There was a round of applause mingled with a few unmistakable Bronx cheers—from the audience.

When the dog was safe in the morgue operating room I called Kevin. He came down with a set of old instruments, reluctantly allocated to us by the O.R. staff. I anesthetized the dog with an intravenous barbiturate and we went to work.

There are some professors of surgery who claim you can train a man to be a surgeon by letting him operate on dogs. I don't believe these professors. Dogs aren't people, and no matter how humane he is, a surgeon doesn't operate on a dog with the concern he shows for a human patient. Particularly when, as was our policy, the dog was to be sacrificed, painlessly, with an overdose of the anesthetic after the operation was over. My few weeks of exposure at Triboro cured me forever of any desire to devote my career to experimental surgery in a dog laboratory.

But it is possible to learn a particular technique by operating on an animal and in the next three weeks Kevin became an adept aorta surgeon. He did at least a dozen operations and I watched or helped on all of them. He did the twelfth job with much more finesse and far greater speed than he had done the first.

It paid big dividends. When Rick was ready, the operation went smoothly from beginning to end. After it was over, Dr. Ames said, "Kevin, I think you did that better than I would have done it." I'm sure he didn't mean it—Ames had too much ego to think anyone was as good as he—but I'm inclined to think that in this instance he was right.

Unfortunately, not all our heart cases were triumphs. Some were unmitigated disasters. Ethel Simmons, for example.

Ethel had bad heart disease. Not that there's any such thing as "good" heart disease, but Ethel was in about as poor a condition as a heart patient can be and still survive. She had had problems since a bout with rheumatic fever as a child and she had been getting progressively worse. Now, at thirty-three, she was virtually incapacitated. She led a bed-and-chair existence, and even so, she was in the hospital more than she was out. The medical men gave up on her and turned her over to Kevin. She was admitted to our cardiac ward.

Ethel was an unusual woman. She had been deprived of most of the things we take for granted—childhood games, dancing, swimming, and even marriage. She was an attractive young woman, but as she said, "I was told I couldn't have children—that it would kill me. I didn't want marriage under those conditions." Yet, despite her difficulties and deprivations, she remained serene and cheerful.

One day I commented to her on her attitude. "Dr. Nolen," she said, "I have only two choices. Either I choose to ignore my problems and keep smiling, or I concentrate on them and cry all the time. I'd rather smile." With that she smiled and so did I.

We put Ethel through an intensive evaluation. All our patients with disease of the heart valves had to have both an angiocardiogram and a heart catheterization. Neither procedure was "fun."

The angiocardiogram is simply an x-ray of the heart. One of us—Oscar, Sirry or myself—would put a huge needle into an arm vein and then, at a given signal, shoot in a large mass of dye that would show up on the x-ray plate. In the next few seconds, as the dye circulated through the heart, the x-ray technicians would take a series of pictures at split-second intervals. From these films we could get a reasonable idea of the size and shape of each heart chamber. The only problems that ever arose were of a technical nature. The needle might go through the vein and infiltrate the fat; the x-ray films might get stuck in the chamber; our timing might be off and the films would show the dye either before entering or after leaving the heart. If any of these things happened we'd have to start over; usually it went well the first time.

The catheterization wasn't much more of a problem for the patient. We'd sedate him well, take him to a special x-ray room and, under local anesthesia, pass a small tube into an arm vein. Using the fluoroscope—an x-ray machine through which you can peer and watch what is happening—we'd pass the catheter up into the chest, down a large vein, and into the heart. Through the tube we could take blood samples and measure pressures. It helped us evaluate the rigidity of the valves.

Ethel's heart valves were extremely rigid—probably, we thought, calcified. This happens to patients with long-standing valvular disease. We decided to go ahead anyway. Ethel knew it was dangerous but she wanted to take the gamble. We agreed it was probably a reasonable choice.

We had the first team in again—Kevin and Dick. Kevin did the operating but Dick kept a tight rein on him. I was interested in what they'd find, and I liked Ethel so much that although it wasn't my turn to scrub, I stood on a stool and watched.

Ethel's heart was enormous. The tight valve, her mitral valve, had caused so much back pressure that one chamber, by itself, was the size of an average normal heart.

"That's going to be a tough valve to crack, Kevin," Dr. Ames said as he looked down at the beating heart. "Let's get going."

Kevin put a purse-string stitch about two inches from the tip of the dilated chamber. Dr. Ames put a clamp across the chamber, below it. Kevin cut off the tip of the appendage, took off his glove and put his bare index finger into the heart. Oscar, who was acting as second assistant, pulled the purse string tight around Kevin's finger. Dr. Ames removed the clamp.

Now Kevin probed in the beating heart for the valve. He

found it and started to press on it, hoping to tear the calcified leaflets apart. After working for two or three minutes, he was soaked with perspiration. Not from the work, from the tension. "They won't budge! I can't get anything going."

"Mind if I try it, Kevin?" Dr. Ames asked.

"Not at all. I wish you would." Kevin withdrew his finger. Oscar tightened the purse string so as to close the hole, and Kevin and Dr. Ames changed places.

When Dr. Ames was ready the clamp was again released and he put his finger through the hole in the heart. He worked for five minutes, then looked up and said, "It's no use. That valve is like a rock. We'll have to cut it."

This was a technique in which, instead of the operator's finger, a bladed cutting instrument was used to cut the valve. It was reserved for difficult cases because it was a blind cut and potentially dangerous.

"Come on over here, Kevin," Dr. Ames said. "You do it." They changed places again. Kevin put the knife into the heart.

"Feel the valve?" Dr. Ames asked.

Kevin nodded.

"Fine, now cut between the leaflets." The mitral valve has two leaflets. In disease these stick together.

Kevin put the knife in position and worked the blade. "How does it feel?"

"Better, but not good enough."

"Make another cut."

Again Kevin put the knife in position. Then, as he pushed on the handle that worked the blade, all hell broke loose. Blood poured from the back of the heart, covering Kevin's hand in seconds.

"Goddamn it," he said, "I've gone through the back wall."

"Pour in the blood," Ames said to the anesthetist. Even as he spoke he reached into the chest, flipped the heart on its axis and brought the back wall of the heart into view. The blood was spurting through a gash about half an inch long.

"Give me a one silk," he said, quite calmly, to the nurse. He took the needle holder, quickly put the stitch into the heart and tied it. The bleeding stopped. He let the heart slip back into its normal position.

"How did she take it?" he asked the anesthetist.

"For twenty seconds that was the wildest looking E.K.G. I've ever seen"—we took continuous tracings on all our heart patients—"but it doesn't look bad now."

"Kevin," Dr. Ames said, "let's get out of here. You've cut that valve about as much as it can be cut. Any deeper and I'd have lost part of my finger."

Kevin grinned, but not very broadly.

I'd like to be able to say that Ethel Simmons did beautifully; alas, she didn't. She recovered, all right, and went home, but her valvular disease was too far gone to be remedied by the operation. A month after her discharge she came back into the hospital in severe heart failure and died. She was a damn fine woman.

That's the way it went, unfortunately. We lost patients a few years ago that would come through with ease now. Cardiac surgery has made giant strides in the few years that have elapsed since we were doing "blind" mitral-valve surgery at Triboro. But I suspect that in 1980 we'll look back on the current sorry state of heart transplants with the same chagrin that I now look back on our results at Triboro.

I hope so.

15

North Shore: Private vs. Public

City hospitals and private hospitals are as different as night and day. Not only for the patients, but for the interns and residents as well. Going from Bellevue and Triboro, both city hospitals, to North Shore, a private hospital on Long Island, was like traveling from heaven to hell; or vice versa, depending on your taste.

The first differences that struck me when I rolled into the hospital for a six-month stint were the physical ones.

North Shore was a new hospital situated in a nice community. It was a wealthy hospital, as hospitals go, and the administrator could afford to do things right. The well-heeled clientele of the hospital expected first-class service, and they got it. The rooms were clean and spacious; the meals were varied and delicious; there were maids and nurses' aides to keep the water pitchers filled and the patients comfortable.

Physically, in comparison to Bellevue, North Shore was paradise. But in other respects, from a resident's point of view, North Shore left a lot to be desired. Take my job: I was second-in-command, as far as the house staff was concerned, and alternated nights on duty with the chief resident, Jorge Castillo. Any time an emergency arose, the nurse in charge would call one of the junior residents, Bob Knudson or Russ Smith, who, like me, had come from Bellevue to North Shore for six months; if necessary, they called me. I would then decide whether to handle the problem myself or call the attending. In the case of anything more serious than an ingrown toenail, it was expected that the attending be called. I made no major decisions, nor did I perform any complicated procedures on my own. I had no real responsibility. None of us did.

This came as a blow to me. At Bellevue every patient that came into the hospital "belonged" to the house staff. We had attending surgeons assigned to each ward, but they took responsibility in name only. We ran the place. Not so at North Shore. There, 95 percent of the beds were private. A token two or three were allocated to charity patients, but much of the time even these few were vacant.

This meant that virtually every patient admitted to the hospital had a private doctor. And the attitude of a private patient is almost universally: "Look, Dr. Loudon, I'm paying you to fix this hernia and you'd better do it yourself. I don't want any beginners practicing on me." So it was the private doctor who examined the patient in his office, ordered the x-rays, made the diagnosis, and decided whether or not to operate. Once admitted to the ward, the orders that directed the patient's management were written by the attending surgeon. The job of the house staff was, essentially, to follow the attending surgeon's directions. It doesn't sound like an attractive arrangement, and it wasn't. You can't teach a man to operate unless you let him use the knife, but on whom, in a private hospital, are you going to let him cut?

There is no good answer. Either the surgeon does the operation as the patient, and frequently the referring doctor, wishes, or he lets the intern or resident do it as he and the intern or resident would like. Either way you run into problems.

What, then, were we there for? Aside from the rare

acute emergency when we'd have to take action in the absence
of the attending, we were there to assist. There were four
operating rooms, busy most of each day, and one or two
assistants were required on each case. What profit we got out
of our time at North Shore was going to depend almost
entirely on how we spent those hours in the operating room.

As chief resident Jorge Castillo had the prerogative of
deciding who would scrub on which cases. Late every afternoon he would check the operating schedule for the next day
and select the cases on which he wanted to scrub. I would
then pick from what was left, and we would assign a junior
resident, Smith or Knudson, to the rest. Theoretically this
didn't sound as if it would work out very well for the junior
residents, but in practice it wasn't a bad system.

The surgery cases that appealed most to Jorge were major
operations scheduled by attendings who might let him take
over. I was interested in these cases too, so there was some
conflict, but often there were double bookings—two bowel
operations, for example, scheduled in different rooms at the
same time, and since Jorge couldn't be in both places simultaneously, I'd get one by default.

Smith and Knudson, who were in their first year as assistant residents, weren't interested in "major" cases. They
knew that no attending was going to let them do them. They
preferred to scrub on hernias, appendectomies, and the like,
and I was content to forgo them. The major cases, like the
stomach, bowel and chest cases, were the ones I wanted. If
Jorge chose the only big operation that was apt to be given
away, I would elect to assist on another big case, even though
I knew the attending wouldn't let me do it. Not only did I feel
it was unfair to take small cases away from Smith or Knudson;
I felt that I could learn more by assisting on a major operation,
done by a capable surgeon, than I could from doing a minor
case myself. This, in fact, was one of the big advantages that
North Shore offered to us residents.

At Bellevue the system of training was "Watch one; do

one; teach one." It wasn't quite that bad, of course, but it was true that we learned technique from the man one year ahead of us in training, and he in turn had learned from the fellow one year ahead of him. It was an inbred system.

At North Shore the attendings were all fully trained surgeons. Some had been in New York, some in Minnesota, others in Canada—virtually all the major training centers were represented—and from each of these attendings, by assisting and observing, the alert resident could learn something. So the key to a successful and profitable six months at North Shore lay in identifying the surgeons who could teach us best, who would let us take the most responsibility, and then spending as much time as possible with them.

It's not, of course, a matter of the surgeon simply turning the patient over to the intern and then going off for a smoke while the tyro fixes the hernia. The attending scrubs, acts as first assistant and leads the intern or assistant resident through the case. If the operation is more complicated than anticipated, the attending takes over. In fact, the patient who has his operation done by the intern or resident, with the attending acting as first assistant, gets a job that is at least as good as, and often better than, if the attending operated alone. The attending pays more attention and sweats more when he's helping someone operate on his patient than when he's doing it himself.

Some surgeons won't give anything away; they are too afraid of antagonizing the referring medical man and/or the patient.

Some surgeons give virtually every case away; they don't give a darn what the medical man thinks and they don't worry about the patient's opinion. They know they aren't doing anyone a disservice.

Most surgeons tread a middle ground. They'll let the intern or resident do some operations, they'll do some themselves. Their policy in any individual case depends on the attitude of the referring medical man, the personality of the patient, and—this is most important—how well they like and trust the intern or resident with whom they are working.

Obviously the resident who fares best at a private hospital is the one who works the hardest at his job and, consequently, gets along best with the attendings.

It didn't take long to identify the three key men. They were John Grove, Marlon Steele and Jeff Loudon. They were the surgeons who were most interested in teaching and training residents and who had the self-confidence to know that they didn't have to wield the scalpel themselves to assure their patients a good operation. Nor did they give a damn what the medical men thought. They were sufficiently good at their craft, and had sufficiently large practices, not to have to worry about referrals. Let the medical man bitch, if he wanted—let him send his patients to someone else; they'd survive. (None of the medical men ever dropped one of these three. A medical man might not be able to tell a deft operator from a clumsy one, but he could recognize good results when he saw them. The patients who were referred to these men did well; that was all the referring doctor could reasonably ask.)

We all wanted to stay on the right side of the "big three" and we worked hard to do so. We had to.

Loudon, for example, made his rounds sometime around six or six-thirty in the morning. He did much of his surgery at a New York hospital, even though he was the chief at North Shore, and he had to be in the city to start operating at eight.

Every night before I turned in, I'd stop at the nurses' station on the surgical ward and tell the charge nurse, "When Dr. Loudon shows up, no matter what time it is, call me."

At six-fifteen or so, just as he was stepping in to see his first patient, I'd materialize at his elbow.

"Good morning, Dr. Loudon."

"Well, hello, Bill. Up early, aren't you?"

"Just wanted to tell you about Mrs. Patterson. When I changed her dressing yesterday I noticed her incision was a bit red at one end. You may want to take out a stitch or two."

"Let's have a look," he'd say, and I'd complete his rounds with him. It not only earned me Brownie points but I also had the benefit of listening to his comments as he saw his patients. It was like having the chief of surgery as a private tutor.

Grove, a short, wiry man with a nose like a hawk, was at the other extreme. He never showed up in the morning. He always tacked on his cases at the end of the O.R. schedule. If he wasn't operating, he'd make his rounds sometime between eleven at night and two in the morning.

When he did arrive, he'd come in like a whirlwind, running down the corridor as if he hadn't a moment to spare. "Been tied up all day," he'd mutter to himself. "Goddamn nitwit over at Coney Island sent me a patient with a ruptured bowel he'd had for a week. Couldn't get away." Half the time I think these stories were fictitious. He was, quite simply, a night owl. But I didn't mind because he was such a great teacher. Sometimes too great. He'd spend so much time teaching in the O.R. that the patient would be under anesthesia an hour longer than necessary. Mrs. Andrews with her gall stones was a case in point. Some of them had worked their way into the common duct, which runs from the liver to the bowel. Grove put her on the schedule for three o'clock one afternoon.

Jorge had planned to scrub on this case himself, but fortunately for me, at three o'clock he was still tied up on a chest case that turned out to be more complicated than he had anticipated. I scrubbed in.

It was, of course, bad manners to step to the operator's side of the table before you were asked. I took my position on the left side.

Grove walked around to the patient's right side and picked

up the scalpel. Then he looked at me. He must have seen the disappointment in my eyes. "All right, Nolen—goddamn it, come on over here." We changed places.

This was the first case I had ever done with Grove, and it was hell from start to finish.

I had no sooner picked up the scalpel than he began shouting at me, "For Christ's sake, Nolen, don't you even know how to hold a knife? Here." He took the scalpel out of my hand and moved my fingers. "That's more like it."

I made my incision through the skin and fat. I was about to go deeper when he put a gauze pad over the cut, bringing the operation to a complete halt. I looked up at him.

"Nolen," he said, "what the hell do you think we're doing—taking off a wart? You'll never get those mitts of yours in there. Make a hole you can be proud of. They heal from side to side, you know, not end to end."

I added another inch to either end of the incision, but he wasn't satisfied. "Here, you sissy. Cut here," and he indicated a point three inches across the midline.

We had already been operating for ten minutes and were only down to the fascia, which I started to cut for the full length of the incision. He threw the pad into the wound again.

"Nolen," he said, "did you ever dig a hole? Don't answer, it's obvious you haven't. Well, let me tell you something. When you dig a hole you make it wider at the top than you do at the bottom. It's easier to make it that way.

"Not only that, but the hole you make when you operate (and that's all a goddam incision is—a hole) you have to close later. Layer by layer. It's a helluva lot easier to close it if you can see what you're doing, and you can see what you're doing by making the cut in the deep layers shorter than the cut in the skin."

That's the way it went for three long hours. He wasn't satisfied with the way I tied knots, or the method I used to free the artery leading to the gall bladder, or the way I sutured the gall bladder bed. When I used the scissors to cut the gall bladder duct, he fairly screamed, "For Christ's sake, Nolen, you're a surgeon, not a veterinarian. Use a knife. Give me those goddamn scissors." He grabbed them out of my hand and threw them on the floor. "Now get back to work."

When the case was over I was limp as a rag. I could have strangled the man with my bare hands, but when I saw him sag into the chair in the dressing room—this wiry little guy who was tough as nails—I realized he was as tired as I was. When he said, "Not too bad, Nolen—I'll make a surgeon out of you yet," my resentment melted away.

There were times in the months at North Shore when I thought Grove was about to crack. Some nights—he was great at finding cases to do at two in the morning—he seemed barely able to stand up at the table. But make one false move, and *wham!*, he'd rap my knuckles with a clamp, a favorite trick of his. He might be down, but was one hell of a long way from out.

Grove was full of pearls. He had forgotten more about operating technique than most surgeons ever knew. He was a slow operator, and there were times when I questioned his judgment, but I never doubted his ability to perform, or help me perform, an operation. He was a great technician, and he could teach. I learned more technique from him than anyone I ever encountered.

I paid a price, of course. He would sometimes disappear for two or three days without letting me know where he went, and I'd have to calm his irate patients.

"Dr. Grove is operating in Garden City, Mrs. Andrews," I'd say. "I'm sure he'll be in to see you tomorrow"; "Mr. Wright, Dr. Grove phoned and asked me to tell you he's ill with the flu. I told him you were doing fine and he sent his regards." I'd make up story after story, and I'd watch his patients very, very carefully. He expected me, or whoever had done the case, to supervise the postoperative care. And he expected his patients to do well.

Then, after a three-day absence, he'd walk in at two in

the morning. I'd meet him on the ward, summoned by my spy system, and we'd talk about his patients.

"How's Andrews doing?"

"I took out her drain today. Wound looks fine."

"Wright?"

"No problem. Eating, and his bowels are working."

"What about Clarke's path report?"

"Cancer. She'll need a bowel resection."

"Did you grab some operating time?"

"Not yet. I didn't know when you'd be back."

He'd grab his head in both hands. "Goddamn you, Nolen, can't you do anything right?" And he meant it.

The mystery of Grove's three-day disappearances was solved not long before I left North Shore. The betting had been (1) that he went on benders, and (2) that he had a mistress. It was neither.

"Nolen," he said to me one day, "my mother's coming in tomorrow. I want her in 218, the private room on the quiet end of second. And I want her to have nothing but the best—that's your job."

"What's the problem?"

"Cancer, I think. She's been living alone up in northern New York. She's refused to leave home till now. I've been going up to see her whenever I could. But she can't manage any more, so I've brought her here." He looked at his watch. "Goddamn it, Nolen, I can't stand here talking to you all day," and he tore off down the corridor.

It was odd to watch Grove with his mother. He was a different man. Never swore, soft-spoken, as gentle with her as he was rough with us. She, on her part, treated him like a young boy. "Johnny," she said one day while Bob Knudson and I were in her room, "I hope you're nice to these boys. They're taking good care of me."

"He treats us just fine, Mrs. Grove," I said. "Don't you worry." Even Grove had to smile.

Steele, the third member of the "big three," was like

Grove in only one respect: he let the residents do all his cases. In everything else they were poles apart. Steele always seemed relaxed. He didn't race down the corridor like Grove; he sauntered. He never seemed to be in a hurry to go any place or do anything. He was about Grove's height but stockier, and he dressed in clothes that looked as if they had come from Goodwill Industries. He'd wear the same baggy suit with shiny trousers for a week at a time. Grove, who was a very stylish dresser, always kidded Steele about his appearance on the rare occasions when the two met. Which wasn't often, because Steele stuck to a schedule. He made rounds at seven in the morning, and again at about four in the afternoon. He saw each patient twice every day. He preferred to operate in the morning, the earlier the better. He was even-tempered and never swore at his assistant.

In the operating room he was as fast as Grove was slow, as gross as Grove was meticulous. When I was doing a case with Grove I was careful to put my hemostat on nothing but the bleeding vessel. I'd tie it with fine silk. Steele would grab a vessel and with it a big glob of the adjacent fat. "Meatball it," he'd say, and I'd tie the whole bundle off with a piece of catgut thick enough to strangle a moose. Silk, which meticulous and delicate surgeons generally use whenever possible, was anathema to Steele. "I don't have silk privileges yet—I'm not old enough," was one of his favorite lines.

One morning he had a hemorrhoidectomy on the schedule. The scrub nurse got upset when Steele didn't bother to clip sterile towels around the patient's anus. "Dr. Steele," she chided him, "that's not good sterile technique."

"Listen," he said laughing, "on a case like this we ought to just throw a few newspapers on the floor. In two minutes we'll have shit pouring into the wound so we won't be able to see, and you're worrying about sterile technique! On hemorrhoidectomies we ought to scrub after, not before we operate." Steele was a realist.

On another occasion I was repairing an incisional hernia

for him and asked the nurse for a pair of Martin forceps, an instrument I thought might help me do a more elegant job.

"Nolen," he said, "cut the crap. You're from Bellevue, aren't you—what do you want with fancy instruments? If you can't do this case with a rock and the top of a tin can, move over and let some guy in who can." I let the Martin forceps go.

The anesthetists loved Steele because he was so fast. He'd have poor-risk patients on and off the table, when Grove would still be backing up for a good start. Grove used to say of his worst cases, "That guy is so sick you'd kill him if you cut his hair." Steele could take the stomach out of a patient in that precarious category and pull him through.

I remember one case in particular because it demonstrated so clearly that Steele firmly believed the patient would do as well with him assisting the resident as if he wielded the scalpel himself. Mr. Cappa was the eighty-year-old father of Dr. Joe Cappa, the chief of orthopedics. The old man had had his gall bladder out three months earlier but was now back in with jaundice. Steele ordered some x-rays and blood studies and then spoke to Dr. Cappa. I was with him at the time.

"Joe," Steele said, "it looks like I screwed up the first time around. I left a stone in the duct. We better go back after it."

"Okay, Marlon," Dr. Cappa said. "Good luck."

"We'll need it. That abdomen is going to be a mess."

I scrubbed on the case. Jorge let it go because this was, after all, a doctor's father. Moreover, Dr. Cappa was going to come in and watch. Steele would have to do this one himself. I took my place on the left side of the table as Steele walked into the O.R.

"What are you doing, Nolen?" he asked as he put on his gown. "Don't you know where the common duct is? Or are you going to show off and do this case from the wrong side? Come on now, I don't want any fancy stuff. Joe might get mad. Get over where you belong."

I was dumbfounded, but I did as he said. With Dr. Cappa

breathing down my neck I took the knife, and under Steele's guidance, went to work.

Steele was right. The abdomen was a mess. The cholecystectomy done three months before had been for an acute gall bladder inflammation, and the entire right upper quadrant was a mass of adhesions. Steele would pick up tissue, say "Cut," and I'd cut. Bit by bit we worked our way down to the common duct. "All right, open it," Steele said.

I did, stuck in a stone forceps and pulled out a rock the size of a marble. It was a high point in my career.

Dr. Cappa stepped off the stool on which he had been standing. "Nice job, Nolen," he said. "Even with Steele messing you up, you got the job done."

Steele laughed and said, "Get out of here, Cappa, or I'll tell Loudon on you. This isn't one of those bone cases you can do with a hammer and chisel. We only want surgeons in here." Dr. Cappa left and we closed the abdomen.

Again, unlike Grove, Steele preferred to manage the postoperative care himself, although he'd say, "You guys know too much for me; I'm just a simple surgeon. I don't understand all these fancy fluids and drugs. They confuse me." But in a serious moment he once told me, "Nolen, any jackass can learn to cut and tie. What makes the difference between success and failure is how you handle the patient before and after those few hours in the operating room. I never start worrying about a case till the wound is closed. Then I worry like hell."

He had a good point. For example, whenever Grove's patients got into trouble it was not because of what he had done in the O.R. but because he neglected them so badly postoperatively. We'd do our best to manage them, but we lacked his experience and judgment. We made errors that were sometimes costly. Once, for example, when he had disappeared for three days, I pulled the rubber drain out of a patient on whom he had done a gastrectomy. The next day the patient started running a fever, and as luck would have it, Grove picked that day to come back.

"How's Bailey?" he asked me.

"He's running a fever."

"For how long?"

"Since yesterday."

"Damn it," he said, "I'll bet that stump is leaking. Is there much drainage?"

"I took the drain out."

"You what?" he said, rising out of his chair. "You took his drain out?"

"Yes, I did. You weren't around and there wasn't much drainage so I thought it was time."

"Nolen, Nolen, Nolen!" he said, holding his head. "What in the hell do you use for brains? I put that goddamn drain in there because I didn't trust the stump closure. Never, never, never take out a drain without asking me. Now we're up to our ass in trouble."

The fact was that I had pulled drains many times without asking his permission. I'd even been chewed out for not pulling them, when he had come back after a three-day disappearance. There was no way I could win. It's also true, however, that Grove had more experience and training than I, and if he had been around he could have averted the troubles he occasionally had. Steele's patients, under his personal care, rarely had problems in the postoperative period.

Sometimes I had the impression that Grove actually enjoyed problems. He loved to sit up at all hours and plan ways to get a patient out of the mess he was in. The best thing about it was that he would usually come up with the right answer. He might let them get into trouble, but he invariably got them out.

Steele was no slouch as a diagnostician. He was one of those surgeons who have a sixth sense about symptoms and could learn more about a patient in five minutes than most doctors do in an hour. I took him to see one of our rare service cases, an eight-year-old boy admitted for possible appendicitis. Steele spent two minutes with him and we stepped back into the corridor.

"Did you notice the way he kept his right knee bent? Did you see that he wasn't moving his abdomen at all when he breathed? Did you get a look at how dry his tongue was? That kid's got peritonitis. Put him on the schedule."

"But his white count is only nine thousand and his temperature is normal," I objected.

"Nolen, let me tell you something," Steele said. "Try looking at the patient instead of the chart. The chart isn't sick."

The boy had a ruptured appendix with peritonitis.

Steele approached the postoperative management of his cases with the same no-nonsense attitude. "Please don't order all those chemistries on Mr. Ross, Nolen"—he had just removed Mr. Ross's stomach—"he can't afford them and I don't understand them anyway. In two days he'll be eating and drinking and he won't get into any trouble in that short a time." Reluctantly I canceled the orders I'd written, and Mr. Ross did very well without a hundred dollars' worth of lab studies.

This business of ordering unnecessary laboratory studies was a trap into which it was very easy for a city-hospital-trained surgeon to fall. At Bellevue we never thought about expense. Our patients didn't pay for anything, so why not order everything? It was routine to get a full battery of blood chemistries—about fifty dollars' worth—each postoperative day for about five days after every major operation. Half the time we never even bothered to look at the results. It was a habit I'd have to get rid of before I went into practice, and Steele got me started on the road to breaking it.

There were, naturally, individual preferences that developed during the months we spent at North Shore. Bob Knudson got along particularly well with an attending named Boles, who would give him cases that he wouldn't give to Russ Smith. Smith had a personality that made for good rapport with Loudon, who gave him two gall bladders. Jorge Castillo hit it off very well with a chest surgeon named Vasho.

On the other hand, Jorge did not do very well with some of the attendings because he couldn't learn to keep his mouth shut. Jorge had spent two years at Memorial Hospital, a cancer center in New York, and as a result had become excessively cancer-conscious. He was oriented to the view that every patient had cancer until proven otherwise and, by God, you'd better get it all out, even if it meant throwing out most of the patient with the tumor. He couldn't get it through his head that this philosophy was acceptable at Memorial, where all the patients had major cancer problems, but that it just didn't apply in a general hospital where hemorrhoids were seen a helluva lot more often than tumors of the colon. "What you doing, Dr. Monson?" he would ask as Monson prepared to cut across a stomach. "You leaving too much stomach. What if that turns out to be cancer? Then what?"

"Yes, Jorge—but it doesn't look like cancer, nor does it feel like cancer. I'm not going to make this man miserable by taking out his entire stomach just on the remote possibility that this thing is malignant. It looks like an ulcer to me, and I'm going to do an ulcer operation."

"Okay, Dr. Monson, but don't say I didn't warn you."

Monson would glare at Jorge and then go on, but was it any wonder he never gave Jorge a case?

One of the men with whom I had developed a close rapport, and with whom I scrubbed frequently, was a doctor named Ben Levin. Al Johnson had told me in a discussion we had before I left Bellevue, "Ben is a good man to scrub with. He won't give you any cases, but he's a good operator and you can learn a lot just watching him."

Ben had a big practice. He did more surgery at North Shore than any other attending, chiefly because there was one big group of internists who referred everything to him. And he was good, there was no mistaking that fact. He worked with a scalpel rather than scissors most of the time, a skill he had picked up in Toronto where he had trained, and he used the knife deftly. He never made a false move.

Al was partly right—I did learn a lot from him, but he was wrong as far as his not giving me surgery was concerned. The first radical breast I ever did was on one of Ben's patients, a Mrs. McGraw, and the next week he let me do a gall bladder on a Mr. Riley. In short order he turned over a tendon repair on a Mr. Duncomb and a perforated ulcer on a fellow named Cook. These were only a small percentage of Ben's total cases but they kept me more than happy.

It suddenly dawned on me, as I was going over the operative records near the end of my stay, that there was a curious pattern to Ben's cases. About 85 percent of his patients were Jewish, as was he, and these patients he always did himself. The other 15 percent, the gentiles, he had let me do. I decided to call him on it. Since I got along very well with him—he always requested that I help him when I could—I didn't think he'd mnid.

"Dr. Levin," I began as we were changing after a case, "I've noticed that you often let me do the gentiles, while you always operate on your Jewish patients. That seems curious."

He laughed. "I wondered if you'd notice that, Bill. I'm rather embarrassed that you have, but I expected you might. Let me explain.

"I've got a good practice, as I'm sure you're aware, but it wasn't always this good. The reason I'm doing well now is that I'm getting all the referrals from a group of internists, all of whom happen to be Jewish.

"You may also have noticed that one or the other of the group usually drops in when I'm operating. They want to make certain I'm doing the case and not just assisting.

"They're not sold yet on the idea of letting residents do their surgery. I'm working on them, trying to convince them that it won't hurt the patient in the least, but until I can make my point I've got to play ball. I have to make a living. That's why I can only give you the cases I get from Tom Murphy, who believes in the residency system—and all his patients are gentiles."

Which cleared up the mystery.

Everyone loved to scrub with Chet Berg. Chet was a plastic surgeon with a special interest in hand cases. There's hardly anything more incapacitating than a deformed hand, and hand reconstruction is one of the most challenging forms of surgery. Chet was a master.

He gave everything away. I scrubbed with him through a series of cases in which we moved a toe from a little girl's foot onto her hand to serve as a thumb, a reconstructive procedure far beyond my technical abilities at that stage of my training, and in the entire series of operations—four of them—Chet never so much as put in a stitch. He would say, and often did, "Nolen, you dumb bastard, move that flap here, not there," and point out my error, but he never took the knife or the needle holder away from me. He didn't need to; he was good enough for both of us.

There was one surgeon we all wanted to scrub with because not only would he give us cases, he'd let us do them any way we wanted. His name was Sam Marity. He had been trained in a university hospital and knew surgical theory cold, but he was frightened to death of operating. He gave his cases to us because he was afraid to do them himself. How and why he had ever gone into surgery I'll never know. He must have been constantly miserable, dreading the possibility that someone would send him a difficult case. This hardly ever happened. All the surgeons, and the medical men, knew that Marity was no operator, and he hardly ever saw a patient with anything more complicated than a simple hernia. He liked it that way. On one occasion, however, a new pediatrician who didn't know Marity's reputation referred to him a six-year-old boy who had swallowed a spike.

Generally speaking, it's safe to watch most foreign bodies that reach the stomach. They will usually make their way along the intestinal tract and emerge in the stool. If there's any sign of trouble, or if x-rays show that the foreign body is stuck, there's time enough then to operate. But this was a spike, about six inches long, and there was absolutely no chance that it could pass through the small intestines of this little boy.

I wasn't aware of the case until Don Fitch, the radiologist, called it to my attention. He caught me one morning as I was walking by the radiology department, and showed me the film. "Dr. Marity has had this kid in for three days," he said. "Every day he gets an x-ray, and every day the spike is in the same place. I'm no surgeon, but I think someone should go after that thing."

I agreed wholeheartedly. But this created a delicate situation. I could hardly tell Marity what to do—after all, I was only a resident—but someone had to persuade him to operate. I decided to work through Loudon. When he came that evening to make rounds I caught him in his office.

"Got a minute, Dr. Loudon?" I asked. "I'd like to show you an interesting film."

"Sure, Bill. Come on in."

I mounted the x-ray.

"Man, that kid sure likes hardware," Dr. Loudon said, laughing. "Have you got that spike with you?"

"No, I haven't Dr. Loudon," I answered. "It's still in his stomach."

He frowned—and Loudon really knew how to frown. "Did he just come in?" he asked.

"He's been here three days."

"I see," he said. There was no levity now. "Whose patient is he?"

"Dr. Marity's."

Loudon picked up the phone and dialed Marity's office. "Sam? Jeff Loudon. Say, one of the residents was just showing me an interesting x-ray—that kid with the spike. That's a beauty, isn't it?" There was a pause as, I presume, Marity agreed.

"I was wondering," Dr. Loudon continued, " if you were planning to take that out tonight or first thing in the morning. I'm kind of betting you plan to do it tonight. Am I right?"

Pause.

"That's fine, Sam. I'd like to hang around and watch, but we've got dinner guests. Ask the resident to show it to me tomorrow." He hung up and smiled at me. "You've got yourself your first stomach case, Bill. Have fun."

Admittedly I had been a bit sneaky, but it had to be done.

At North Shore I observed, for the first time, the intense economic competition between the various surgical specialists. The gynecologists, the thoracic surgeons, the pediatric surgeons, the proctologists—all the subspecialists—fought like tigers to protect their respective domains from infringement by outsiders.

On one occasion, for example, Ben Levin did a radical breast operation on a patient with cancer. When the pathology report showed that the tumor had spread to the glands outside the breast, Ben decided to remove the woman's ovaries. This is sometimes done to slow down the spread of the cancer. He put the case on the schedule—and all hell broke loose.

The chief of gynecology called Dr. Loudon two hours after the case was scheduled. One of his "boys" had called him. "What's Ben Levin doing operating on the ovaries?" he asked. "He's no gynecologist."

"I know, I know," Dr. Loudon said, "but all he plans to do is take them out. Surely he can do that."

"I know he's capable of it—that's not the point. Ovary surgery is gynecology. He ought to refer this patient to a gynecologist. We don't go around taking out appendices."

"All right," Dr. Loudon said. "I'll speak to him."

Ben called in a gynecologist to do the case—a twenty-minute operation that any general surgeon could do with ease. It kept peace in the family.

The saddest aspect of this sort of thing was that it cost the patient more money. The woman in this case had to pay a gynecologist as well as a general surgeon; her total bill would have been much less if Ben had done both operations.

No one bucked the system. One young surgeon, Tom Blake, tried, and it almost cost him his practice. It was all completely inadvertent. A six-year-old boy came into the hospital after falling out of a tree. He had a ruptured spleen and a broken wrist. Tom operated on the boy, removed the spleen, and then, while the boy was still asleep, reduced the fracture and put it in a cast. He had trained in a city hospital like Bellevue, and had had extensive experience in fracture management.

The orthopedic surgeons raised hell. They didn't give a damn how good a job Tom had done on the wrist; he was a general surgeon, not an orthopedist, and he had no business setting a fracture. He should have called an orthopod.

Tom apologized to the chief of orthopedics and to every orthopod on the staff. He didn't want to but decided he had better, otherwise he would be done for. No orthopod would ever refer a case to him, nor, in all probability, would the gynecologists, internists, or others. The man who stepped outside his specialty was a threat to all the other specialists. You played the game—or else.

Ostensibly, of course, the system was devised "to protect the patient." Only specially trained men could operate on specific portions of the body. If the rule had been applied with reason it might have had some merit. But it wasn't—not at North Shore, at any rate. There it was enforced rigidly and unreasonably, not for the protection of the patient, but for the protection of the specialists who were in greater supply than the demand warranted. They had to protect their narrow domains to ensure themselves of healthy incomes.

It was always the patient who paid.

There was another aspect of surgical practice to which North Shore gave me my first exposure. To put it in the vernacular, the ass-kissing. Some of the surgeons, particularly the young ones who had little to do, were so flagrant in their courting of the medical men that it made me want to vomit. When you listened to them talk to a potential source of referrals you'd think the medical man was a cross between Socrates and Jesus Christ, incorporating only the best features of both. Steve Boscomb was, by all odds, the worst. Admittedly, Steve had a tough row to hoe. He had specialized in cardiovascular surgery, not yet a well-established subspecialty, and he needed referrals from a wide area to make a go of it. Moreover, he had trained in Minnesota, so he didn't know many of the doctors on the staff who could send him patients.

One of his best potential sources of referral was a pediatrician named Owen Detrich, who also specialized in cardiovascular problems, but from the medical point of view. I was helping Steve do a patent ductus (an operation in which a small vessel just off the heart, which should have closed after birth but didn't, is tied off) and Owen was in the room. Steve's chatter was incessant.

"Owen, your diagnosis is right on the button, even to the size of the ductus. See?" He pointed at the ductus in the depth of the wound. Owen, standing on a stool behind him, couldn't possibly see it.

"But, then, what else should we expect from the best pediatric cardiologist in the state? Not just the state—the East. Hell, why deny it—in the country!"

Owen didn't deny it.

I am not exaggerating. He went on like that for the entire three hours. It was difficult not to laugh; I couldn't believe

Owen would swallow all that hot air. I thought Steve was killing himself with all this bullshit. Apparently not. It's hard to overestimate the capacity of a human being for flattery. Owen kept right on sending Steve patients.

There was another reason why I didn't like either Steve or Owen. It was based on a conversation between the two which I overheard one morning as I was scrubbing to help him do a relatively minor vascular case. Steve was washing at the sink next to mine and Owen was standing in the corridor behind us, thumbing through a chart.

"I'm doing a septal defect over in Queens tomorrow," Steve said. A septal defect repair is a major heart operation, fraught with danger.

Owen looked up. "You are? You seem awfully nonchalant about it."

"Not worried a bit," Steve answered.

"Well, you ought to be. I'll bet you won't get the patient through."

"Maybe not," Steve agreed. "But I'm still not worrying."

"Oh, now I get it. You're doing a mongoloid."

"You guessed it—a six-year-old." And they both laughed.

From that point on I never had any respect for either of them. Any doctor who could laugh about, or even take lightly, a heart operation just because the patient happened to be retarded—mongoloid children have a high incidence of congenital heart problems—was a bastard in my book. And still is.

Steve Boscomb, much as his tactics revolted me, was at least building a practice. Jerry Pollins, on the other hand, was going nowhere fast.

There's a great misconception among the general public that there is a crying need for doctors in this country. There is an element of truth in this. G.P.'s and some specialists—radiologists and ophthalmologists, for example—are in short supply. A man in one of these fields can go almost anywhere and build a big practice in no time. General surgeons, on the other hand, in the big cities and their suburbs particularly, are a dime a dozen. At North Shore we had far more surgeons on the staff than we needed to take care of the patients the hospital could accommodate. The competition for patients and operating time was vicious. This was why guys like Steve Boscomb, who were just starting out, had to be "nice" guys.

Jerry couldn't get this through his head. He thought that since he was well trained, knowledgeable and a reasonably good operator, the referring doctors ought to beat a path to his door. He went around with an air of "Here I am, boys, God's gift to the internists. Get in line with your offerings." No one got in line.

Instead of improving his attitude and tactics, Jerry turned bitter.

Checking the schedule in the O.R. book one morning, he said to me, "Damn it, Bill, look at this. Ray Harman scheduling a portacaval shunt. Do you know where he trained? Bronx City—a little rathole of a private hospital. He has no business doing a shunt. The credentials committee should get down on him."

Another time Ben was his target. "Look at that schedule," he said. "Levin, Levin, Levin. The bastard is in the O.R. all the time. You know why, don't you?"

"No," I said. "Why?"

"He splits fees, that's why. He kicks back half of every surgical charge to the guy who sent him the patient. If I wanted to play that game I'd be doing as well as he is. Mark my words, though; we'll catch him yet."

Jerry was damn near paranoid about his situation. Grove was his pet hate. "He's mad, Bill," he said to me one day. "The guy is absolutely off his rocker. He comes wandering onto the wards at all hours of the night and then he disappears for three days. Half the time he's so tired out that he can barely stand up to operate. If Loudon had any sense he'd kick him off the staff."

It was sad to see Jerry, a capable and intelligent surgeon, wasting away his time. I didn't intend to emulate Steve Boscomb when I went into practice, but I wasn't going to model myself after Jerry, either.

Besides teaching me surgical technique, North Shore gave me many lessons in the business of surgery. Some of them were distasteful. I learned, for example, that every surgeon wasn't always honest. It came as a kind of shock to me. At Bellevue, and at Triboro, we never thought about money. Whether we did a hemorrhoid or a stomach resection, the pay was the same. Not so in private practice. The insurance companies, and the patients, paid a lot more for a big case than they did for a small one. And it influenced what some of these men did, or said they did.

One morning, for example, I was scrubbing with Dr. Small on a lung case. Small never gave anything away and he wasn't much of a teacher, but a senior man was expected to scrub on major cases and I was elected.

We opened the chest and found that the cancer was widespread. Resection was impossible.

"Hopeless, I'm afraid," Small said. "Can't get it out." I thought he'd close right up, but no—first he resected a small segment of lung.

"Why are you taking out that piece, Dr. Small?" I asked. "That certainly isn't going to help the patient."

He laughed. "Something for the pathologist, Nolen. Insurance companies pay better for lung resections than they do for in-and-out cases. We've got to be able to show some lung tissue. Don't worry. It won't hurt Mr. Francis any." It didn't, but that hardly justified the procedure.

On another occasion a patient came in with bowel obstruction due to widespread cancer. The man was obviously terminal and any operation was bound to be futile. I knew it and so did Dr. David Lund, whose patient he was. I couldn't believe it when Lund said, "Put him on the schedule, Nolen. We'd better have a look."

"Gee, Dr. Lund, do you really think it's necessary? I can feel tumor all over his abdomen." I knew I was sticking my neck out, but I had decided to chance it.

"Look, Nolen," he said angrily, "you haven't been around long enough to start advising me. If there's a thousand-to-one chance we can help this man, it's worth taking."

I didn't bother arguing. So we opened, could do nothing, and closed. The patient died the next day. The whole case took forty-five minutes. Lund charged the family three hundred dollars. The bastard.

One of the side effects of having a house staff at North Shore was that in some instances when the attending surgeons might have been tempted to lie, we kept them honest. We residents never had anything to hide—we weren't financially involved in the patient's illness—so we could look at problems objectively and speak frankly. If the emperor wasn't wearing any clothes, we didn't hesitate to say so.

Like the case of John Myers, who needed an operation for the poor circulation in his legs. We used to do many sympathectomies at Bellevue—many more than were done at North Shore—since our derelict patients often had circulation problems. Through an incision in the lower abdomen a segment of sympathetic nerve—the nerve which controls spasm in the blood vessels of the leg—is excised. Hopefully the vessels will then function better.

Ben hadn't done many sympathectomies. I'd probably done more than he had, at least in the last few years. I assisted him on the operation.

When we were down near the spine, in the region where the sympathetic chain lies, Ben grabbed some nondescript yellowish-white material in his clamp and started to excise it.

"I don't think that's the sympathetic chain, Dr. Levin," I ventured.

"Sure it is, Bill," he answered. "See the ganglia?"

The sympathetic chain doesn't look like much. It's about three inches in length, stringlike, with two or three bulbous areas about one quarter of an inch in diameter, called ganglia, along the chain. It can be difficult to differentiate from pieces of muscle, other nerves or glands. Surgeons have even removed segments of the ureter under the impression that they had the nerve. The genitofemoral nerve, which has nothing to do with circulation in the leg, has been mistakenly removed on so many occasions that it has come to be known as "the fool's sympathetic nerve."

"Those don't look like ganglia to me," I said. "They're too big."

"I'm right where the chain ought to be. I'm sure this is it."

I wasn't, but I'd said my piece.

When the pathology report came back it read: "Lymph nodes; no nerve seen." I caught Ben on rounds the morning the report came back. "What are you going to do about Mr. Myers?" I asked.

"Send him home," Ben said. "He's doing fine."

"Did you see his path report?" I knew he had. I'd seen him reading it.

"No."

"You didn't get the nerve."

"I didn't? Damn it!" He paused to consider. Then he said, "Okay, let me talk to him. We'll do him again in a few weeks if he'll sit still for it."

Ben was a nice guy and basically honest but he would never have told Mr. Myers about his error if I hadn't been in on it. As H. L. Mencken said: "Conscience is that little voice that tells us someone may be watching."

Everyone was watching John Rankin after he operated on Mrs. Fleischer. John had left a sponge behind and he was really sweating it out. He hated to tell her, but he had to. The sponge had shown up on a postoperative x-ray, and every doctor and nurse in the place knew about it. You can't keep something like that quiet. Bad news travels fast in a hospital.

If he hadn't had the x-ray—if we hadn't all known about it—he probably wouldn't have said a thing. Her wound was healing well and the sponge didn't seem to be causing any trouble. He gave her ten days—time to recover from the operation and begin to feel like herself again—and then he broke the news. I was in the room with him at his invitation. I guess he wanted a witness.

"Mrs. Fleischer," he said, "I hate to tell you this but when I operated on you I left a sponge—a piece of gauze—in your abdomen. It hasn't bothered you and I don't expect it will, at least not for a while. But I think in a month or two, when you feel stronger, I ought to remove it. I'm sorry to have to put you through this, but it won't be a big operation and I think you should tolerate it very well.

"These things happen occasionally. They shouldn't, but they do. I was concerned about removing your tumor, and when I had it out I got careless. We count all our sponges before we open and as we close the incision. Somewhere along the line the scrub nurse should have noted the error, but she didn't. However, I'm not blaming her; the responsibility is mine."

"Thank you for telling me," Mrs. Fleischer said, "I respect you for it. And please don't worry. I'm not going to sue you. I came to you because I wanted you to save me from dying of cancer. Hopefully, you have. I'm not going to let a little piece of gauze diminish my gratitude for what you have done."

Mr. Myers had been just as understanding when Dr. Levin broke the news on the sympathectomy. These episodes, and others like them, taught me that patients realize we doctors are human, and if we are honest about our errors, aren't inclined to be vindictive. I could understand that both Dr. Levin and Dr. Rankin were tempted to lie—under similar circumstances I'd have been so inclined myself—but perhaps because they had no choice, they were honest and it worked out all right.

It was a valuable lesson.

16

First Assistant Resident: Next to the Top

You could tell when you made first assistant resident because suddenly there were more people asking you what to do than there were telling you what to do. When I came back from North Shore to Bellevue, Jack Lesperance was chief resident, and one of the first-A.R. jobs was mine. I've mentioned it before in passing, but perhaps a brief review of what the post entailed might be in order.

The two first assistant residents are the right hand men of the chief resident. They take responsibility in decision making when he isn't available. Jack might, for example, be tied up in the operating room or be over in the medical wards, discussing a case at conference, when a man with a crushed chest was admitted. If I, or Walt Kleiss, who was the other first A.R., were around, we would be the ones to say, "Trache him," if we thought it was indicated.

We made rounds for Jack on the mornings when he was in the O.R. I'd take one ward; Walt would take the other two. It was our job to see to it that the A.R. and the intern weren't missing anything.

One morning, for example, I was making rounds when we came to Dick Curtis, a thirty-eight-year old fireman who had had a perirectal abscess drained two days earlier.

"How's it coming?" I asked Charlie Schultz, the A.R. on the ward.

"Kind of slow, Bill," he answered, "not much drainage but it isn't closing in very fast."

I didn't always look at wounds (if the intern had already dressed them I hated to tear the dressing off, memories of my internship still being fresh in my mind), but I decided I'd have a look at this one.

"Sorry, Dick," I said as I yanked the tape.

"Forget it, Doc. Can't be helped."

The wound didn't look healthy. There was nothing specific; it just didn't look like a drained abscess should.

"Let me see his chart." Charlie handed it to me and I thumbed through it.

"That's odd," I said "his white count was twenty thousand when he came in, but he didn't have any temperature. Better repeat that white count," I said to Mike Rantala, the intern, "and get a differential." A differential would tell what kind of cells these were. Mike wrote the order in his scut book.

That night at card rounds when Jack came to Curtis' card I interrupted. "What did that white count show, Mike?"

"I almost hate to tell you," he said. "All immature cells. I took the slide over to medicine and had the resident look at it. Curtis has leukemia."

That case of leukemia might have gone undiagnosed for a long time if I hadn't caught it on rounds. It wasn't that Charlie and Mike were stupid and I was smart. It was just that I had had more experience than they. I had seen more abscesses and knew more about how healing wounds should look.

I also had the advantage of not being involved in the day-to-day care of the patient. Curtis, to Mike, was "the rectal abscess in bed six," a wound he had to dress every day. Charlie looked at Curtis as a patient for whom he was expected to write regular progress notes. To both of them Curtis represented work. I, on the other hand, could consider Curtis *in toto*, order studies that I wouldn't have to carry out myself and see him only once a day. Charlie and Mike had to concentrate on the trees; I could see the forest. I was less apt to miss things.

This system of checking and double-checking paid dividends on many occasions. Making rounds one morning I came to Pepi Weich, a little man who had been admitted from the O.P.D. the day before with a diagnosis of duodenal ulcer. He looked pale to me.

"Mike," I said, "what's Mr. Weich's hemoglobin?"

"Twelve grams"—about normal.

"When did you do it?"

"Yesterday." Mike was a good intern.

"How do you feel, Mr. Weich?" I asked him.

"Not bad," he answered, "a little weak, that's all."

"Weaker than yesterday?"

"Maybe a little."

"Mike," I said as we walked away, "you go do a hemoglobin on Mr. Weich now. Charlie and I will finish rounds."

Before we had seen five more patients Mike came back down the ward. "His hemoglobin's down to six," he said. "He must be bleeding."

"Stick a tube down and see," I told him.

Bright red blood came back from Pepi's stomach.

The only tip-off in this patient had been his pallor. I saw it; Mike and Charlie hadn't. Why? First, because I'd been around longer and had been burned more often than they had. Second, because I hadn't seen Pepi for twenty-four hours. The change in his appearance seemed acute and obvious to me. If I had watched his color change gradually I might not have noticed it.

. . .

Jack, as the year began, did all the big operations. The stomachs, the colons, the chest cases. This was payoff year and until he had all he wanted and needed he wouldn't pass anything much down to Walt or me. When it was my turn as chief I'd do the same.

Sometimes Walt or I scrubbed with Jack on big cases, but most of the time we didn't. The ward A.R.'s needed the experience, and unless the case promised to be particularly difficult, Jack would manage very well without our help. But while we were waiting for Jack to send things our way, we got in plenty of O.R. time. On any case that an intern or A.R. was doing, either Walt or I acted as first assistant. I was in the O.R. every other day. Now I could appreciate what George Walters went through the night I did my first appendectomy. Helping an inept intern through a case requires nerves of steel and the patience of Job. It's most harrowing.

The one intern I most dreaded helping was Bob Lang. I had watched him sew up lacerations in the emergency ward and he was almost unbelievably clumsy. He dropped so many instruments on the floor that the E.W. nurses finally made a routine practice of providing two minor-surgery trays every time Lang had a cut to suture. But though he couldn't walk and chew gum at the same time, he was a good intern. He drew blood, did dressings, worked up patients—did all the menial intern tasks promptly and conscientiously. He could stay up all night and still report efficiently and thoroughly at card rounds the next afternoon. If any one of the interns deserved a reward, in the form of an operation to perform, Lang was the guy.

As fate would have it, I was on call the night his first appendectomy came in. He called me down to the E.W. to see the patient.

"Bill, this is Mr. Franseen," he said. "Mr. Franseen has had a pain in his belly for the last twenty-four hours and it's getting worse. His temperature is one hundred degrees and his white blood count is sixteen thousand."

I examined the patient. There was no doubt he had an acute appy. "Get him seen, signed and prepped, Bob," I said. "There's a Caesarian section going now, but we'll be next. Shouldn't be more than an hour."

We got into the O.R. about midnight and now it was my turn to go through the same sort of ordeal George had suffered with me six years earlier. Lang did everything wrong. He broke ties, dropped clamps, let bleeders get loose. When we got into the abdomen I gave him five tries at delivering the appendix and finally did it myself. It was agonizing.

He didn't cut the appendix too short or break the purse string, as I had (I was wary of these problems after my own initiation and watched like a hawk as the intern performed these maneuvers), but in another respect he did me one better. Before the case ended he had cut me with the scalpel, not once but three times. The case took an extra five minutes just because I had to change gloves so often.

When it was over and we were loading Mr. Franseen on the stretcher I almost choked, but I managed to say what he wanted to hear: "Nice job, Bob."

"Gee, thanks, Bill," he said, all smiles. "I thought it went pretty well myself." He actually believed me!

This guy was going to be tough to discourage.

As the year wore on Jack passed much of the major surgery down to me, since I was to be the next resident, but one kind of case he refused to give me—a portacaval shunt. The reason he wouldn't pass one down was simple—not one of Jack's patients had survived the operation. He was hardly in a position to give these cases away.

A portacaval shunt is done on patients with cirrhosis of the liver whose disease is so bad that it blocks the portal vein. This vein, about the size of a thumb, normally carries all the blood from the intestine to the liver, but when it becomes obstructed, the pressure increases to levels many times normal. The blood backs up, and one of the places it goes to is the esophagus. Patients with advanced cirrhosis develop varicose veins of the esophagus which tear easily, with resulting hemorrhage.

In a portacaval shunt a communication is constructed between the portal vein and the inferior vena cava, a big vein that is unaffected by liver disease, and relieves the back pressure on the veins of the esophagus. This is always a very bloody operation. The back pressure is so high that even the slightest injury may cause the veins to bleed vigorously. It's not unusual for a patient to lose twenty pints of blood in the course of the surgery.

Patients who needed this operation were terrible risks. Most of them were men, or women, who ate little and drank much, mostly cheap muscatel. When they came to the hospital they were not only bleeding; they were also suffering from jaundice and malnutrition.

During the years preceding the shunt operation—it was relatively new—treatment had been medical. Transfuse the patient, place a balloon in his esophagus and blow it up to stop the bleeding with pressure, and hope for the best. The best, in about 90 percent of cases, was death. So now we were shunting all these patients, often at night. Jack did them, and Julius Norton, an attending with a particular interest in the problem, helped. I'd usually drop into the O.R. and watch.

We did all the patients under hypothermia. We'd cool them down before surgery to about 86 degrees F.—this protected the liver—using a blanket through which ice water was circulated. After surgery we'd warm them up by circulating warm water through the same blanket.

Jack must have done a dozen cases as resident, and his mortality rate was 100 percent. It wasn't Jack's fault. The operations went as smoothly as could be; it was just that our patients were too damn sick. (Even in private hospitals with well-fed patients, surgeons were reporting mortalities in the 60–70 percent range.) I mention these bad results only to emphasize that at Bellevue we were continually fighting against overwhelming odds, much greater than we would eventually face as surgeons at private hospitals.

My opinion that this was so was reinforced one day when we were visited by Dr. Edward Stevens, the brother of Dr. Russell Stevens, the director of our division. Edward Stevens was professor emeritus at a well-known medical school and a world-renowned authority on surgery. We gathered the house staff together and he made rounds with us. When we had finished he turned to us and said, "Boys, if you can take good care of these patients, as you are obviously doing, have no fear. When you get out into practice you will find the problems much simpler."

That was the best news I'd heard in a long, long time.

17

Death

As a medical student I couldn't have been convinced by anyone that I would ever want a patient to die, but the time came when I did.

The first patient whose death I desired was a thirty-five-year-old man named Jim Adams. Jim had been on a drunk for several weeks, a drunk which ended when he fell asleep smoking in a Bowery flophouse and set his bed on fire. He came in with 80 percent of his body burned, most of it third-degree.

I took care of him. I dressed his burns, started his intravenous fluids, checked his medications. He was conscious from the first day and knew he was in serious trouble. Every day when I came to work on him he asked me how he was doing and I'd give him an encouraging answer: "Not bad at all, Jim. Your temperature's normal today"; "Looking better; we'll probably start feeding you soon"; "Wouldn't be surprised if the hand burns turned out to be only second-degree."

And for a while—the usual two weeks—he didn't do badly. Then infection set in. His burns began to peel, and pus got into the raw areas. His temperature soared, and all our dressings and antibiotics couldn't get him under control. He lost weight and strength and was in constant pain. It was obvious he was going to die; the only question was when.

Still I persisted in treating him. Remove the dead tissue, put on clean dressings, start the I.V.'s; like a mechanical man.

Even when he was too weak to ask about himself and could barely whisper when I hurt him, I stuck to it. Day after day after day.

Then one morning when I opened the door to his room, I realized for the first time that I wanted Jim Adams to die. I was sick of doing his dressings, sick of causing him futile pain, sick of treating a hopelessly ill patient. I had trouble getting myself to admit it and would have denied it if anyone asked me, but it was the unvarnished, undeniable truth; I wanted this man dead.

I did nothing about it, of course. If anything, because of my guilt feelings, I worked harder to keep him alive. But when he died, about a week later—one month after he had been admitted—I was relieved. Happy he was gone; happy I didn't have to work on him any more.

It was the first time I wanted a patient dead, but it wasn't the last. Patients suffering with terminal cancer, who weren't any good to themselves or others, I often wished would die, and to be brutally honest, not just for their own sake but for mine as well. Visiting them every day, giving them false cheer and futile sustenance, got to be such a burden that I wished it were over, and the only way it could end was with the patient's death. Not a praiseworthy desire, to be sure, but a human one.

A logical question of course is: if a patient was suffering, if his condition was hopeless, if he was a burden to his family and if they were in constant anguish from watching him suffer, then why did I, or any doctor, persist in our efforts to keep him alive? The answer lies in the word "hopeless." I don't know the origin of the adage "Where there's life there's hope," but I can testify that whoever coined it sensed something deep within the soul of man. I might know by all the norms and standards of scientific medicine that Jim Adams would be dead within a week; still I didn't *know* it. The odds might be 2 million or 5 million or 10 billion to one that he would soon be dead, but as long as there was one chance, no

matter how remote, that he might live, did I have the right
to deny life to him? I'll answer the question: No.

After all, what is the alternative? Perhaps death would
come as a welcome relief from his suffering; perhaps, if he
believed in an afterlife he would actually look forward to
it, but I could never assume the responsibility of imposing
death upon him. I couldn't play God.

But what about the patient; if he chose to die, if he asked
for death, shouldn't I respect his wishes? Surprisingly, this
never occurred during my residency, nor has it happened in
the years of practice since. What usually happens is that the
patient doesn't desire death, in fact clings to life until he
reaches a point where he is no longer capable of making a
reasonable request or a rational decision. By the time it should
be obvious that his death is imminent and unescapable he
really doesn't care what happens. He has either become stu-
porous or delirious. As Longfellow said, "Whom the Gods
want to destroy they first make mad." Longfellow was right.
I suppose, theoretically, a doctor could say to a patient,
"Look, you are going to be dead in a week [though the doctor
would not really know this]; all you have to look forward to
in the days that remain are pain and gradual deterioration.
Would you like me to help you die now?" Theoretically, I
say, a doctor could ask this question, but I've never met anyone who had the nerve to ask it.

I learned, the more I dealt with dying patients, that it
didn't matter much whether you were an intern or a professor
of surgery; the responsibility for deciding a patient should die
was one you avoided with all the resources at your command.
It's one thing for a layman to say, "If I were a doctor I'd never
let a hopeless patient linger"; quite another to be that doctor
and to walk over to the respirator, pull out the plug, and
watch the patient die. The responsibility is awesome and
more than most doctors are willing to bear.

At the risk of belaboring the issue, I'd like to mention one
other factor that ought to be emphasized, since it represents

an aspect to which the layman is probably not quite as exposed as the doctor. Miracles—I use the term to signify phenomena that we simply can't explain—do occur.

Consider one of the children we operated on, eighteen months old with a large tumor in the abdomen. We opened him up, found that the mass had so involved vital structures that it couldn't be removed, biopsied it, and closed. It was a neuroblastoma, a tumor which had arisen from a primordial nerve cell—a malignant tumor. We told the parents that there was nothing we could do, that the boy was beyond our help, that their child's life was, so to speak, in the hands of the Lord.

The boy made an uneventful recovery. Five years later he was alive and well without a trace of the tumor. Why? I don't know, nor does anyone else, including the surgeons who specialize in pediatric diseases. This sort of thing happens occasionally, particularly in the case of neuroblastomas. Once in a while one will go away spontaneously. In twenty children the tumor grows, spreads and kills them; in one, no different from the others as far as anyone can tell, the tumor melts away. And so it will happen with other growths and diseases in adults as well as in children. There is hardly a surgeon of any experience who hasn't on at least one occasion given a patient up for dead only to find that the patient makes a complete recovery—one that is inexplicable, in terms of scientific knowledge.

Is there any wonder that, in the face of such experiences, a surgeon is reluctant to "pull the plug"? Is it any wonder that he hesitates to "play God"?

18

Mutual Lack of Admiration

At Bellevue, we had one of the few artificial kidneys available anywhere in the country. The machine was a big, bulky affair and its use was supervised by Virgil Lewis, a medical attending on the Cornell Medical Division. Patients were referred to Second Medicine for dialysis—treatment with the artificial kidney—from hospitals all over the city.

The medical men would have liked to run this machine without the help of the surgeons, and we surer than hell wished they could, but it was impossible. To run a patient on the machine you had to first put one catheter into an artery and another into a vein, and this kind of surgery, "minor" as it might seem, was often difficult. The room in which the kidney was kept was not well lighted—the instruments that were put in the "kidney packs" were discards from the O.R.—the patients were often restless and unco-operative, tough to control under local anesthesia.

On top of that there were always a dozen medical men breathing down our backs as we worked, making snide comments on how long it was taking us just to "slip a couple of catheters in." I hated these calls to the kidney unit but I had to go; the surgery was much too difficult for any internist to attempt.

I'll have to qualify that: On every medical division there is at least one frustrated surgeon, one fellow who wished he were a "cutting doctor" but who for one reason or other wound up a medical man instead. On the Cornell Medical Division, Bert Yates was the guy.

One night I got a call from Virgil Lewis asking me to come over to Second Medicine immediately. They had a patient with salicylate poisoning—she had swallowed something like two hundred aspirins—and they wanted to get her on the machine immediately.

"Gee, Virgil, I'm sorry," I said, "but I can't get there for at least forty-five minutes. We're just about to do an appy and I can't leave. If you can't wait I'll send Russ Smith over. I'm sure he can handle it."

There were a few seconds of muffled conversation and Virgil got back on the wire. "Never mind sending Smith, Bill; Bert has watched you several times and he says he can do it. We'll just go ahead."

I had to smile. "Fine, Virgil," I said, "if you need me later I'll be in the division library."

I'd have given a good share of my worldly goods to have been a fly on the wall of that dialysis room for the next two hours. It was that long before Virgil called me back, as I damn well knew he eventually would. "Say, Bill, maybe you'd better take a look in here, at that. Bert seems to be having a bit of trouble." Which, as far as I could tell, was the understatement of the year. When I arrived, Bert had more blood on his white suit than most surgeons would acquire taking out a lung. He had enough instruments strewn about to do a heart transplant. His shirt was wringing wet and I could see from the distribution of the drapes that he had given up on sterile technique at least an hour earlier.

"I've almost got it, Bill," he said as I peered into the wound. "The only problem is this damn artery. It seems to be blocked." I couldn't bring myself to tell him that the "artery" into which he was trying to thread the catheter was the tendon to the thumb.

"Let me get some gloves on, Bert, maybe I can give you a hand." I dug out the artery from beneath the tendon, put a tie around it and said to Bert, "Let's try this one. It seems to be in better shape." The catheter slipped in easily.

Bert had realized, as soon as I took over, that he had missed the artery completely. I kept my mouth shut and didn't let any of the other medical men know he had blundered. I was Bert's friend for life. He, of course, was cured. He never tried to go it alone again.

Medical men don't think much of surgeons, and vice versa. In medical school we used to say, "Internists know everything but do nothing; surgeons know nothing but do everything; pathologists know everything and do everything, but too late."

Surgery attracts a different sort of person than does medicine. The guy that goes into surgery is the fellow who doesn't want to sit around waiting for results. He wants the quick cure of a scalpel, not the slow cure of a pill. What he lacks in patience he makes up for in decisiveness.

The surgeon is more of a gambler than is the medical man. I can remember, as a medical student, watching the house staff at a hospital play poker in the evening. It was always dealer's choice. I quickly learned to tell what specialty the resident or intern was in by the game he called and the way he played it. The surgeons played things like "no peek," "fiery cross" and "baseball"—games with seven cards, most of them wild. The medical men always played five-card draw or five-card stud. The surgeons would bet the maximum on a low pair; the medical man wouldn't risk a nickel unless he had the pot cold.

Medical men regard surgeons as technicians: not too bright, but show them what has to do done and they may have the dexterity to do it. Surgeons look upon medical men as doctors who lack decisiveness. Internists hem and haw for hours over whether to give a patient penicillin or aureomycin; they'd be lost if they had to make up their minds in minutes whether or not to open an abdomen.

Despite this mutual lack of admiration it was imperative that we surgeons get along with our counterparts on medicine, and they with us. There was no telling when one of our postoperative patients would have a coronary and we'd need the help and advice of an internist; they couldn't be certain that their patient with pneumonia wouldn't develop appendicitis. For that matter, either of us might require the services of a neurosurgeon if one of our patients fell out of bed and sustained a fractured skull. All of us, doctors from every discipline, were interdependent when it came to providing complete care for the patient.

But there was always an undercurrent of mutual disdain and sometimes it seemed to be warranted. More than once I ruefully had to call for the help of a medical man when I discovered one of our patients had gone into severe congestive heart failure because I had failed to spot early evidence of the disease; on the other hand, once I became a surgical consultant, I not infrequently would be called to see a patient with a perforated ulcer or acute appendicitis hours, or even days, after the event had occurred. One of the unattractive side effects of the shift from general practice to specialization is that each specialist has some "blind spots." (Another saying from medical school: "The general practitioner is a guy who knows less and less about more and more, until eventually he knows nothing about everything; the specialist is a guy who knows more and more about less and less, until eventually he knows everything about nothing.")

You didn't become a consultant in surgery until you reached the first-A.R. level—the fourth year of surgical training. By that time it was expected not only that you had enough experience and enough knowledge to give sound advice to the doctors who requested counsel, but that you were mature enough to give this advice in an inoffensive way. By the time you reached the first-A.R. level you had usually made enough mistakes of your own to take a charitable attitude toward the mistakes of others. Instead of saying to an internist, "You damn fool, a first-year medical student would have known this guy had appendicitis, and here you've been calling it 'intestinal flu' for the last three days," you'd say, "Appendicitis in the elderly is often difficult to diagnose. I can certainly understand your inclination to suspect an intestinal infection. However, even though I can't be certain, I think it might be good judgment to take the patient to the operating room and just make sure that his appendix is okay."

We kept a "consultation book" at the nurses' station on Sharon's ward, and any doctor from any other service who wanted a consultation would phone in his request. The nurse or ward clerk who answered the phone would make a note of the patient's name, ward and presumptive diagnosis. If the doctor requested an emergency consultation for an acute surgical problem, she would notify either Walt Kleiss or me, and as first A.R.'s, whichever of us was free would go and see the patient. If the consultation was not urgent, then we'd see that patient later that day or the next. One of us always checked the consult book each day.

Usually the consultations were neither challenging nor demanding. I might see some patient recovering from pneumonia who had an incidental hernia. I'd write: "Refer patient to surgical O.P.D. for hernia repair when lung problem has cleared completely." Or perhaps the patient might be a man with a coronary who had developed phlebitis, inflammation of the leg veins. My note would read: "Continue treatment with anticoagulants, apply wet pads to leg, and call back if the patient throws an embolus. We would then consider tying off his vein." No real problem.

But once in a while something would come up that really tested my judgment. One evening I was called to see John Muchler as an emergency. George Vachon, the resident on the medical ward, met me at the nurses' station. George was, in my opinion, a good sound medical man—a rare bird.

"Bill," he said, "this is a tough problem. Muchler is fifty-two years old. He's had bad heart disease for twenty years. We admitted him last week in failure up to the eyeballs and we're just now getting him so he can breathe without bubbling.

"Yesterday he vomited blood. We put a tube down him, sedated him and gave him a couple of pints. When it didn't stop, we got some x-rays and they show a helluva big gastric ulcer. He's a lousy risk but I wonder if you shouldn't do him."

I looked at the films. The ulcer was big, the size of a half dollar, but at least it was on the greater curvative, the part of the stomach that's easiest to get at. My initial impression was that we should indeed do him.

Then I went to see Mr. Muchler. He was propped up in bed on three pillows and still breathing with difficulty. He was ashen. He looked, as Grove would say, as if we'd kill him if we cut his hair. I decided after seeing him that we shouldn't operate.

"I don't think he can take it, George," I said. "You'd better keep transfusing him. Maybe he'll stop."

"Come off it, Bill," George said, "he isn't going to stop. He hasn't yet and it's almost twenty-four hours. Besides, we're really on thin ice with the transfusions. One pint too many and we'll have him in failure so we'll never get him out; one too few and he'll bleed to death."

"You've got a point, George," I said. "Tell you what—let's ask Jack what he thinks."

So Jack Lesperance came over and the three of us went over the case again. "We're damned if we do and damned if we don't," said Jack. "Let's do him."

I made a special trip to the O.R. to make certain we got the best anesthetist on the staff, explained to him how precarious the situation was, and about ten o'clock we got started.

Frank Jenkins, the attending who had given us the go ahead, came in at Jack's request, but he didn't scrub.

"You don't need me, Jack," he said. "You can handle it. I'm just going to stand by and applaud."

We did the fastest gastrectomy I'd ever seen. We used a midline incision, not a favorite on our division because of its inherent weakness, but one that can be quickly made, and we closed the abdomen with a single layer of through-and-through wire sutures. We were done in less than an hour.

Mr. Muchler made it. It was touch and go for a few days, but with his bleeding stopped, George and his associates were able to get his heart failure back under control. The success of that case raised our stock sky-high on medicine.

The only time we had contact with the psychiatric division, other than when we were trying to "bug" someone (to "bug" means, in Bellevuese, to transfer to psycho), was when we had a patient who was senile or disoriented and upon whom we had to operate.

These patients were obviously unable to take the responsibility for signing the permit slip themselves. We were supposed to call the psychiatrist, get him to sign a statement saying the patient was mentally incompetent, and then go to one of the medical superintendents who would authorize surgery and sign the permit.

All this rigmarole was time-consuming, and time at Bellevue was too precious to be squandered on unessentials such as legal technicalities. So we used a different routine.

When I had a patient, like Mr. Price, who was obviously out in left field, but just as obviously needed an operation—for cancer or bleeding or some other catastrophe—I'd walk over to the bed with my intern and say, "Mr. Price, you're bleeding. We're going to take your stomach out if that is okay with you. Do you have any objection?" Mr. Price was eighty-six years old and back in his second childhood. I might as well have been talking to the wall. I gave Mr. Price ten or fifteen seconds to speak up—I wanted to be fair—then I said, "As long as you have no objection, would you please sign this slip?"

There was, of course, no response.

I then picked up Mr. Price's hand and said, "Here, let me help you." I put the pen in his hand and moved it until we had an X. I witnessed the signature, the intern counter-signed it, and we ran Mr. Price up to the O.R.

Not completely legal, perhaps, but it saved a lot of time and an occasional life. At Bellevue you learned to be practical, if you learned nothing else.

If a patient had attempted suicide we could, if we thought he might try it again, transfer the patient to the psychiatric ward. The psychiatrists would almost invariably accept these patients. It was too risky to leave them in the general hospital, where supervision was often minimal.

But when you couldn't make an ironclad case, when the patient wasn't obviously off his rocker, it was tough to get a patient to the psychiatric ward. Take the case of Abe Fredman, a fifty-year-old man who had been admitted from the outpatient department because he had had blood in his stools. He looked healthy and I thought the eventual explanation would prove to be hemorrhoids.

Abe had cancer phobia. While he was waiting for his barium enema, which was scheduled a week later, he kept after me about it. "How can you be sure it isn't cancer? What if they don't find anything—they might just miss it. My father died of cancer and his symptoms were just like mine." He went on and on, and no matter what I said I couldn't re-assure him.

Then the ward nurse told me she had noticed that Abe was crying. Two or three times a day he'd go into the linen closet and bawl. This was too much. Cancer phobia is rela-tively common—we all have it in a mild form—but Abe was going to extremes. He was getting into a depression.

"Call the psychiatrists," I said to the intern, "you'd better have them take a look at Abe. He's getting a little squirrely."

The psychiatric resident came over that afternoon, spent about fifteen minutes talking to Abe, wrote a consultation note and left.

I walked over to the nurses' station and read it. "This man is concerned that he may have cancer. However, he is oriented in all spheres (knows who he is, where he is, and what day it is) and though he is in a depression, it is a mild one. There is no need to transfer this patient to the psychiatric service. I recommend sedation with phenobarbital 30 mgms three times a day. Thank you"—and he signed his name.

We started Abe on phenobarbital for his "mild depression" that afternoon. The next day, while we were making rounds, he walked to the window and jumped out. When we reached the parking lot we found him lying dead on the smashed-in roof of a '54 Chevrolet.

The psychiatric service was chronically overloaded with patients and was routinely understaffed. Every doctor on the service had to supervise more patients than he could handle. Naturally, they were wary of accepting more. Sometimes, however, they refused patients like Abe Fredman, whom they might have helped.

To prevent being swamped with alcoholics, whom we frequently tried to transfer, the psychiatrists had a hard and fast rule that no one would be accepted unless he was actually hallucinating. Anything short of snakes and pink elephants on the wall, the patient stayed on the general ward.

I'll never forget one man we had, a guy named Steve Reynolds. He was a fireman and he had broken his leg when he fell down the pole hole in a strange firehouse—a kooky enough thing in itself. His leg was shattered. It was so bad that there was no way to hold it in a cast or even to hold it together with screws and plates. So we chose a third alternative, we put him in traction. Bascially what it amounts to is that weights are used to pull the fractured bones into alignment. In Steve's case we attached the weight to a pin through his heel.

The third day of his hospitalization it was obvious that Steve was getting restless. It's routine to ask any patient about his drinking habits, and it's equally routine for the heavy drinkers to lie. Steve had admitted only to "an occasional glass of beer."

But on rounds that morning it was obvious that Steve was going into the D.T.'s. He was picking at his sheets and talking to his wife, who, of course, wasn't there.

"Get the psychiatrist over," I said. "We'd better 'bug' this guy before he gets into trouble."

But, as luck would have it, when the "bug" doctor arrived Steve was temporarily back with us. He knew his name, the date, and even remembered my name.

I told the psychiatrist how Steve had been that morning, but no dice. "He's not hallucinating now," he said. "You can keep him."

That night Steve pulled his leg out of the traction apparatus and ran down the ward trying to get away from the snakes. We could probably have "bugged" him the next day, but we didn't try—his fracture was now too much of a challenge.

Once in a while we'd run into a consultation problem that was sticky not only from the surgical point of view but diplomatically as well. I saw one dandy on the genitourinary service. The resident, with the help of a G.U. attending, had done a case in which an artificial bladder was constructed from a segment of intestine. After isolating this segment, putting the ureters into it and bringing the new bladder to the abdominal wall, you must of course do an anastomosis—sew the two ends of the intestine back together.

Strictly speaking, bowel work lies in the domain of the general surgeon. G.U. men don't have occasion to work with intestine very often; most of the problems they see have to do with the kidneys, bladder and reproductive organs. On the other hand, most G.U. men have had a year or two of general surgery. They may or may not have done some bowel work. Most probably they haven't, but they have at least seen it done.

The attending on this particular case apparently thought he knew enough about general surgery to do the job. Certainly he hadn't asked any of us to scrub in and help, an option that was open to him. I wasn't asked to see Mr. Jarvis, the patient, until seven days after the surgery. Even then the consultation wasn't categorized as an emergency. The note in the consult book read simply: "Jarvis, genitourinary ward, possible bowel obstruction, nonemergent." So I leisurely wandered over to see Jarvis that afternoon.

Pete Lemke, the G.U. resident, saw me on the ward examining Mr. Jarvis. He came up to me and said, "Sorry to bother you with this one, Bill, but you know Allard. He was the attending on the case and he's antsy. I'm sure Jarvis here just has a few early adhesions that should break up soon."

Jarvis' abdomen was blown up like a balloon. I asked him if he was passing any gas.

"You mean, am I farting, Doc?"

I nodded.

"Not since my operation, and I was always one for doing it." He seemed to be in the best of spirits.

"Have you got any films?" I asked Pete.

"Got some this morning. Haven't seen them yet. Let's take a look." We put the films up on the view box. The small intestine, for half its length, was enormously distended. There was no gas in the lower portion of the small bowel, nor in the large intestine.

"Where did you get the bowel for your new bladder?" I asked.

"Somewhere around the middle I guess," Pete said. "Why?"

"Oh, nothing—I was just wondering."

I went back and listened to Mr. Jarvis' abdomen. His bowels were in an uproar.

"Well, what do you think, Bill?" Pete asked. His concern was now evident. "Shall we give him a few more days and see if he opens up?"

Now was the time to be careful. "I'll tell you, Pete, I'm a bit concerned. It's just possible that somehow that bowel has twisted right about at the point where you sewed it back together. I think maybe we ought to take a look. It may be a big false alarm, but Jarvis seems to be in good shape, and even if I'm wrong I don't think we'll hurt him."

"Well, if you say so, Bill," Pete said, "but I think you're jumping the gun a little."

We did Jarvis that evening, and to the surprise of absolutely no one on the general surgical service, we found that Jarvis' bowel had been sutured completely shut. The stitches the G.U. surgeons had put in had been so deep that they had caught both sides of the bowel. Jarvis could have stayed in bed till doomsday without ever spontaneously becoming unobstructed. Pete and Allard were, naturally, chagrined. I didn't rub it in, of course, not with all the skeletons in my closet, but we had to let them know what we found. The next time they did a similar case they invited me to scrub.

Pete's reluctance to have me re-explore Mr. Jarvis is far from an uncommon attitude among surgeons. Anyone hates to admit there's even a remote possibility that he has blundered. There's a great temptation to rationalize, long past the time when it's reasonable to do so, that the problem is only a temporary one and that time will take care of it. When this happens, when you're so emotionally involved in a case that you can't think rationally, that's the time to call in a new and objective observer. It's painful, but it's the only course to follow. Anything short of that is unfair to the patient.

In order to maintain good relations with the medical service it sometimes became necessary to make a decision for or against operating on grounds other than purely scientific ones. I recall one case when I was chief resident that illustrates this point particularly well.

Mr. Navarone was a forty-year-old man suffering from disseminated lupus erythematosus, a disease that can cause problems in any or every organ of the body. He had been on the medical service for two weeks when the episode occurred. At the time, the patient was receiving high doses of cortisone. This was the treatment for his medical disease. On this particular day he complained of abdominal pain and vomited once or twice. The medical resident felt that Mr. Navarone had probably developed an acute ulcer of the stomach—a complication that sometimes occurs when large doses of cortisone are used—and that this ulcer had perforated. He asked us for a consultation.

Walt went over to the medical ward to see the man, examined him, looked at the x-rays and decided that there was no perforation—that Mr. Navarone simply had an upset stomach. He recommended medical treatment.

Half an hour later I received a call from the chief medical resident. "Bill," he said, "would you mind taking a look at Mr. Navarone? I know Walt doesn't think it's a surgical problem but I do, and so does the attending on the ward. We'd appreciate it."

I had been content to accept Walt's appraisal, but since an attending was now involved, I obliged and went to see the patient myself. He was sitting up in bed, reading. On questioning he complained of severe pain in the abdomen, but on examination there was no evidence of the tenderness and muscle spasm that ordinarily comes with a perforated ulcer.

I called the medical resident and told him I agreed with Walt's diagnosis. He thanked me and said he would go ahead with the medical treatment.

One hour later, sitting in the surgical library reading about disseminated lupus, I got another call. This time it was the medical attending himself. "Dr. Nolen," he said, "I realize you're in charge over there but I am convinced that Mr. Navarone has a perforated ulcer. Would you kindly ask one of your attending surgeons to see him?"

This was extraordinary behavior. Attendings rarely contacted house staff members of other services directly. It simply wasn't done. But once it was done, once the request was made, there was nothing to do but honor it. I was upset, but I got hold of Bill Starr, explained the situation to him, and brought him to the medical ward to see Mr. Navarone.

Starr spent a half-hour talking to and examining Mr. Navarone. When we were through he took me aside and said, "Bill, I agree with you. I don't think this man has a perforated ulcer. But from what you tell me, the medical people feel very strongly that he does.

"Now," he continued, "it is just possible that they are right. Cortisone can mask symptoms. At any rate, the medical people are stuck. They want him operated on—and they can't do it. You have to do it for them, if it's to be done at all.

"Neither of us thinks the man has a perforation but I guess we had better look, as a courtesy to them. If they're right, we'll help Mr. Navarone and we'll learn something; if they're wrong, I don't think we'll have hurt Mr. Navarone much and the medical people will have learned even more."

So we operated on Mr. Navarone. The chief medical resident and the attending came up to the operating room, something medical men rarely do, to see what we'd find. I could tell they were ready to gloat, and I admit I had begun to doubt my own judgment.

There was nothing to fear. Mr. Navarone's abdominal cavity was clean. No ulcer, no perforation—nothing. We opened him, looked around and closed. A thirty-minute job.

I never heard a word directly from the medical attending, but I learned from the chief resident that from that time on, whenever the medical residents and interns said disparaging things about surgeons—a game medical men frequently play— he kept his mouth shut.

Our operation hadn't been a total waste.

Learning to maintain good rapport was an important part of our training. Once we got out into practice we'd have no captive referrals. We would have to rely on the good will of the medical men for patients. Better to learn diplomacy now when we weren't under any pressure than to develop bad habits that could give us some lean years later on.

19

The O.R. Team

Every operation is a team event. A surgeon can no more operate on a patient by himself then can a general fight a war alone. An operation, like a battle, is a co-operative venture.

The surgeon is the boss. He's the one who takes the responsibility, legally as well as practically, for whatever is done to the patient during the time he's in the operating room. The surgeon decides where to make the cut, what operation to perform, how to close the incision. He may ask his assistant for an opinion, but the ultimate decision is the surgeon's alone.

Since the bulk of this book is about the surgeon and his assistant it might be well to mention here the other members of the team—the circulating nurse, the scrub nurse and the anesthesiologist.

The circulating nurse is the one who makes the preparations for surgery. There are standard pieces of equipment that are used on every operation—hemostats to clamp vessels, scalpels for cutting, sponges for mopping up blood; but there are other instruments and implements that are used only in specific operations. For example, the surgeon needs a screwdriver and a drill to fix a broken hip; he doesn't need them to take out a gall bladder. To take out a gall bladder he needs clamps with the tip bent at a right angle; he doesn't need these clamps if he's going to remove a stomach. It's the circulating nurse's job to see that all the instruments the surgeon may need for a scheduled operation are available and sterilized.

Most of the time, even if there's only a remote chance that a tool may be needed, the circulating nurse will put it in. There is nothing that makes a surgeon erupt more quickly than the discovery that an absolutely essential piece of equipment is not available. It takes twenty minutes to sterilize some tools, and sitting around doing nothing for twenty minutes in an operating room with the patient asleep and the abdomen open seems like an eternity.

At Bellevue we often had student nurses circulating, so the wise surgeon learned to check all the equipment before the operation began. There was a list available of all the instruments routinely used in each type of operation, but it was always possible that an inexperienced nurse would provide the wrong tools. The surgeon who double-checked avoided this possibility.

The scrub nurse is the nurse who actually works with the surgeon as he performs the operation. She's the one who hands him the instruments he needs while he's operating. The classic story is of the surgeon who inadvertently said "Scissors" to the nurse when he actually wanted a clamp. He held out his hand and she slapped the scissors into it. He took one look at what he was holding and threw it on the floor. "God damn it, Miss Johnson," he said, "don't give me what I ask for, give me what I need."

A good scrub nurse, one who has worked with a surgeon many times, will do just that. She keeps one eye on the wound at all times and learns to anticipate what the surgeon will want next. He just holds out his hand and she'll put into it a ligature, a clamp, a scalpel—whatever is indicated. He doesn't have to say a word. A scrub nurse in that class can chop minutes off an operation.

At Bellevue we had a great many experienced scrub nurses. Sometimes they knew more about the operation than the surgeon who was doing it. When that situation arose it was imperative that she be extremely diplomatic.

I was helping an intern do an appendectomy one night, with Miss Danvers, who was one of the best, scrubbed in. When the intern started to close the abdomen—it had been a very messy, infected appendix—he asked Miss Danvers for silk sutures. A surgeon never uses silk in a dirty wound if he can help it. It's a nonabsorbable suture and in an infected wound it won't be tolerated. The patient will "spit" silk from his incision for months. "Silk?" she said. She looked at me. I said nothing.

"Yes," the intern answered. "Why not?"

"I just thought that with all that pus around, you might prefer catgut." Catgut is absorbed by the body after the two or three weeks it takes for a wound to heal.

He paused for a minute. "You know," he said, "that's a good thought. Why don't you give me catgut instead." He was smart too; he wasn't too pigheaded to take the advice of an experienced scrub nurse.

Many of them, however, were inexperienced. Then, if the team was to function smoothly, the surgeon would try to be a step or two ahead of himself. Removing a stomach, I might say, "Now, Miss Dean, I'm going to divide the tissue between the bowel and the stomach. I'll need two clamps, one after the other, then the scissors to cut between them. After I've used about ten clamps, I'll stop and tie. I'll need number 2-o silk."

Knowing what I planned to do would help the scrub nurse prepare before I actually needed the equipment. While I was clamping and cutting she'd make certain that the silk ties were available. I'd help her stay one jump ahead of me so that we wouldn't have any of those awkward little delays—me standing and waiting while she got the stitches threaded on the needle—that would break up the rhythm of the operation. We had enough unavoidable hindrances to smooth surgery at Bellevue; we couldn't afford any unnecessary ones.

The anesthesiologist, the final member of the team, is in many ways the most important to the success of the operation. Even, and I say this with reluctance, more important than the surgeon.

For while the surgeon, the assistant and the scrub nurse are concentrating on one specific portion of the patient's anatomy—the gall bladder filled with stones, the ulcer in the stomach or the tumor in the colon—the anesthesiologist is thinking about the patient as a whole. He's the one who is making certain that the heart keeps beating, the lungs continue to function and that the patient's blood chemistries remain in satisfactory condition. If he doesn't do his job properly, then it's possible to wind up two hours of surgery with that horrible contradiction: a successful operation and a dead patient.

The anesthesiologists at Bellevue always evaluated the patient prior to surgery. On elective cases they'd go to the ward the night before surgery, look over the chart and talk to the patient; in critical situations they'd visit the patient in the emergency ward, if there was time, or see him as soon as he arrived in the operating room.

Most of their interest focused on the heart and lungs. The anesthesia they chose to use would depend to a large extent on the condition of these organs. They would also check for allergies a patient might have, in case there was a history of an allergy to a certain anesthetic, and would question the patient closely about any medication he might be taking. Certain medicines, antihypertensive drugs and cortisone for example, might cause the patient to overreact to one anesthetic or another; if he was alerted to this possibility the anesthesiologist might choose either a different anesthetic or a smaller dose of the one he had elected to use.

If the anesthesiologist was considering spinal anesthesia, which is particularly useful in patients with bad hearts or lungs, he had other factors to weigh. First, the site of the operation. Spinals are safest for operations below the waist—

hernia repairs, appendectomies, and the like. Second, the condition of the patient's spine; it can be extremely difficult to push a needle into the spinal canal of a patient with bad arthritis. Last, but far from least, the mental attitude of the patient. Any patient who was convinced that he'd have bad headaches after a spinal, or who "knew a friend who had a spinal and was paralyzed ever after," would not be a good candidate. That kind always had postanesthetic problems, usually imaginary. So the anesthesiologist had to do a bit of psychiatric evaluation to rule out these poor risks.

As I write specifically about anesthesia I'm making a point of calling the men who administer the anesthetic anesthesiologists rather than anesthetists. There is a reason.

The "gas passers"—as we'd call them when there were none around—are very sensitive about the label given to them. An anesthesiologist is a physician, an M.D., whose specialty is anesthesia; an anesthetist is anyone who gives anesthesia and in many hospitals this includes specially trained nurses. The M.D.'s don't like to be grouped in with the nurses, and really they shouldn't be. We had no nurse anesthetists at Bellevue, since the hospital had an excellent training program for anesthesiologists, but where the two coexisted, the nurses always worked under the direction of the anesthesiologist. In small hospitals, I learned later, nurse anesthetists often worked alone, and most were damn good at their job. Anyway, M.D.'s who specialize in anesthesia are sensitive about the label, and where I've slipped and called them anesthetists I apologize.

I always made a point of talking to the anesthesiologist as soon as we had all assembled in the operating room, before we did anything to the patient. I might say, "Watch out for this one, Charlie, he had a coronary last month."

"Yeah, I know. His electrocardiogram looks like hell. I'll stay away from the cyclopropane." Cyclopropane was a gas that occasionally aggravated irregular heart rhythms.

Another time the patient would be a diabetic. "Better give him some insulin with his fluids," I'd suggest. "He didn't get any on the ward this morning." The chances were excellent that whoever was giving the anesthetic knew the patient was a diabetic, but I always liked to make certain.

During the operation decisions to give blood to the patient were made jointly. The anesthesiologist might say to me, "Bill, his blood pressure's down to eighty over sixty. Think we should give him a pint?"

"I don't think we've lost much blood yet, Charlie. How's his pulse?"

"Ninety and steady."

"Why don't we wait till I stop tugging on his stomach? His pressure drop may be reflex. I'm pulling pretty hard."

"Fine. I'll keep you posted."

So we'd postpone the transfusion temporarily. No sense in giving valuable blood, to say nothing of exposing the patient to the risk of a transfusion reaction, unless we had to do so.

I'd always try to keep the anesthesiologist posted on how things were going at my end of the table, he'd warn me of any problems he noted. If a bleeder got loose I'd say, "Shoot the blood to him, Charlie. We're losing it fast in here." If he noted any irregularities of the pulse he might ask me to stop for a minute so he could give the patient digitalis or some other supportive heart medicine. We needed to help each other if we were going to help the patient.

One of the simplest and most important ways in which a surgeon could help an anesthesiologist was in noting the color of the blood. Most of the major cases were done under controlled respiration. The anesthesiologist would put a tube through the mouth into the patient's windpipe, after he was put to sleep either with an intravenous medication or with a gas, and then the anesthesiologist would rhythmically pump a bag to inflate the lungs and breathe for the patient. With this kind of control he could then paralyze the patient with a muscle relaxing drug so that the surgeon could operate more easily.

The danger inherent in using this technique was that the anesthesiologist might not pump the bag often enough or hard enough to keep the patient's blood well supplied with oxygen.

In white people the danger was not very great. The anesthesiologist always had the patient's face in view and if he wasn't getting enough oxygen the skin would get cyanotic—blue. But in black people the skin-color change was not noticeable. Unless the anesthesiologist were careful, he might overlook early signs of poor oxygen supply. However, black or white, too little oxygen was quickly obvious in the blood. It would go from bright red to a dark crimson color. Whenever I saw dark blood in a wound I'd immediately call it to the anesthesiologist's attention. Usually a few good pumps on the bag would turn the blood bright red again. If not we had a more serious problem on our hands.

I'll never forget one case in which this happened. The patient was a six-year-old black boy with a cystic hygroma of the neck (a thin-walled, fluid-filled tumor). It isn't a cancerous growth; most often it's removed either for cosmetic reasons—it creates an unsightly bulge—or because it crowds the other structures of the neck and interferes with breathing.

The tumor can be difficult to remove, since it is closely related to a great number of important blood vessels and nerves. Stan Rollins, a plastic surgeon, was doing this case and Mort Weis was the anesthesiologist.

The case took almost five hours. Several times in the course of the operation Stan asked Mort, "How's he doing?"

"Fine," Mort answered. "Blood pressure and pulse are okay."

"Tell me if you have any problems," Stan said. "I can always quit and finish the case in a second stage."

"Go ahead," Mort said. "Everything's all right."

In the recovery room after the operation we learned everything wasn't all right. The boy had brain damage, presumably because he'd gone too long with poorly oxygenated

blood. He never woke up. The hell of it was that this anesthetic death could easily have been prevented if Stan or Mort
had watched more carefully the color of the blood.

Whenever we had a particularly tough case to do, some
patient with bad heart or lung disease who needed emergency
surgery but was an extremely poor risk, I always called the
chief resident on anesthesia to make certain that he either
did the case himself or assigned us a capable resident. The
anesthesia residency program was a three-year one; poor-risk
patients were not the proper responsibility of some first-year
man. It would be like letting a surgical intern take out a
stomach.

The anesthesiologists had to start somewhere, however,
and this often gave us problems. These tyros were just as in-
secure and frightened of their job as the budding surgeons
were of theirs. Consequently the beginners would not give
the patient enough anesthesia to relax the muscles fully and
the intern, who would have a hard time getting at the appendix under the best of conditions, would have a tight
abdominal wall to contend with.

It's amazing how much difference good anesthesia makes.
On one occasion, as first A.R., I had explored the abdomen
of a man who had been stabbed in the belly, looking for an
injury to the bowel. I thought I had a sufficiently long incision but for the life of me I couldn't get the bowel up
where I could see it. Jack walked into the O.R. while I was
working.

"How's it going?" he asked.

"Terrible," I replied. "I can't get at the colon."

He looked over my shoulder. "For Christ's sake," he said
to the anesthetist, "Put this guy to sleep."

"Isn't he relaxed?" the anesthetist asked in a hurt tone.

"He's relaxed like a block of cement," Jack answered.
"Don't even try to get that bowel up," he said to me.
"You'll break your wrist. Wait till he gets him down."

The anesthetist shot a muscle relaxant into the patient,

and within two mintues the entire situation had changed. I delivered the bowel with ease. I found out later that the guy who had been giving anesthesia was a dentist. The dental residents rotated through Anesthesia so that they could learn how to use anesthesia in their practice. The only problem was that I wasn't trying to pull a tooth.

It was a vicious cycle of sorts. The anesthetists were afraid to put the patient too deeply asleep because the surgeons were so slow; and part of the reasons the surgeons were so slow was because the anesthesia wasn't sufficiently deep. Now that I was chief resident, the anesthetists figured I'd be reasonably quick, so they would usually put the patient down. When I thought the patient was getting too tight, I'd bend over the head end of the drapes and ask, "I hope I'm not hurting you too much." The anesthetist invariably got the point.

I can hardly say enough about the team concept of surgery. A surgeon had to be able to get through a case with a clumsy assistant, an inattentive scrub nurse and an apathetic anesthesiologist—and I could. But when any part of the team was faulty the entire operation creaked. All the fun, all the pleasure, went out of doing the job. It became plain hard work. When we all worked together, when we could feel that things were going right, we shared equally in the joy of a job well done.

20

Dr. Stevens

The man who really ran the Second Surgical Division—and about this there was no doubt in the mind of anyone—was Dr. Russell Stevens. He wasn't actually in the hospital much of the time, he had many other commitments, but the force of his character was such that his influence was felt for days after a single visit.

When he walked onto a ward or into the library, everyone came to attention. Not literally, of course, but mentally. You'd suddenly become aware that your white pants were dirty, that there was blood on your shoes, that the fracture room hadn't been straightened up.

He'd never say, "Your white pants are dirty," or "When did you last clean the fracture room?" He didn't have to. It was just that he always seemed so well organized, so meticulous himself that he made you realize your shortcomings and resolve to do something about them.

Just as in the Army the whole tone and spirit is set by the man at the top, the general, so the tone and spirit of the Second Surgical Division was set by Dr. Stevens; and, like a general, he never fraternized with the troops. Many of our attendings would drop in occasionally, sit around in the library drinking coffee and chewing the fat with us about cases on our wards or about patients they had in other hospitals. When we reached the first A.R. level we'd even call them Floyd or Dick or Al and they'd call us by our first name. But I think I'd have fainted on the spot if I had ever seen Dr. Stevens buddying up to the house staff; and I'd have dropped dead if I had ever heard someone on the house staff call him "Russ." He just wasn't that kind of a person. Not, at any rate, with us.

Besides his routine attendance at the hospital twice a week, on Mondays and Thursdays, Dr. Stevens made visits at other times, often on Sunday mornings, but these were unannounced and unscheduled. He had a very busy private practice and had to take time out for Bellevue whenever he could.

Monday evenings he made rounds from six to seven on one of our three wards. At five minutes to six I'd stop by his office, with Walt Kleiss and Larry Evenson if they were free, and we'd escort him to whichever ward held the most interesting cases. Everyone on the house staff, whether on or off duty, was expected to attend these rounds. Dr. Stevens was a practical surgeon, not a research man, and the pearls he dropped were most apt to be those he had learned through experience than through research or reading.

"What sort of an incision did you use to do Mr. Perez's gastrectomy, Bill?" he asked one night as we moved from Perez's bed to the next.

"Muscle splitting, Dr. Stevens," I answered.

"Is that so?" A pause. "Why?"

"Well, it's a little faster than retracting the muscle."

"Yes, it is," he said. "It can save you five minutes now and then. I used to use it a lot myself, years ago.

"I don't use it much any more, though. I find it's weaker than a muscle-retracting incision and the wound is more likely to break down. Now, what have we here?" We were at the next bed.

He never hammered his point home. Just offered it casually and hoped you'd pick it up. He knew that as the resident became more adept he was apt to take pride in how fast he could operate—even to the point of taking dangerous shortcuts. I stopped splitting the muscle.

The intern whose ward we were visiting was expected to have all the appropriate x-rays available and his charts up to date. It was his neck if he didn't, and he knew it. He also answered all of Dr. Stevens' questions, except for those directed specifically to me. This was Dr. Stevens' idea. It was on these rounds that he had his only direct contact with the interns. Since he was ultimately responsible for reappointing or dropping them from the program, he used these occasions to get a personal insight into just how well each of them functioned. He could learn enough in five minutes to decide whether the man was worth keeping for five years.

It was the intern's chance to shine, his opportunity to score the points he needed for reappointment and neither I nor anyone else interfered unless he was obviously passing out a large pile of misinformation.

We had one intern who would occasionally do this. If he didn't know the answer he'd make it up. He was a smooth operator, and he got away with it for quite a while, but one night he got his. The patient who led to his downfall was a man named Garth Olson. Garth had been admitted to the ward to have his gall bladder removed, but in the course of his work-up we had noted that he had intermittent hypertension of rather marked severity and were in the process of evaluating this before we operated on him.

Dr. Stevens took a notion to go into this hypertension business quite thoroughly. He would often do this, dwell on things that we expected him to ignore and ignore problems that we expected him to dwell on. Frankly, I hadn't taken much interest in Olson's hypertension. I had been content to let the medical consultant evaluate it for us, so I was pleased that Mike Rantala, our glib intern, seemed to be right on top of the problem.

"How's Mr. Olson's kidney function, Dr. Rantala?" Dr. Stevens never addressed anyone lower than a first A.R. by his given name.

"Fine, Dr. Stevens. His urine specific gravity has been

running about one-point-oh-two-four and his blood-urea nitrogen is twelve." I didn't know whether Mike was bluffing or not, but since Dr. Stevens wasn't thumbing through the chart I wasn't worried.

"What about his electrocardiogram?"

"We had one done yesterday. According to our medical consultant, it shows a slight left ventricular strain, otherwise nothing unusual."

"His eyegrounds?"

"Both perfectly normal. No papilledema, no hemorrhages." Rantala had to be bluffing. I knew he'd never check Olson's eyegrounds.

"Very interesting," Dr. Stevens said thoughtfully. "With such a marked elevation of his blood pressure, I'd have thought possibly he might have some retinal hemorrhages. Have you an ophthalmoscope? I'd like to take a look."

Mike ran to the front of the ward and came back with the instrument. Dr. Stevens stepped to Mr. Olson's bedside.

"Just look at that curtain over there a moment, would you please, Mr. Olson," Dr. Stevens told him.

"Sure, Doc, glad to oblige." Dr. Stevens looked into his right eye. "Correct, Dr. Rantala. No hemorrhage." I breathed a sigh of relief. "Now, just turn your head so I can look into your other eye."

"No sense looking into this one, Doc," Mr. Olson said. "I lost it in a car accident years ago. This here's glass."

Rantala turned white, I turned crimson, and Dr. Stevens simply moved on to the next bed. He knew all he'd ever need to know about Dr. Rantala.

Dr. Stevens was basically conservative. He was not the sort of surgeon who was always first with the latest. I was eager to try all the new things, all the recently developed procedures. Dr. Stevens knew that many of these new operations were worthless fads that wouldn't stand the test of time.

He also knew that if he said no to me, as he had every right to do, I'd not only resent his interference but would always suspect that perhaps the operation would have been a good one to perform. So he'd find some less direct way of persuading me. He might, for example, remind me of some bit of surgical history. Often that was enough.

I showed him a woman with a breast cancer one night. "I think I may do a supraradical mastectomy on this patient, Dr. Stevens," I said. "It was written up in *Surgery* last month."

"Yes, Bill," he said. "I saw the article. It sounded quite impressive. Of course, the author didn't have many cases, nor did he have a very long follow-up. Before you make your final decision, why don't you look up the work Dr. Bloodgood did on this problem about twenty years ago?"

I did. Bloodgood had decided that the operation killed more patients than it cured. I didn't do it. Within a year, in *Surgery*, the author published another article saying he had given up the procedure.

Dr. Stevens was a great one for biding his time. One of the hardest things in the world for a surgeon to do is to do nothing. When he has a patient who is in the soup it's very difficult to sit and wait for things to improve. There's a great temptation to take a knife and kill or cure him in a few hours.

Mr. Simon was such a patient. He had been transferred to Bellevue from a private hospital a week after an operation on his bowel. The surgeon who had done the case had damaged the duodenum, and through a drain site in the side of the abdomen, Mr. Simon continually poured out bile, intestinal juices and anything he ate or drank. We had had him on the ward for a week, feeding him intravenously and dressing his wound. The drainage was as copious now as it had been the day he came in. Mr. Simon looked like hell.

After the intern had given him the pertinent data, we stepped away from the bedside and Dr. Stevens asked me what I planned to do.

"I'm going to operate tomorrow," I told him. "His drainage is as heavy now as it was a week ago. I don't know if we can close the hole but I think we'd better try."

"Is he worse now than when he came in, Bill?"

I paused. "Not worse, really, but not much better."

"Is he a little better?"

"Perhaps. His blood chemistries are back to normal and he isn't as septic."

"It's a tough case, all right," he said. "The mortality on lateral duodenal fistulas is high, no matter how you treat them. You've been watching the case, so you do as you think best. But my own inclination, if he's even the least bit better, would be to wait. These things always take about three weeks to close."

I waited. Every day I was tempted, but I resolved not to operate unless Mr. Simon lost ground. He never did and three weeks after his operation, to the day, the fistula closed spontaneously.

Dr. Stevens taught me not only how to manage patients but how to manage families and friends. After rounds on Monday evenings I'd walk back to his office with him. "Any problems, Bill?" he'd ask. Usually my answer would be no. Occasionally I'd mention some particular case, the management of which was bothering me, and we'd discuss it at length. He was a busy man, but never too busy to give his assistance when asked.

One night while we were talking, the phone rang in the outer office. I answered it. The caller identified himself as the minister of the church to which Sophie Michaels, one of our patients, belonged. Sophie was a problem. She had had at least a half-dozen operations on her abdomen for a variety of complaints. As soon as she was over one thing she'd come down with another. We knew she was neurotic but she also had organic pathology, so we kept operating.

Now she was in with a hiatus hernia, a hernia of the stomach into the chest. Almost 10 percent of the population has this condition to some extent, but 90 percent of those have no symptoms. Only rarely is it necessary to operate.

We had discussed Sophie's case at conference and had finally decided to do her. Her symptoms were classical and we hadn't been able to relieve them with medication. If pressed, I'd have to admit there was another reason why we were doing her; I wanted to do the operation. Chest cases weren't common and I hated to let Sophie out without operating on her.

After he had introduced himself the minister asked to speak to Dr. Stevens. "I want to tell him that I don't think you should operate on Mrs. Michaels," he said. "I don't think you'll help her."

"Look," I said. "Dr. Stevens is a busy man. He has discussed this case with me many times. Not only that, we've discussed it at conference with ten other experienced surgeons. We've made up our minds. I don't think you have the background to be offering Dr. Stevens advice. At any rate, he's too busy to talk right now. If you want to discuss the case further, stop by and see me tomorrow afternoon."

I hung up and returned to Dr. Stevens' office. I explained what had happened. "Sometimes these people really get pushy," I added. "It's tough to get rid of them."

I could see that Dr. Stevens was upset. "Bill," he said, "you have a lot to learn. I don't like to be critical, but you handled that very poorly. Who knows what will happen when you operate on Mrs. Michaels? This minister may be perfectly right. Now, if she doesn't do well, he will not be on your side. You've made an enemy where you might have made a friend.

"Let me give you some advice. Always listen to the opinions of lay people—families, friends, ministers—and consider them. It will be tedious at times, but try not to be impatient. It won't hurt you and occasionally you'll learn something.

Don't ever forget that medicine is an inexact science. You're going to make many errors in your career as a surgeon. You'll need all the friends you can find."

When I had to criticize the interns or A.R.'s, my approach was not as subtle as Dr. Stevens'—not with the interns, at any rate. It was easy for an intern to slip into bad habits, like getting to the ward late in the morning, disappearing for an hour after lunch, failing to keep his charts up to date. Walt or Larry would notice these things, but they'd leave it to me to raise hell. As first assistant residents they had to live with the interns more intimately than I.

Bob Card had become an offender, so I decided to get after him. I wasn't operating the next morning and got to Bob's ward at seven forty-five, hoping to arrive before Bob. I did. I sat in the kitchen drinking coffee as I waited to attack. Bob arrived at five minutes after eight.

"Where do you think you are," I began, "at the New York Hospital? You think we're running this place to suit your convenience? What's the idea of getting here after eight o'clock? Where the hell have you been?" I gave him both barrels.

"I'm sorry, Bill," he said. He was visibly shaken and I wondered momentarily if I'd been too tough on him. "I was on my way here at seven-thirty. I'd been down to the emergency ward and took the elevator. When we got to the third floor, the damn cable broke and we fell three floors. It shook me up so I lay down for twenty minutes. I'm sorry."

For a fleeting moment I considered apologizing. Then I reflected that no self-respecting intern at Bellevue rode up fewer than five flights or down ever. I chewed him out again.

The elevators in Bellevue were the worst I've ever seen. Half of them were inoperable at any given time, and the other half should have been. It was actually dangerous to ride most of them. The operators were supposed to keep the loads limited to a certain weight but it was pure guesswork on their part. I never felt safe in them, and even our attendings, some of whom were well into their sixties, would walk four flights to avoid riding in them. They are the one aspect of Bellevue about which I've never felt the least bit nostalgic.

About Tuesday of each week I'd begin to worry about Thursday's general surgical conference. Ten or fifteen busy surgeons took time off from their practices to attend this conference and Dr. Stevens, who knew how important time was to a practicing surgeon, didn't want them wasting theirs. He presided at the conference and he depended on the resident to make certain that the cases were interesting, well prepared and efficiently presented. There was nothing that made my day happier than to have Dr. Stevens say, when the last case had been discussed, "Very interesting conference, Bill."

Larry, Walt and I would sit around the library kicking the possibilities around.

"How about Hall? He's an interesting case."

"Interesting, all right, but can you imagine what Dr. Stevens will have to say about that midline incision? No thanks. I want that guy out of here before the boss even knows he exists." Dr. Stevens hated midline incisions; they were easily and quickly made, but notoriously weak.

"How about Rodriguez, the one with the pancreatitis?"

"No good. We talked about pancreatitis last month."

"Stillman?"

"Not bad. I'd like to hear how Falren feels about esophageal cancer. Put him down as the first case."

There were many things to consider. Number one—in my book, anyway—was to avoid presenting some case I had really screwed up. I didn't hide my mistakes but I didn't advertise them, either. I liked to let sleeping dogs lie.

A second consideration was, "On which cases do we need help the most?" This was the one occasion in the week when we'd have several experienced surgeons simultaneously available to give us advice. It would be foolish not to avail ourselves of it. Each of the attendings had one or two fields in which he was particularly well informed. Falren in esophageal surgery, Jones in hand problems, Baker for vascular cases. We picked their brains at the conferences whenever we had suitable patients.

The third factor I always considered was controversy. There was nothing worse than presenting a case and asking for opinions, only to find that there was unanimous agreement as to how the problem should be managed. It was a waste of the attendings' time as well as ours. Happily, with the attendings on our staff, this rarely occurred. We could almost count on Floyd Moyer to disagree with Dean Voss, Jeff Loudon with Dick Ames, and Frank Jenkins with one and all.

It would probably shock a layman to sit in on one of these sessions. Most patients assume, or would like to assume, that for every surgical problem there is one specific answer and that every surgeon knows what that answer is. Ten minutes in one of our conferences would quickly have disabused the listener of that notion.

"Voss must have been the attending on that case," Floyd Moyer would say. "He's still back in the middle ages. I haven't done an eighty percent gastrectomy for a duodenal ulcer in ten years."

"Maybe you ought to go back to it," Dean would answer. "You might cure a few patients. That operation you do leaves them worse than they were."

"You're both wrong," Al Johnson would chime in. "This guy shouldn't have been done at all; good medical treatment was all he really needed."

Frank Jenkins was always advocating something kooky. He did it, I think, just to rile the other attendings, but he'd argue his case as if he meant it. Sometimes it was hard to tell if he was serious. At conferences it didn't matter too much.

After the discussion had gone on for ten or fifteen minutes Dr. Stevens would sum things up and give his opinion. If he thought Frank was way off base he'd say so, nicely, and that would be the end of it. We'd then go on to the next case.

These summations of Dr. Stevens' were always impressive. He didn't make a big thing out of quoting from the literature, as some surgeons did, nor did he refer to the numerous similar cases he'd seen, as was the policy of other senior men. Instead he would choose, neatly and succinctly, from all the data we'd presented, the item which seemed to him most pertinent to the case in question. He would briefly review the arguments that had been presented for or against specific diagnosis or modes of therapy, and show how these arguments did or did not apply to the situation. He would then give his opinion, and almost every time each of us would say to himself, "Why of course, that's only logical." When he had finished such a summation it was always obvious to us why Dr. Stevens, of all the surgeons in the room, had been appointed director.

But Frank Jenkins was anything but logical, and one night one of his wild ideas got us into a peck of trouble—trouble that even shook Dr. Stevens' usually imperturbable equanimity. Jack Lesperance was resident at the time and I think it was the low spot in his year. It was a distasteful episode, but interesting. Frank, who was the attending on a surgical ward, wandered in around five o'clock on this particular evening. He occasionally did this when he was on service and Ray Hogan, the A.R. on the ward, took him on rounds. They stopped to see one very sick patient on the ward at the time, a Mrs. Swan. She had had a bowel operation for cancer ten days earlier and had now developed staphylococcal enteritis, which is a virulent form of diarrhea. The patients often lose so much fluid from their intestinal tract that electrolyte imbalance (a distortion of the normal chemical equilibrium in the blood) occurs and they die. The cause of the malfunction, as in Mrs. Swan's case, is loss of the normal bacteria of the bowel. Antibiotics given before and after surgery kill them off, the staphylococci which are resistant to the antibiotic grow in great numbers, and the bowel wall becomes inflamed. If the normal bacteria count is restored, the diarrhea will stop.

"What are you doing for her?" Frank asked Ray.

"The usual. Intravenous fluids, cheese, vitamins. We're using neomycin to see if we can kill off the staph."

"There's an article in the *Annals of Surgery* this month," Frank said. "Talks about giving the patient normal stool by mouth to get the bacteria back. Maybe you ought to try it."

Now, if Frank had made this suggestion to Jack, me or any other man on the house staff except Ray, we'd have nodded and forgotten about it. Not Ray. He liked wild ideas.

As soon as Jenkins left, Ray went looking for fresh stool. Unfortunately, no one on the floor had had a recent bowel movement, so Ray started calling other wards. He finally located some fresh stool on Third Surgery, collected it in a cardboard cup and took it back to the interns' lab. He mixed it in chocolate milk, chuckling all the while, took it to Mrs. Swan and fed it to her.

It was only when I found him later, giggling to himself in the library, that I learned what he had done.

"Hogan, you damn fool!" I yelled. "When the hell are you going to learn? Don't you know Frank gets wild ideas? If Mrs. Swan doesn't make it and anyone hears what we've done, we'll be castrated. Don't write a word on the chart about this and keep your mouth shut."

I called Jack and told him what had happened. "Jee-sus," he said. "Wait till the boss finds out!"

He did, in less than twenty-four hours. Smith's phone calls had given the episode all the publicity that was needed to bring it to the immediate attention of the medical superintendent, who in turn got to Dr. Stevens. The next day he made an emergency trip to the hospital and called Jack to his office. They were closeted for half an hour. When Dr. Stevens had gone, Jack and I went to his room for a sip of Chivas Regal.

Jack kept a bottle for crises, and this certainly qualified.

"It was awful," he told me. "I've never seen Dr. Stevens so goddamn mad. He was ready to shoot Jenkins, Hogan and me."

"Did you give him the details? About the milk and everything?"

"I did like hell. I think he'd have thrown me out the window if I had. I told him Hogan had collected the stool in a sterile container, took it to the laboratory and made a solution with sterile saline, put it in a centrifuge and then gave the patient only the surface fluid free of all particles. I made that drink sound like the nectar of the gods. I'm sure he knew I was lying through my teeth, but he needed a story for the medical superintendent and it was better for me to be the liar than he."

"What's going to happen?"

"Nothing, as long as Swan gets better; if she doesn't, who knows?"

Fortunately Mrs. Swan got better, so nothing happened. Except, of course, to Hogan. He was dropped from the program when the year ended. Dr. Stevens would never have felt safe with a wild man as resident.

Near the end of my five years at Bellevue I had yet to see Dr. Stevens operate. His patients weren't hospitalized at Bellevue; they had money. He did all his surgery at the New York Hospital.

I hadn't even seen him assist. He never once helped me operate, nor had I ever seen him scrub with any of the residents that preceded me. He could tell by seeing the end results of the surgery (the patients in the postoperative phase) how good or bad a surgeon the resident was.

But I did, finally, get a chance to watch Dr. Stevens operate. The medical service sent us a woman with chronic heart failure due to mitral valve disease (the same sort of heart problem that we had dealt with at Triboro), and we decided to operate on her.

I had never done a case. Neither had any of the attendings except Dr. Stevens, and he had done only two or three. Since I didn't plan to do any heart surgery in practice, there was little to gain from doing just one case as a resident. All things considered, it was decided that Dr. Stevens would perform the operation.

It was an interesting experience. He was a deft operator and it was a pleasure to watch him work. There was no waste motion and it was obvious he knew his way around the chest, so I had no problem assisting him. He was surprisingly relaxed. I had heard from the residents at the New York Hospital that he hummed continually as he worked, and it was true. "Home on the Range" seemed to be one of his favorites. As luck would have it, I was to see what a really cool operator he was.

Briefly, to recapitulate the main points of this particular procedure: the surgeon puts his finger into the appendage of the beating heart and fractures the valve; then, as he withdraws his finger, the assistant pulls tight the purse-string suture which he has been holding snugly around the operator's finger as he works, to prevent blood from leaking from the heart.

The stitch that we used to purse-string the appendage was #O silk, a very strong suture material. Not, however, quite strong enough. As Dr. Stevens withdrew his finger from the heart, I pulled the purse-string suture tight and put in the first knot.

"Tighter, Bill," Dr. Stevens said. I snugged it up a bit more as Dr. Stevens watched.

"Tighter yet, Bill," he said. "I don't think the stitch pulled up properly."

The stitch felt tight enough to me, but I didn't think it was my place to argue. I gave it just the smallest bit more pressure and the goddamn thing broke. Through the open hole in the heart, almost an inch in diameter, blood poured out as I had never seen it pour before. It's not often that anyone sees a one-inch hole in a beating heart.

Dr. Stevens never lost his poise. Before I had time to pick up a clamp he reached into the chest and pinched shut the appendage of the beating heart, discontinuing his humming of "Sweet Sue" only long enough to say, "Would you mind putting in another purse string for me, Bill? I don't like to let go of this heart."

I guess that must have been his understatement of the year.

By keeping a certain distance from us, being friendly, helpful and courteous but never buddy-buddy, he gave our division, at least in our minds, a decorum that the other divisions lacked. We felt he was the best director of surgery at Bellevue, and since he had chosen us for his house staff, we were naturally better surgical interns and residents than any others in the hospital. It may not have been true, but it was a good way to feel and we owed it all to Dr. Stevens.

21

Chief Resident: Final Responsibility

The day that Dr. Stevens called me into his office and told me I was to be the next chief resident ranks with the day I received my acceptance at medical school, and if my wife will excuse me, my wedding day, in my personal list of great moments.

In our pyramidal system, with seven interns, twenty or so assistant residents, and only one chief resident, those of us who wanted the job as chief lived in a perpetual state of anxiety: Will I ever get to be chief resident? The question wasn't always foremost in our minds, but it was there all the time. Now I had the answer—the job was mine. I felt ten feet tall.

Dr. Stevens never announced his decisions until the last minute; he told me I'd be the next chief resident only two weeks before the appointment went into effect. I think he felt that if he waited long enough, attrition would solve most of his problems. Somebody would decide to go into a sub-specialty, another candidate might transfer to a different hospital, a third might get into some sort of trouble. If he waited long enough, it became easier for him to decide which one would get the appointment. After watching the turnover in personnel for five years, I had to agree that he was right. One potential resident left to go into neurosurgery, another moved over to a V.A. hospital, one was even lost because he developed tuberculosis. Time and again personnel problems solved themselves.

Occasionally they didn't. When the time for appointing a new chief resident was upon him, Dr. Stevens would find himself with two capable candidates for the job. Once, before I came to Bellevue, he had tried appointing two men as co-residents, but he didn't like the way it worked out. Authority was not as central as it had to be to keep the service running smoothly. Nor did either man get the full year of responsibility that Dr. Stevens felt was necessary to make a good surgeon.

Subsequently, when faced with this dilemma, he would make his choice and offer the other candidate the opportunity to stay around an extra year, and then take over as chief. Some men preferred not to wait the extra year and Dr. Stevens would then find them a job as chief resident in another hospital. Others chose to stick it out.

This is, in fact, what happened when I became chief. Walt Kleiss was also eligible for the job, but I was older, had interned at Bellevue and had put in two years in the service. These were the reasons, as far as I could tell, why I got the job first; Walt was to follow me.

I succeeded Jack Lesperance as chief resident with mixed emotions. It was the job for which I had been working so long and hard and I was elated to finally have it, but the responsibility that went with it put the fear of God in me. At Bellevue, in a program like ours, the chief resident is king. What he says goes, and no one—not the attending surgeons, nor the director of surgery even—will interfere with the way he runs the show, provided the patients do well.

This is the key. If the resident were to insist that every man on the staff operate left-handed, no one would say a word as long as all the operations went smoothly and the patients were cured. But let the division start running a 10 percent mortality on cases in which nothing over 5 percent is acceptable, and that resident would be in trouble. Nor would it matter if all of the patients who died were operated on by one intern who was all thumbs—it would still be the fault of the chief resident. It was his responsibility to make sure that everyone else on the staff did his job. Dr. Stevens had neither the time nor the inclination to continually evaluate every member of the house staff. He left that to his chief resident, and it was with the chief resident only that he dealt.

I was fortunate in having two damn good first A.R.'s, Walt Kleiss and Larry Evenson. Walt and I had worked together often and had about the same philosophy in dealing with surgical problems. I trusted his judgment without reservation. Larry Evenson was Canadian-trained. He was very much an academic surgeon. He had a filing cabinet full of articles on surgical subjects, and he could dig out facts and statistics on any problem in a matter of minutes. All he was short on was experience. I remember well one case early in my year as chief resident. Larry had helped one of the A.R.'s do his first gall bladder and when the case was over, Larry dropped into the surgical library where I was sitting smoking a cigar and perusing an article on an operative procedure I had on the schedule for the next day.

I looked up when he came in. "How'd it go, Larry?"

"Smashing," he said, a hangover from his Canadian training, "no problem at all. In fact, the gall bladder bed was so dry when we finished that we didn't even bother to drain it."

I shut my book. There is an unwritten law in general surgery prescribing that every gall bladder case be drained. No matter how dry the bed looks when the surgeon is ready to close the abdomen, there are always a few small ducts that leak bile postoperatively. If they leak much, and there's no drain leading to the outside, the patient may get a bile abscess.

Larry sat down with his cup of coffee.

"You're kidding me, Larry," I said, "you're pulling my leg."

"No, honestly," he said, obviously delighted with himself. "Pete did a beautiful job."

"I don't mean that part, Larry. I mean the part about the drain. You're kidding me, aren't you? You did drain him?"

"No, we didn't, Bill. Honestly, he was dry as a bone. Why should we have?"

"Larry," I said, "everyone drains gall bladders. I don't give a goddamn if the liver bed is as dry as the Sahara Desert—it should be drained. Start praying, brother. If that patient gets into the soup it's our ass." It would really be *my* ass, but I didn't want Larry to feel left out.

Larry disappeared quickly and, I'm sure, ran to his filing cabinet. Half an hour later he was back.

"You're right, Bill," he said. "Sorry."

"Forget it. The guy probably won't turn a hair." He didn't, but Larry—and I—sure sweated it out.

The house staff—the A.R.'s and interns—were good boys. Our division regularly attracted top-quality graduates. But how well they would do their job was going to depend in large measure on how well I did mine. The standards are always set at the top, and I was determined to keep ours high.

As chief resident my day began either with an operation or with ward rounds, depending on what we had on the schedule. If it was a big case, a stomach, bowel or chest case, I did it, usually with the A.R. from the ward assisting. Occasionally, during the first few months, I'd ask the attending on the case to scrub. I could have done almost any case by myself, but at this point I was mature enough not to let false pride bother me. I wasn't concerned about my "image" any longer. I knew I had become a pretty good surgeon. I also knew that there were attending surgeons on the staff better than I was, partly, at least, because of their extensive experience. I didn't mind asking them to help.

Sometimes, however, when they thought I was asking for help I didn't really need, they'd agree to come in and then not show, or show too late to do me any good. This happened on the first chest case I did as resident. It wasn't a big case as chest cases go—just a vagotomy, an operation in which two nerves on the esophagus are cut to cure, or help cure, a recurrent ulcer of the stomach. I thought I probably could handle it, but since I'd never done a chest case alone before, I asked Bill Starr to help me. I set the case up for eight o'clock in the morning.

I waited fifteen minutes for Bill to show up and then went ahead. I didn't want to tie up the O.R. all day—we had a big schedule. At nine-fifteen Bill walked into the O.R. "Sorry I'm late—traffic tie-up on the Drive. How's it going?"

By this time I had the chest open, the esophagus mobilized, and was about to cut the nerves. "Fine, Bill," I said. "I'm about ready to cut the nerves."

Bill looked into the chest. "Looks great," he remarked. "I don't see any point in me scrubbing. I'm late for a case uptown as it is. Nice job. See you," and he walked out.

There had been no traffic tie-up on the Drive. Bill had come in late purposely. He knew I could do that case alone and he felt it would build my confidence to do so. He was right.

On rare occasions an attending would scrub on a case when I didn't want him. We had one attending, Lorny Swenson, a young fellow just two years out of training, who did this with some frequency. He hadn't built much of a practice yet, so if there was something big coming up from his ward when he was on service, as in the case of Mr. Rocco, he'd say to me, "You won't mind if I scrub in, will you, Bill? I'd like to see what that tumor is like." Actually, he just wanted to get into the O.R. He probably hadn't done a private case in two weeks.

The worst of it was that he was a lousy assistant. Some surgeons are like that. They're good operators, but when it comes to helping someone else they can't keep their hands to themselves. Put the knife down for ten seconds and before you know it they've picked it up. "Just wanted to free this bowel up for you a bit more," they'll say. If an intern did that I'd rap his knuckles, but with an attending it wasn't possible. So Lorny scrubbed in to "help" me on Mr. Rocco.

Rocco had a cancer of the lower end of the esophagus, just above the stomach. Removing a tumor in that location is a big job. It requires an incision that begins in the abdomen and runs up into the chest. Things went along pretty well. I managed to keep the knife in my hand most of the time, and after a couple of hours the tumor was out. I planned to bring up the lower end of the stomach into the chest to do my repair. I was working on the left side of the patient and had to reach over to his right to mobilize the lower end of the stomach. Finally I thought I had freed it up enough to get it where I needed it. I put down the knife and gently pulled the stomach up into the chest. It was a bit tense.

"Won't quite make it yet, Lorny," I said. "There must be something down there still holding it." Lorny had a better view of the lower end of the stomach from his position than I did.

"Yes," he said, "there's a band just below the liver. Here, let me cut it for you."

Before I could get at the knife he had it in his grasp and made a quick cut. Immediately I heard him say, "Oh, my God!"

I looked down into the wound. He had cut the common bile duct in half.

We spent the next hour repairing the damage Lorny had done with one quick slash. That was one case after which I think the attending sweated more than I did. If that patient had died of complications related to that cut common bile duct, Lorny would have gone into acute depression. Fortunately, Rocco made it in good shape, but I wish I could say that this experience cured Lorny of picking up the operator's knife. I'm afraid it didn't; that particular disease is incurable.

I scrubbed, now, only on the cases I did myself or on those cases that Walt or Larry were doing for the first time. I left the assisting of the interns and A.R.'s up to them. One year of that had been quite enough. I always did my elective cases at eight o'clock—the hour when elective surgery began. Rank has its privileges; I could put my cases early or late, as I chose, and since I always preferred to operate early, when I was fresh, I did.

At ten or eleven, or whenever I was finished, Walt or Larry would come to the O.R. to help on the next case and I'd go down to the division library. Whichever first A.R. had not been in the O.R. would meet me there. We'd sit and drink a cup of coffee and discuss what was happening on the wards, as Larry and I did one typical morning.

"How's Marietta doing? Did you take out his levin tube?" Marietta was a patient whose stomach I had removed three days earlier.

"I told Morris to clamp it and check the residual in four hours," Larry replied. "If there's no more than sixty c.c., we'll yank it."

"How about Rollins? Is his temperature down?"

"Just one hundred this morning, and it didn't get above a hundred and one last night. He has less pain too; I think we can ride him out." Rollins was a patient with an acute inflammation of the gall bladder. We were hoping it would subside without surgery. We could then remove his gall bladder electively later, under better conditions.

"Watkins?" Charlie Watkins had poor circulation, the result of arteriosclerosis, and he had been admitted because of changes suggesting early gangrene of the leg.

"I'm worried about him," Larry said. "He's started to run

a slight temperature. I think he's getting toxic. Maybe we'd better take his leg off." I told him I'd go down and see Watkins after I finished my coffee. After Larry brought me up to date on our other critical patients, I walked down to see Mr. Watkins.

"How you feeling, champ?" I asked Mr. Watkins, who had been a boxer years before. He was now seventy-eight.

"Not bad, Doc. Toes are sore, that's all."

I examined his foot. It had been dark the day before, when he was admitted; now it was black. There wasn't a trace of pulse below his groin. The leg was virtually dead. "This foot doesn't look good, champ. No blood getting to those toes. It may be that we'll have to take it off, otherwise it might make you awfully sick."

"Jeez, Doc," he said, "don't do that. How'd I get around?"

"We'd fix you up with an artificial leg, don't you worry. You'll get around a lot better than you can on a leg like this one."

"Let's wait and see Doc, okay?"

"Sure, Charlie," I said. "You think about it, but we can't wait too long."

Larry was sitting at the nurses' station. "Put him on for Wednesday," I ordered. "We'll have to take it off above the knee." This was a Monday. The next day I'd speak to Charlie even more emphatically. By Wednesday he'd be ready to accept the necessity of the amputation.

It's impossible to rush a patient in such a situation. No one, naturally, wants to part with a limb until every other choice is ruled out. The best approach, in a nonemergent situation, is to plant the idea early and let it grow. The amputation then becomes less of a shock, mentally, for the patient.

This was one of those bits of knowledge I had acquired through experience; one of those things that I realized I hadn't known five years before; one more bit of evidence that I might now be ready for the most important aspect of a chief resident's job—making decisions.

22

Decisions

Removing a stomach, a gall bladder or an appendix can be a difficult job. If the ulcer is stuck to the pancreas, the gall bladder acutely inflamed, the appendix ruptured, it takes a smooth technician to do the job safely. Still, a reasonably intelligent, moderately adept individual might learn to do any of these jobs in a few months. If you can cut, sew and tie knots, you can operate. When you get down to fundamentals, that's really all there is to the mechanical phase of surgery.

Then what is there about surgery that makes it necessary for a doctor to study for five years? The answer, in a word, is "judgment."

It takes a long time and a lot of hard work for a doctor to acquire sound surgical judgment. Every time he sees a patient he has to be able to assess and evaluate the history of the patient's illness, the findings on physical examination, the chemical studies of the blood, the results of x-rays and a multitude of other factors; and after weighing all these factors, he has to decide whether to operate or not, what procedure to use, whether to do the operation immediately or later. And he has to be right. It takes at least five years for a doctor to acquire the knowledge and experience he needs to do the job. It's much more difficult to decide if a patient needs to have his stomach removed than it is to do it.

Decision making is, consequently, the chief resident's chief function. This includes of course an obligation to relegate authority to certain members of the house staff, but always with the understanding that on any critical case the final decision will be the direct responsibility of the chief resident. He is expected to be the man on the house staff with the best surgical judgment.

When I became chief resident, the tough decisions were passed to me all along the line. There the buck stopped. I was the boss and I was expected, both by the house staff I supervised and by the attendings who supervised me, to make them. My batting average had to be high in the decision-making department—if not 1,000 (no one can be that good), at least in the 900 range—not only because the patients' well-being was at stake, though this was the primary concern. Another reason was that if I made many mistakes, Dr. Stevens, who always found out about sins and omissions, would ask himself if he had erred in giving me the job. He might not have fired me, but he might have taken away some of my responsibilities by asking the attendings to play a more active role in running the service. He had done this to one resident; I didn't want him to do it to me.

One decision over which I sweated blood involved an eighteen-year-old Puerto Rican boy named Pedro Rodriguez, who was admitted about eleven o'clock one night. He had been sick, with stomach pains and vomiting, for almost forty-eight hours before coming to the hospital. He was a stranger in the city, living alone, and hadn't known where to go.

Walt Kleiss was the first A.R. on duty. Mike Rantala, who was the intern, asked him to come to the E.W. and see the boy. Walt looked him over, concluded that he probably had a ruptured appendix with peritonitis, but decided not to operate immediately. He felt that eight or ten hours of intravenous fluids and antibiotics would make him a better surgical risk than he was at the moment.

The next morning at seven-thirty Walt called my room and asked me to stop by the E.W. He met me there and told me Pedro's story. Then I examined him. There was no doubt he was a very sick kid. He looked like hell; his eyes were sunken, his skin dry. He had a temperature of 103 degrees, and his abdomen was distended and tender everywhere.

"Brother," I said to Walt, "this kid is in tough shape. I'll bet he's been sick longer than forty-eight hours."

"Could be," Walt said. "His English is lousy and it's hard to get a good history. What do you think we ought to do?"

"I think we'd better open him up, and now. I can see why you might not have wanted to do him last night, but I think he's had any benefit he's liable to get from fluids and antibiotics. If we don't get that appendix out, we're going to lose this kid."

Walt called the O.R. and substituted Pedro for our first case, an elective gall bladder. He was on the table half an hour later.

"You do him, Walt," I said. "Morris may get sore, but tell him he can have the next appendix no matter what ward it goes to. This kid is too sick to take an extra five minutes of anesthesia. It's not an intern's appendix." Our diagnosis was correct. Pedro had a ruptured appendix with pus all through his abdomen. He must have been sick much longer than forty-eight hours.

Postoperatively Pedro didn't bounce back the way an eighteen-year-old should. Peritonitis causes temporary paralysis of the bowel, so we expected we'd have to leave a stomach tube down for two or three days but after almost a week, Pedro's abdomen was still silent. Besides, he was still toxic. His temperature rose to 103 most days, and never got below 100 degrees. He was a long way from being out of the woods.

On his sixth postoperative day he went from bad to worse. He developed a "stress" ulcer of the stomach, which sometimes occurs in patients who are very sick. The lining of the stomach erodes in at least one and often in many places, and these ulcers bleed.

Pedro bled like hell. Over the next two days we gave him fifteen pints of blood and there was no sign of a letup. He was really on the banana peel.

"We're going to lose this kid if he doesn't stop bleeding," I said to Walt. "We've got to do something."

"I agree," he said, "but what? If it's one small ulcer that's going, there's maybe a one-in-ten chance we could stop it and get him through the operation. But if he's bleeding from all over the place, and we have to take out most of his stomach, he'll never survive."

"What about cooling his stomach?" This was a new technique, recently reported in the literature: the patient swallows a balloon through which a cold solution is circulated, which hopefully will cause the vessels of the stomach to go into spasm and thus stop the bleeding. After eight hours or so, the stomach can be rewarmed, and with luck, the vessels will have clotted and the bleeding stopped for good.

"I don't know anything about it," Walt said. "I've never seen it done."

"Neither have I, but Bart Leonard on Second Medicine has been fooling with it. He has a machine he built himself." We decided to talk to Bart and found him willing to give it a try. We sedated Pedro, put him in the side room and passed the balloon.

We were playing a dangerous game. If we had continued simply transfusing Pedro and he died, or even if we had operated and he died, we'd have heard little or no criticism. These were the accepted techniques for treating hemorrhages of this sort. But if we lost Pedro after trying something new, we'd really be in for it and we'd have a hell of a time defending ourselves.

For the first half-hour of cooling nothing happened; the

bleeding was as brisk as ever. Then it changed, We began to get back more clots than liquid blood, and the blood looked darker, older, like coffee grounds. After an hour even the coffee-grounds clots disappeared. The returns from the stomach were clear. Pedro had stopped bleeding.

He wasn't out of the woods yet. For the next six hours Mike Rantala and Bart Leonard stayed with Pedro. When there was no recurrence, Bart cautiously rewarmed the stomach. Still no bleeding, and Pedro's bowel sounds had returned. From that point on it was smooth sailing. We took out his stomach tube, started him on milk, and two days later he was eating solids and gaining strength. He had made it—and so had we.

When we presented Pedro's case at conference the next week we were complimented by several of the attendings on the way we'd managed the case. On the other hand, Jeff Loudon and a few others of the senior men were unconvinced. "He was ready to stop bleeding, anyway," was Jeff's comment. "Just a coincidence." "You should have operated on him," said Dick Ames. "Surgeons are supposed to surge. What the hell are you running here—a hospital or a research center?" We laughed off the criticism. Pedro was alive and well, and that was our entire case. Nothing succeeds like success.

There were occasions early in the year, however, when I both wanted and needed help in making decisions, and I could always get it. On the first big vascular case I did, for example, I asked Floyd Moyer to scrub and he was happy to oblige. The patient, John Brewster, had an aneurysm of the aorta. An aneurysm is a dilated, thin-walled, arteriosclerotic area in the vessel, and the patient who has one lives in constant danger that it may spring a leak—a catastrophe which is rapidly fatal. The operation for this condition consists, basically, of removing the diseased portion and substituting a tube made of some synthetic material.

I was glad I had asked Floyd to scrub. When we got down to the aneurysm we found that it extended to a higher level on the aorta than we had anticipated.

"Damn it, Floyd," I said, "this thing is so close to the renals that I don't think I can get a clamp on below them." I was referring to the kidney arteries, which branched off on either side of the aorta less than half an inch from the point where the aneurysm arose.

"I hate to gamble on shutting off his kidneys for a half-hour. They've got borderline function as it is. Maybe we'd better close."

Floyd looked the situation over. "Bill," he said, "if we leave this thing in, he's going to blow it surer than hell. Let's gamble on his kidneys."

We went ahead with the procedure. It went well, but afterward Mr. Brewster stopped making urine. He died of kidney failure on his fourteenth postoperative day. I felt bad, of course; the old fellow might have lived another two or three years if we hadn't operated on him. The natural course of an aneurysm can't be predicted with certainty. But bad as it was, I would have felt worse if I had done the case and made the decision to gamble on my own. Floyd had done several aneurysms before in his private practice, one or two of whom had died. No one is infallible, and he had been wrong this time. It made me feel better to have him share some of the responsibility for my failure.

But there were times when my inexperience couldn't be covered up. One such case involved a man in his late sixties on the genitourinary service. Larry Evenson, who was the first A.R. on call at the time, was asked to examine the patient because he had developed what the G.U. resident said was intestinal obstruction. Larry also looked at the x-rays, and agreed. He told the G.U. doctors he would clear the case with me but that we'd probably take the man in transfer.

The story, as I got it from Larry a few minutes later, was a simple one. The man had been hospitalized because of a recurrent kidney infection and was undergoing tests to see if the cause could be found. He had been well, except for his kidney problem, until the night before we were called to see him: his stomach swelled up and he began vomiting. X-rays of the abdomen showed marked distention of the small intestine.

The patient's history showed two operations in the past, one for removal of an acutely inflamed appendix, the other for a perforated ulcer. The adhesions after surgery, particularly after operations for inflammatory conditions like these, frequently cause bowel obstruction. I agreed with Larry that it was a cut-and-dry case: the man had intestinal obstruction from adhesions and needed surgery.

We operated a few hours later. Larry did the case and I assisted him. The bowel was distended, all right, but we examined it from end to end and found no point of obstruction. Instead of a mechanical bowel obstruction, the patient had a paralytic ileus—a condition in which the bowel stops working even though there is nothing blocking it. In looking at his chart afterward, I discovered why. He had had a special x-ray examination of the kidneys on the day he developed distention. In some individuals this test will cause the bowel to stop working temporarily. If left alone and treated conservatively, the patient will recover spontaneously. Operations do nothing for these people; they only delay recovery. In my eagerness to operate I had neglected to review the chart personally. Larry was unaware that this pseudo-obstruction develops sometimes and hadn't mentioned the kidney study to me because he didn't consider it relevant. Between us we had submitted a patient to an operation he didn't need. Fortunately, he recovered uneventfully.

The toughest decisions of all were those that meant certain death for the patient involved.

Take Gene Holm's case, for example. Gene was fifty. He'd never been sick a day in his life. He came to Bellevue only because he had felt a "lump in the belly" and he wondered what it was all about.

All our x-rays failed to reveal any definite diagnosis. "I'm afraid he's got a liver loaded with cancer," I said to Larry, "but we'd better make sure. Let's explore him." Gene had a massive hepatoma, a completely inoperable tumor of the liver. It was an open-and-close ("zipper") case.

Postoperatively Gene started to bleed from his esophagus. His tumor had given him massive varices. We did the usual things—put down the balloon, gave him blood, sedated him —but nothing stopped the bleeding.

"What'll we do?" Larry asked me. "He's on his eighth pint and we're getting nowhere. We may as well pour the blood into the sink."

It was a miserable situation. Gene Holm wanted to live as badly as I did, but he had an incurable disease. We were wasting blood and it wasn't doing him a damn bit of good.

"Slow down the blood," I said. "Give him dextrose and water. If he stops, he stops. If he doesn't, let him go."

He died that night.

Tougher still were the cases that wound up on the respirator. We saw a lot of trauma at Bellevue and some of the problems were horrible.

Like Jim Blotley. Jim was twenty-three. He had been tearing down the East River Drive on his motorcycle when he went into a "high-speed wobble," a sort of shimmy, like the shaking a car does when its wheels are out of line. He lost control and smashed into a concrete embankment.

Jim cracked his skull and was unconscious, but we got him instead of the neurosurgeons because he'd also split his liver and was hemorrhaging. We opened his abdomen, got the liver bleeding under control, and brought him back to the ward. He didn't wake up. His breathing stopped and we put him on the respirator. His pupils were dilated and he had no reflexes. Obviously his brain was gone.

Jimmy's mother and father were by his bedside day and

night. For three weeks, with I.V. fluids and then tube feedings, we kept him "alive"—if it can be called that. It was hell on his parents, but of course they wouldn't give up. In this situation, if I had had the guts, I'd have said, "Shut off the respirator. Let him die," but I didn't. Damn few doctors do. Instead I waited for, almost prayed for a complication. It makes the decision easier.

It came. Jimmy got pneumonia. Mike Rantala told me about it at card rounds. "I've got a culture—it's pneumococcus. Shall I give him penicillin?"

"No," I said, "why prolong the agony?" Jimmy died three days later. It's easier to withhold something than to knock out the prop you've already applied.

As far as the house staff was concerned, I made these decisions on my own. Most times this was true; sometimes it wasn't. One of our attendings, Bill Starr, dropped into the office two or three times a week. On these life-and-death things I'd often talk to him. I wondered if I was shirking my responsibility in so doing, and one day I asked him.

"Not a bit, Bill," he said. "There isn't a surgeon I know— a decent surgeon, that is—who doesn't talk over problems like this with someone else. None of us like to play God. When we have to, it's only sensible to share the responsibility."

Decision making in the O.R. could be just as difficult—and here, often, I had to act on my own. I wasn't God by a long shot, but as far as power was concerned, I was closer to Him than anyone else at hand. I had to play the role.

Take the case of Mr. Fletcher—seventy-six years old, mentally alert, physically spry. I opened him up to resect a cancer of the colon and found that it had gone so far that if I were to remove it, I'd have to open not only his bowel but his bladder onto the abdominal wall as well. Even this wouldn't cure him. He had tumor in his liver. At best, the operation might add three months to his life.

As it was, he was reasonably comfortable, getting by nicely for the moment. Would it be better to live three extra months with a messy situation difficult for an old man to adjust to, or to die sooner in relative comfort? I opted for the latter and closed him up without removing the tumor. Another surgeon might have done the resection.

On another occasion I explored a fifty-year-old man, a Mr. Stiles, who had vague abdominal symptoms which we had been unable to diagnose. At operation I discovered a growth in his pancreas, but I couldn't find out whether it was benign or malignant—its location was such that a biopsy was virtually impossible.

The operation which would be required to remove the growth was a very big one and associated with a high mortality rate. If the growth was benign I might kill him unnecessarily in doing the procedure. On the other hand, if it was malignant it would be criminal to leave it behind. I elected to take it out. The operation went smoothly, but even so, the postoperative course was stormy. On the third day Mr. Stiles developed pneumonia and we had to do a tracheotomy on him. On that same day the pathology report came back: "Benign." The massive operation I had performed was unnecessary. Now I really began to sweat. It's one thing to lose a patient after a cancer operation—quite another to lose him after an unnecessary operation for a benign disease.

I didn't leave the hospital once for the next three days. I was in the hair of Mike Rantala, the intern whose ward Mr. Stiles was on, all the time. He got the most intensive of intensive care. It paid off. Mr. Stiles pulled through; and so, with a few more gray hairs, did I.

As chief resident, another decision I had to make repeatedly was what and how much to tell our cancer patients. Some surgeons are very blunt in their dealings with cancer patients, others are extremely evasive. It's often a matter of personality—the doctor's as well as the patient's.

I tried to individualize. In some cases it was advantageous for the patients to know that they had incurable cancer; they needed what time was left to arrange their affairs. I felt that others, without responsibility, would probably be happier not knowing all the harsh facts. Then I'd inform a responsible member of the family but would not tell the patient himself. I didn't lie—I just didn't supply all the pertinent details.

I became convinced that this was a sound policy when a tragedy hit our division. Jack Roberts, one of our first-year A.R.'s, asked Walt Kleiss to remove a mole from his leg. Jack had bruised it a few days before and it had bled easily. He wasn't overly concerned but thought it ought to come off. Walt removed it under local anesthesia in the side room of the male surgical ward and I didn't know about it until the path report came back. Walt showed it to me. It was malignant melanoma—a virulent form of cancer.

"What now?" Walt asked. We were in the library.

"We'll have to tell him," I said. "You got around it, according to the report, but he'll need more surgery. A much wider excision and a skin graft. Where is he now?"

"In the O.P.D."

"I'll call him."

Jack came to the library and I gave him the bad news. He took it well. We put him on the schedule a few days later. Floyd Moyer did the operation and I assisted.

Jack was back on duty a month later. After a few more weeks he came to me one day and said, "Bill, I'm afraid it's spread. I've got swollen glands."

I examined him and found that he was right: the tumor had moved into his groin. All we could do was go after it and hope to get it out. The night before his second operation I stopped in his room to try to cheer him up. By that time he had read every article on malignant melanoma he could find. He knew the odds were against him.

"One thing, Bill," he said, "good or bad, I want to know what you find."

I looked at him. He meant it. "All right, Jack," I said, "I'll tell you."

It was bad—very bad. The spread was too extensive. We couldn't get it all out. I dreaded visiting Jack the next day, but of course I did. We talked about his diet, his antibiotics, the weather. I kept waiting for him to ask me what we had found. But he didn't. Not then, and not ever. I'm sure he knew exactly what the situation was, but now that the operation was over, he had changed his mind. He didn't want the cold facts. He wanted them left unsaid.

If Jack, who was an emotionally stable, well informed, responsible man, preferred it this way, I decided that perhaps the "silent" approach might be a good general policy. It was and, I think, is. I found that it is extremely rare for a patient to ask after an operation, "Doctor, is my cancer incurable?" I suspect the fact that I don't volunteer good news is enough; they prefer not to have the last bridge burned, so I never voluntarily burn it.

Heartbreak, sorrow, despair—they were part of our everyday life and we had to learn to live with them, to confront them, to be defeated by them—to bear them.

It was not easy. The obvious defense against the tragedies we encountered was to become indifferent, to do our job as well as possible and the results be damned. If a severely burned patient died of overwhelming sepsis, if a young man succumbed to a crushed skull, if a mother bled out from a ruptured ectopic pregnancy—it was all part of the day's work. There was no point in dwelling on these things.

But it was equally important that we "care" for our patients in the true sense of the word. If we didn't become emotionally involved we wouldn't do our job as well as we should. We had to be, at one and the same time, compassionate and calloused. It was a difficult line to walk.

We erred in both directions. I can remember stopping into the O.R. to watch an operation on a young man we had sent to neurosurgery. Part of his brain had been crushed beyond salvation, and as the neurosurgical resident scooped the dead fragments of gray matter out of the wound, the assistant resident said, "There go the piano lessons." I suppose it was a funny line, but no one laughed. Not even the man who had said it. He didn't mean to be crude. It was just that the tragedy of the situation was overwhelming and he had resorted to humor in an attempt to dispel the gloom. It hadn't worked.

The other approach—giving in to despair—was worse. It happened to me more than once. A case I remember particularly well involved a young woman, Maria Chavez, who had come in to have her gall bladder removed. She was a cheerful girl, twenty-four years old, who had been in New York for about a year. She was married and had two small children. She had had rheumatic fever as a child and had a heart murmur as a result, but none of us considered it significant. "Do a good job, please, Dr. Nolen," she said as we moved her to the O.R. table, "I want to get home quick to my kids."

"Don't worry, Maria," I assured her, "you're going to do just fine."

On the third postoperative day her tube was out, she was eating and she was beginning to feel well again. "You'll be home in a week, Maria," I told her on rounds.

"God bless you, Doctor," she said. "I'm so happy."

That afternoon a clot broke loose from her heart and lodged in the main artery to her leg, cutting off the circulation. Mike Rantala called me to the ward to see her. After I had examined her I said, "Sorry, Maria, we're going to have to take you back to the operating room. You've got a clot in one of your blood vessels and we have to take it out."

I could tell she was frightened but she only smiled and said, "That's all right, Doctor. You do whatever's best."

From that moment on it was a nightmare. We got rid of the clot, only to have her throw another to her brain three days later. She developed a paralysis involving half her body and could no longer talk. She could only look pleadingly at me as we made rounds. I criticized myself unmercifully. Why hadn't I left her with her gall stones? Why hadn't I recognized the severity of her heart disease? Why hadn't I done things differently? There were no answers to these questions.

I wanted her desperately to live, but it wasn't to be. Ten days after her brain clot she died. I went into a slump that lasted for days. Me—the resident—the one who preached the need for emotional stability to the house staff. I was a fine example to them.

The guilt feelings that go with a patient's death are almost impossible for a surgeon to avoid. No matter what he has done to the patient, there is always something else he might have done; he could certainly have done nothing at all. One of the things I had to learn as resident was not to give in to irrational guilt feelings. I had to learn to accept occasional failure without becoming despondent. I had to learn it over and over again.

23

The Making of a Surgeon

How does a doctor recognize the point in time when he is finally a "surgeon"? As my year as chief resident drew to a close I asked myself this question on more than one occasion.

The answer, I concluded, was self-confidence. When you can say to yourself, "There is no surgical patient I cannot treat competently, treat just as well or better than any other surgeon"—then, and not until then, you are indeed a surgeon. I was nearing that point.

Take, for example, the emergency situations that we encountered almost every night. The first few months of the year I had dreaded the ringing of the telephone. I knew it meant another critical decision to be made. Often, after I had told Walt or Larry what to do in a particular situation, I'd have trouble getting back to sleep. I'd review all the facts of the case and, not infrequently, wonder if I hadn't made a poor decision. More than once at two or three in the morning, after lying awake for an hour, I'd get out of bed, dress and drive to the hospital to see the patient myself. It was the only way I could find the peace of mind I needed to relax.

Now, in the last month of my residency, sleeping was no longer a problem. There were still situations in which I couldn't be certain my decision had been the right one, but

I had learned to accept this as a permanently recurring problem for a surgeon, one that could never be completely resolved —and I could live with it. So, once I had made a considered decision, I no longer dwelt on it. Reviewing it wasn't going to help and I knew that with my knowledge and experience, any decision I'd made was bound to be a sound one. It was a nice feeling.

In the operating room I was equally confident. I knew I had the knowledge, the technical dexterity, the experience to handle any surgical situation I'd ever encounter in practice. There were no more butterflies in my stomach when I opened up an abdomen—a chest—an extremity. I knew that even if the case was one in which it was impossible to anticipate the problem in advance, I could handle whatever I found. I'd sweated through my share of stab wounds of the belly, of punctured lungs, of compound fractures. I had sweated over them for five years. I didn't need to sweat any more.

Nor was I afraid of making mistakes. I knew that when I was out in practice I would inevitably err at one time or another and operate on someone who didn't need surgery or sit on someone who did. Five years earlier—even one year earlier—I wouldn't have been able to live with myself if I had had to take sole responsibility for a mistake in judgment. Now I could. I still dreaded errors—would do my damnedest to avoid them—but I knew they were part of the penance a surgeon recurrently had to pay. I could accept this fact with equanimity because I knew that if I wasn't able to avoid a mistake, chances were that no other surgeon could have, either.

This all sounds conceited and I guess it is—but a surgeon needs conceit. He needs it to sustain him in trying moments when he's battered by the doubts and uncertainties that are part of the practice of medicine. He has to feel that he's as good as and probably better than any other surgeon in the world. Call it conceit—call it self-confidence; whatever it was, I had it.

Confident as I was, or told myself I was, there were still

moments of doubt. Was I right? Was I really good enough? Or was I just an arrogant ass whose ego had grown out of all proportion to his skill? In June I had two cases which confirmed my opinion that perhaps I really was ready to move on.

The first instance involved the grandfather of one of our assistant residents. He was an intelligent, alert man in his middle seventies who had been admitted to the ward with a cancer of the rectum. It was unusual to have a member of the family of one of the house staff on the ward—most relatives had private doctors—but this man had no money and had asked his grandson to arrange his admission.

It was routine, in the few instances when the situation did arise, to ask an attending to do the case. It took the pressure off the resident and off the house-staff member who was related to the patient. Since this case was a touchy one, involving an extensive operation on a man whose age alone made him a poor risk, I was happy to avoid the problem.

"Who would you like to have do the case?" I asked the assistant resident in question. "Bill Starr is on service but I can get one of the senior attendings if you prefer."

"If it's all the same to you, Bill," he said, "I'd just as soon have you do it." It was one of those situations where there was really nothing to say. I'd never had a nicer compliment.

The second case was similar. The father of Tom Lewis, one of the senior anesthesiologists, was admitted to the hospital bleeding massively from a stomach ulcer. Instead of admitting him to the division whose turn it was to receive the next surgical patient, the hospital administrator asked Tom to which division he wanted his father assigned. This was a routine courtesy.

Anesthesiologists are great critics of surgeons. They spend their entire working day in an operating room and they have an opportunity to see all kinds of surgeons at work. They become reasonably good judges of the quality of surgery done. Naturally I was pleased when Tom asked that his father be assigned to our division.

I evaluated Mr. Lewis myself instead of asking Walt or Larry to see him. It was obvious that he would need emergency surgery, so I called Tom and told him what I thought.

"Unless you'd prefer another attending," I said, "I'll have Frank Jenkins look at him too. He's on call tonight."

"Use your own judgment," Tom said. "You know what you're doing."

Frank Jenkins came in and examined Mr. Lewis. He agreed that we should operate immediately.

When we got to the O.R. I took my place on the left side of the table, planning to assist Frank. Tom had come to the O.R. to watch. As Frank was putting on his gown he looked over and saw where I was standing. "What the hell are you doing over there, Bill?" he said. "This is your patient. You can do him as well as I can; probably better. Isn't that so, Tom?" Tom nodded his assent and I did the case. It went smoothly and Mr. Lewis made an uneventful recovery.

I mention these two episodes not to pat myself on the back, but because they marked, as definitely as it can be marked, the point in time when I became, formally, a surgeon.

I use the word "formally" advisedly; a man never becomes a surgeon. He is, rather, continually in the process of "becoming" a surgeon. I knew then, as I know now, that after every operation I performed, every decision I made, every crisis I met, I would be a bit more of a surgeon than I had been. I would continue to learn more of the art of surgery each day that I practiced it. But now, at the end of my five years of training, I had reached the point where the attendings on our staff no longer looked upon me as a "would-be" surgeon whom it was their duty to instruct, but as an equal. It was just this recognition that I had worked so long and so hard to achieve. I could stand on my own two feet in the surgical world. It was time to go out and do something for others with what I've learned. I didn't need Bellevue any more; some other would-be surgeon did.

24

A Last Good-bye

June 30 is always a hectic day at Bellevue. The interns and assistant residents who are leaving have to be at their new assignments, ready to start work on July 1. Sometimes this means a cross-country trip, frequently it means a trip to another state, but even if it's just a move to another hospital in New York City, the resident has to pack up all the clothes and books that he has accumulated in his year or years on the house staff and transfer them to a new home. Any move requires one day, at least, and since one third or more of the house staff may be involved, Bellevue is always short of help on June 30. It's a bad day to be sick.

The June 30 on which I ended my residency was no exception. We were losing three assistant residents to other hospitals and all but two of our interns were leaving for the service. We kept the elective operating schedule to a minimum —just one hernia and a hemorrhoidectomy—but there was no way to slow down the rest of the hospital. The emergency ward, the outpatient department and the admitting office were as busy as ever.

For the last two weeks I had been playing a token role on the staff. I was still operating occasionally, just to keep my hand in, but I had turned most of the responsibility over to Walt. It gave him a chance to take over the reins gradually, while he still had an experienced staff working for him. On July 1 he'd have a bunch of new interns and A.R.'s to break in, and for a few hectic weeks he'd have to keep an extremely close watch on everything that was going on.

The final morning Walt and I made rounds together on all three wards. We discussed briefly what his plans were for each patient, I made a few suggestions—some of which I knew damn well he'd ignore—and I said good-bye to the nurses and aides on each ward.

You'd think that after all these years together the farewells would have been nostalgic and prolonged, but they weren't. We had coffee in each ward kitchen, reminisced for a few minutes and then it was time to get back to work. When I saw Sharon she didn't even sit down. She had three sick patients, all of whom needed close nursing supervision, and she didn't dare leave. After rounds she said simply, "It's been nice working with you, Dr. Nolen. Good luck." I said, "Thanks, Sharon—I appreciated your help"—and that was it.

After rounds Walt and I went down to lunch together. Al Ralston, who was finishing up in medicine as was I in surgery, came over and said good-bye. I sought out some of the residents from the other services with whom I had worked—and fought—over the years and shook hands with them. There was a lot of milling around.

Walt had to go on a consultation and I had some last-minute packing to do, so we went our separate ways after lunch. I'd see him and the rest of the house staff at the four o'clock card rounds when I could say a final thank you and good-bye.

It took me longer than I had anticipated to get my books and clothes packed and loaded in the car, and by the time I had turned in my room keys it was a little after four. I walked over to the library trying to think of a few appropriate final words. I didn't know how emotional to get. We'd been a pretty close-knit group for the last year and I wanted to let them know how much I liked them all, but a "hearts and flowers" routine didn't seem called for. Even as I opened the door I wasn't sure exactly what I'd say.

I needn't have worried. There wasn't a soul in the library —just a note on the conference table. It was brief and to the point: "Bill—Sorry, but I've had to cancel card rounds. Things have hit the fan. The consult turned out to be a guy with a duodenal ulcer who was bleeding like a stuck pig. Those jackasses on medicine had been sitting on the case for three days. I've taken him to the O.R. Larry and the rest of the guys are tied up in the E.W. with two bad burn cases. It's been fun—Keep in touch—Good luck. Walt."

I poured myself a cup of coffee and sat down for a final cigar, alone, at Bellevue.

How appropriate, I thought—typical Bellevue. Start to turn sentimental and you're lost. People get sick—you help them. You win a few, you lose a few, but you always keep trying. You don't stop for good-byes—there isn't time. One resident leaves, another takes over, but the patients go on forever.

As I sat there, smoking and thinking back on my years of training, I found it much easier to recall the pleasant memories, the moments of achievement and triumph, than those of failure and despair. I was looking forward to the challenge of private practice but I knew I would miss Bellevue as long as I lived. These five years had been difficult ones. They had been wearing, physically and emotionally, and I knew I could never go through them again; I wouldn't have had the strength.

But I also realized then, as I do now, that it had been a wonderful experience, one I wouldn't have missed for the world.

I put out my cigar, left the library and trudged down five Bellevue flights for the last time. As I walked out the back door to the parking lot a kid with a suitcase was just getting out of his car. "Excuse me," he said, an eager smile on his unlined, cheery, rested, innocent face, "but do you have any idea where the Second Surgical Division might be?"

I didn't know whether to laugh or cry.